AF607903

LITERARY CONJUGATIONS

Richard T. Gray, Series Editor

LITERARY CONJUGATIONS investigates literary artifacts in their cultural and historical environments. Through comparative investigations and case studies across a wide array of national literatures, it highlights the interdisciplinary character of literary studies and explores how literary production extends into, influences, and refracts multiple domains of intellectual and cultural life.

W. G. Sebald: A Critical Companion
edited by J. J. Long and Anne Whitehead

Speaking Havoc: Social Suffering and South Asian Narratives
by Ramu Nagappan

The Linguistics of Lying and Other Essays
by Harald Weinrich, translated and introduced by Jane K. Brown and Marshall Brown

Missing the Breast: Gender, Fantasy, and the Body in the German Enlightenment
by Simon Richter

The Work of Print: Authorship and the English Text Trades, 1660–1760
by Lisa Maruca

Money Matters: Economics and the German Cultural Imagination, 1770–1850
by Richard T. Gray

Febris Erotica: Lovesickness in the Russian Literary Imagination
by Valeria Sobol

Mind's World: Imagination and Subjectivity from Descartes to Romanticism
by Alexander Schlutz

The Tooth That Nibbles at the Soul: Essays on Music and Poetry
by Marshall Brown

The Little Everyman: Stature and Masculinity in Eighteenth-Century English Literature
by Deborah Needleman Armintor

the little everyman

STATURE AND MASCULINITY IN EIGHTEENTH-CENTURY ENGLISH LITERATURE

Deborah Needleman Armintor

A McLellan Book

UNIVERSITY OF WASHINGTON PRESS
Seattle and London

This book is published with the assistance of a grant from the McLellan Endowed Series Fund, established through the generosity of Martha McCleary McLellan and Mary McLellan Williams. This book is also supported by the University of North Texas.

Printed and bound in the United States of America
Designed by Thomas Eykemans
Composed in Warnock Pro, typeface designed by Robert Slimbach.
16 15 14 13 12 5 4 3 2

UNIVERSITY OF WASHINGTON PRESS
PO Box 50096, Seattle, WA 98145, USA
www.washington.edu/uwpress

LIBRARY OF CONGRESS CATALOGING-IN-PUBLICATION DATA
Armintor, Deborah Needleman.
The little everyman : stature and masculinity in eighteenth-century English literature / by Deborah Needleman Armintor.
p. cm. — (Literary conjugations)
"A McLellan Book."
Includes bibliographical references and index.
ISBN 978-0-295-99087-3 (cloth : alk. paper) — ISBN 978-0-295-99088-0 (pbk. : alk. paper)
1. English literature—18th century—History and criticism. 2. Masculinity in literature. 3. Stature, Short—Social aspects—England. 4. Short men—England. I. Title.
PR448.M37A76 2011
820.9'353—dc22 2011005958

The paper used in this publication is acid-free and 90 percent recycled from at least 50 percent post-consumer waste. It meets the minimum requirements of American National Standard for Information Sciences—Permanence of Paper for Printed Library Materials, ANSI Z39.48–1984.

FRONTISPIECE Detail of *Evening* by William Hogarth (see p. 23).

COVER IMAGE Albert Edward Jackson (English, 1873–1952), *Gulliver walking about on the table at the inn as Glumdalclitch, his "little" Brobdingnagian nurse commanded him,* 1911. Chromolithograph. Courtesy of Art Resource. Photo: Image Select, Art Resource, NY.

CONTENTS

PREFACE

If ever a single body symbolized English masculinity in the popular imagination, it was, and to some extent continues to be, the large and brutish figure of John Bull, famously created by Dr. John Arbuthnot in 1712 and circulated widely in popular print from the eighteenth century through the present day. In his book-length study of English national character, Peter Mandler writes that John Bull was definitively big, "a solid, self-reliant, rather aggressive and rugged individualist." Mandler also notes the incongruity of this icon, remarking upon how "unsuited the image of John Bull was to the modern Englishman: The Englishman did not look like John Bull, and he did not think like him either. Or, sometimes in premonition of dissatisfaction with the whole notion of national stereotypes, perhaps he represented only one element in the national make-up. John Bull was not a worker—that is, the average Englishman—but, significantly, he was not a gentleman either."[1]

By the 1920s, writes Mandler, the war-weary country decided that the "national figure of John Bull" should be "redrawn" to accommodate a kinder, gentler view of national manhood.[2] The cartoonist Sidney Strube proposed replacing John Bull with an antithetical figure called "Little Man," a quaint and small-statured English gentleman, created as "an imaginative compound of the City gent and the 'man in the street,' dressed in bow tie and bowler hat and armed with tightly furled umbrella, but, as Harold Nicolson said in proposing him as the national symbol, 'small, kindly, bewildered, modest, obstinate, and very lovable.'"[3] Although Strube's "Little Man" prototype never quite supplanted John Bull, it suggests that the antidote to the brutish image of the Englishman as John Bull lies in its physical antithesis. It is quite likely, in fact, that Arbuthnot invented the John Bull image in 1712 as an antidote to *its* physical antithesis, the pre-Strubean little man, which, by 1712, already played a prominent role in the early-eighteenth-century English imagination. Its prominence was only magnified by the publication of Jonathan Swift's *Gulliver's Travels* in 1726, after which the term "Lilliputian" became commonplace and the little man became an even more familiar male type than his John Bull opposite.

This book investigates the various manifestations of this eighteenth-century idea of the "little man" while tracing its historical trajectory from the aristocratically identified spectatorial rhetoric of court-dwarf portraiture to the more modern idea of the little "man of feeling." Because the present study takes as its subject a particular kind of non-normative human body, it is indebted to the work of critics of disability and monstrosity studies such as Lennard J. Davis and others who have detailed the "remarkable appearance of the disabled person in print as author and character" between 1750 and 1800.[4] As Katherine Park and Lorraine J. Daston have written on the fascination with abnormal bodies and so-called human monstrosities in the period:

> In the early years of the Reformation, the tendency to treat monsters as prodigies—frightening signs of God's wrath dependent ultimately or solely on his will—was almost universal. By the end of the seventeenth century only the most popular forms of literature—ballads, broadsides and the occasional religious pamphlet—treated monsters in this way. For the educated layman, full of Baconian enthusiasm, and even more for the professional scientist of 1700, the religious associations of monsters were merely another manifestation of popular

> ignorance and superstition, fostering uncritical wonder rather than the sober investigation of natural causes.[5]

Rosemarie Garland Thompson has discussed how the Enlightenment shifted the discourse of non-normative bodies from a matter of divine or satanic intervention into one of intellectual "curiosity":

> What was once ominous marvel now becomes gratuitous oddity as monsters shift into the category of *curiosities*. Curiosity fuses inquisitiveness, acquisitiveness, and novelty to the ancient pursuit of the extraordinary body, shifting the ownership of such bodies from God to the scientist, whose Wunderkammern, or cabinet of curiosities, antedate modern museums. Simultaneous with the secularism that finds delight in nature's corporeal jokes arises the contrasting empiricism that creates the knowledge used to drive fancy from the world.[6]

This premise is the starting point for a recent encyclopedic study of the phenomenon, *Curiosity: A Cultural History of Early Modern Inquiry*, by Barbara M. Benedict, who is quoted throughout this book and to whose work this study owes a considerable intellectual debt.[7] Like other scholars of disability and monstrosity, Dennis Todd has noted that small-statured people made up a fundamental component of this eighteenth-century culture of curiosity. In addition to the public exhibition of dwarfs, which came into being at this time, "[m]iniature people, as well as miniature landscapes, could be seen in one of the most popular diversions in London, the peep-shows, which were enclosed boxes containing scenes made out of painted boards, paper flats, and glass panels and given the illusion of depth by mirrors and magnifying glasses," and "'Pygmy Actors' moving in diminutive settings could be seen daily in the London puppet shows."[8] Although a general fascination with little bodies in literature, art, and culture of the 1700s has been acknowledged by such recent critics—particularly within the pages of scholars Felicity Nussbaum's and Helen Deutsch's recent anthology *"Defects": Engendering the Modern Body*, alongside which this book positions itself as an intervention in early-modern disability studies—this volume is the first attempt to analyze the matter at length, reading fictional little men alongside representations of real ones and mapping out the phenomenon's shifting trajectory over the course of the century.

Conceived as both a contribution to and a departure from the aforementioned comprehensive studies of non-normative bodies, this book begins with the odd, and oddly unanalyzed, fact that English literature and art of the eighteenth century abounded in miniature men of diverse kinds: dwarfs (defined rather vaguely both then and now as people significantly below average in height, typically with normal-size head and torso and disproportionally short arms and legs, "whose short stature involves a medical condition"),[9] small-statured non-dwarfs (for whom the derogatory term "midget" is sometimes used to describe unusually short persons who are "otherwise well-proportioned"), normal-size men made little in the context of giants, and even anthropomorphic male sexual props forced to please their gigantic female users.[10] Before the 1700s, by contrast, little-men representation was restricted primarily to the specialized artistic genre of court-dwarf portraiture. The predominance of normal-statured individuals was widely understood as proof of God's sovereignty and the brilliance of his design that man be neither too small nor too tall; neither must man be portrayed, devolutionarily and blasphemously, as small or shrinking. A popular 1657 tract titled *An History of the Constancey of Nature*, for instance, argues that "Mans stature and strength within these three thousand years, are not decayed."[11] In 1688, William Derham's *Physico-Theology* similarly contended in a chapter on "the Stature and Size of Man's Body" that

> As in the Figure, so in the Stature and Size of Man's Body, we have another manifest Indication of excellent Design. Not too Pygmean (1), nor too Gigantick (2), either of which Sizes would in some particular or other, have been incommodious to Himself, or to his Business, or to the rest of his fellow Creatures. Too Pygmean would have rendered him too puny a Lord of the Creation, too impotent and unfit to manage the inferior Creatures, would have exposed him to the Assaults of the weakest Animals, to the ravening Appetite of voracious Birds, and have put him in the Way, and endangered his being trodden in the Dirt by the larger Animals. He would have been also too weak for his Business, unable to carry Burdens, and in a Word to transact the greater Part of his Labours and Concerns.[12]

If before the 1700s, the existence of dwarfs threatened to contradict the perfection of a God who favored utility and statural balance in his creations, in the eighteenth century, the general interest in emphasizing man's normative non-Pygmean height shifted into a fascination with its

"Pygmean" antithesis. This is because little men—typically featured alongside enormous women—were found by many to be a perfect metaphor for the perceived devolution of Englishmen in the face of several significant eighteenth-century developments: (1) the commodification of literature and the movement of both dwarfs and writers from the courts to the public sphere in the beginning of the century (simultaneous movements embodied by the famously dwarfish poet Alexander Pope), (2) the contemporaneous increase in female consumerism and the commodification of scientific instruments, (3) the emergence of companionate marriage in the early-to-mid 1700s, and (4) the rise of the cult of feeling in the mid-to-late 1700s. These developments were occasioned by the well-documented rise of the middle class, the devaluation of the aristocracy, and the emergence of women as potentially powerful actors in a new bourgeois social economy that had come to characterize the arrival of "modernity." It is worth noting here that, for these and other reasons, little men proved to be more relevant cultural signifiers than male giants, who also played a role, albeit a significantly lesser one, in the eighteenth-century cultural imagination. From Hogarthian satirical engravings of metaphorical little men, to the publication of Swift's *Gulliver's Travels* (1726), with its depiction of the comparatively little Lemuel among the giants, to the subscription-only sale of Josef Boruwlaski's *Memoirs of the Celebrated Dwarf* (1788), tiny male bodies both real and imagined had seemingly captured the imagination of a newly bourgeoisified English culture. Henry Fielding's Tom Thumb plays (1730 and 1731) drew packed crowds, while public "freak shows" advertised male dwarfs as paragons of English masculinity. Bawdy popular poems featured diminutive men of their own, and conservative intellectuals of the time characterized the relationship between "the moderns" and "the ancients" as that of dwarfs standing on the shoulders of giants. Over the shifting course of a century, it remained an age of little men.

The five chapters in this book are organized chronologically and show how the modes of little-man representation both changed and persevered throughout the century along with the culture's ideologies and anxieties, moving from a primarily visual rhetoric of aristocratic spectatorship to an increasingly literary and anxiety-ridden discourse of bourgeois identification. Chapter 1 articulates a sort of visual prehistory of the representation of dwarfs and non-dwarf little men in pre- and early-eighteenth-century visual culture, from Van Dyck to Hogarth, as the little man moved from a spectator-substitute aristocratic dependent to a representative little man of the people. Chapter 2 takes several steps away from the term "dwarf" in order to explore the use of the concept of the non-dwarf little man in literature of and about the famously height-impaired early-eighteenth-century poet Alexander Pope, transforming the aristocratically inflected discourse of dwarf representation into a more modern and bourgeois mode of representation while retaining residues of its dwarfish origins. As Pope and his numerous critics both understood, the dwarf's move from the courts to public exhibitions was an apt parallel for writers' simultaneous move from patronage to the allegedly free literary market. Departing from the dwarf theme entirely, chapter 3 shows how Swift's representation of Gulliver as a little man in Brobdingnag satirizes the perceived commodification and feminization of scientific observation in the eighteenth century, by which the enlightened man of science was reduced to a pocket microscope–cum–sexual prop in the hands of enormous consuming female virtuosos. Chapter 4 analyzes Fielding's Tom Thumb plays alongside the remarkable eighteenth-century genre of anthropomorphic dildo poetry and examines how ideologies surrounding the emergent cult of companionate marriage led to imaginings of the modern companionate husband as an emasculated little man who labored to serve the sexually counter-normative desires of modern consuming women. Chapter 5 and the concluding chapter show how the emergence of the cult of feeling in the mid-to-late century engendered an association of small-statured men with sentiment that contributed to the rhetorical advantage and disadvantage of real and imagined feeling and "felt" little men of the time in the writings of Christopher Smart, Laurence Sterne, William Hay, and Boruwlaski. Boruwlaski's *Memoirs* strategically, albeit unsuccessfully, incorporates each of the transforming modes of little-men representation within the tradition's hundred-year trajectory, from early aristocratic court-dwarf portraiture to the bourgeois mid- to late-century little man's association with sentimental spectatorship.

Not unlike Boruwlaski's *Memoirs*, this volume is not without its rhetorical limitations. In limiting its scope to little men and male authors, for instance, I have focused on the emergence of little-men representation in the period as the articulation of men's concerns about masculinity—with the notable exception that, given the number of anonymously authored texts in this study, "Anon.," as Virginia Woolf famously posited, might very well have been a woman. Although I found that the vast majority of texts about little people in this period were male-authored and about little men, women writers of the period were not uninterested in the subject, nor was there an absence, in literature and life, of small-bodied females. Eliza Haywood, for one, in 1733 wrote *The Opera of Operas*, an adaptation of Henry Fielding's Tom Thumb plays that was almost as popular as Fielding's work (although Haywood's version reads differently as a political allegory, its sexual satire of the little male husband is, for the most part, a faithful retelling of Fielding's). Other examples of women-authored tales of little people and female dwarfs include the dwarfs in Sarah Scott's proto-feminist utopia *Millenium Hall* who "find refuge from the tyranny of those wretches who seem to think that being two or three feet taller gives them a right to make them a property";[13] Sarah Fielding's popular children's chapbook *The Story of the Cruel Giant Barbarico, the Good Giant Benefico, and the Little Pretty Dwarf Mignon* (1749), in which an evil male giant enslaves a helpless female dwarf; Eugenia in Frances Burney's *Camilla*, whose beauty and sexual maturation are stunted by her facial disfigurement; and the second part of Aphra Behn's comedy *The Rover*, in which a wealthy Jewish female dwarf is paired up with a comparatively big man while her giant sister is coupled with a comparatively little man. Actual female dwarfs from and around the period, though lesser known than their male counterparts, include the seventeenth century's Anne Shepherd, well-known page and confidante to Lady Mary Villiers (they were commemorated side by side in a portrait by Van Dyck), and the nineteenth century's Mary Rutherford Garrettson, a prominent theologian and author of children's books.[14] Such texts, characters, and historical figures are all fascinating in their own right, but because they entail a different set of gendered considerations that would be better developed more fully in another context (not to mention the period's primary focus on little men and male-authored representations of small male bodies), they are not included here.

Another caveat: Among the little men I have chosen not to include are the dwarfs of William Beckford's *Vathek* (Beckford was one of the last English gentlemen to "own" a dwarf, whom he kept at Fonthill) and the abundance of little men in other gothic fiction of the period, such as William Godwin's *Caleb Williams*, whose servant protagonist is portrayed as both physically and socially small compared to his large and powerful master-antagonist. Ellen Brinks's book on gothic masculinity has so masterfully discussed the gothic theme of enormous female dominatrices paired with comparatively little passive men that I do not see the need to elaborate on the point further.[15] Nor, out of my reluctance to stretch the category too broadly, do I classify male children as little men, even though this is precisely the period when children were just beginning to be represented as individuals—that is, little men and women in their own right (as epitomized by the nineteenth-century novels of Louisa May Alcott, to which my title alludes). The newly developed genre of the children's periodical, for instance, which, as Janis Dawson notes, emerged in the eighteenth century and epitomized the new idea of the child as consumer, was launched by a 1752 John Newbery creation called *The Lilliputian Magazine*, which featured a dog-riding miniature male protagonist called Tommy Trip, described as "not much bigger than Tom Thumb, but a great deal better."[16] The magazine's subscribers became members of the Lilliputian Society, a miniature society of reader-consumers comparable to the imagined community of tiny writer-producers satirized (as discussed in chapter 2) in Pope's Short Club.[17]

By limiting this study to a carefully circumscribed examination of little men represented by eighteenth-century male authors, my intention is to delineate a history of transforming modes of short-bodied masculinities that both reflected and intervened in the fundamental shift in English culture from an ideology of patronage, elitism, and aristocracy to the brave new—and, as much of the little-men-oriented art and literature of the period make clear, potentially emasculating—worlds of consumerism, companionate marriage, sentimentalism, and other supposedly democratizing principles of the new bourgeoisie. My secondary objective is to establish real and imagined eighteenth-century little men—as Betty Adelson does so effectively for real-life dwarfs in her historically sweeping *The Lives of Dwarfs*—as a cultural category and literary genre related to, but standing apart from, more general discussions of non-normative bodies of the period.[18] I hope that any little men, women, or authors whom I have omitted will become the subject of future study on this important literary, artistic, scientific, and popular form of gendered eighteenth-century representation. It is the story of how the little man moved from antiquated court dwarf to paradigmatic new man of feeling and became, for a century, an Everyman.

ACKNOWLEDGMENTS

This book would not have been possible without the unflagging support of two very important Jacquelines: Jacqueline Foertsch, my strongest advocate and most valued colleague at the University of North Texas (UNT), and Jacqueline Ettinger, my brilliant editor at the University of Washington Press. The invaluable comments and critiques from series editor Richard Gray and two anonymous readers have helped to improve this book in ways too numerous to list. This project has also profited immensely from the input of my wonderful North Texan colleagues, especially my dear friend and mentor Alexander Pettit, and our fellow *dix-huitièmistes* Marilyn Morris, Bonnie Blackwell, and Kelly Wisecup. My colleagues and comrades Robert Upchurch, Evan Horowitz, Stephanie Hawkins, Ian Finseth, Nicole Smith, Walton Muyumba, Jacqueline Vanhoutte, and Marshall Needleman Armintor also provided indispensable advice as they read various permutations of my manuscript along the way. Members of the C18-L listserv were essential in offering suggestions at the earliest stages of this project, as were participants and respondents at various regional and national meetings of the Society for Eighteenth-Century Studies. My talented research assistant, Eliscia Kinder, provided invaluable help in this project's final stages. The fantastic students at UNT have given me more ideas for this project than they know, and have made coming to work every day an absolute joy.

Thanks are also due to my anonymous readers at *SEL: Studies in English Literature 1500–1900* and *The Eighteenth Century: Theory and Interpretation*, and to the editors of those fine journals, for sharing their suggestions and allowing me to reprint material from two previous articles. Robert C. Leitz of the James Smith Noel Collection at Louisiana State University in Shreveport gave me time, funding, and access to study Boruwlaski's *Memoirs*, and Phillip Sloan graciously hosted me at the Replica Rara collection of usable antique microscope replicas at the University of Notre Dame. The UNT Study of Sexualities/GLBT Studies Program, the UNT Junior Faculty Summer Research Grants, and the UNT Small Grants were of great intellectual and financial assistance. I am also grateful to the National Gallery of Art in Washington, D.C., the National Portrait Gallery in London, the Lewis Walpole Library at Yale University, the British Museum, ProQuest, the Library of Congress, Science Heritage Limited, Art Resource, Corbis, Eliscia Kinder, and the James Smith Noel Collection, all of whom generously provided permissions to reprint the illustrations that appear in these pages.

On a sentimental note, neither this book nor my career would exist without the graduate mentorship of Edward A. Snow, whose intellectual guidance was one of the greatest gifts I have ever received; the influence of my other graduate mentor, Colleen Lamos, for whose groundbreaking queer theory seminar I wrote the "dildo paper" that launched this project; and the inspiration of William Flesch, my undergraduate mentor at Brandeis University, who first taught me the joys of reading closely and against the grain. My wonderful parents, Wanda and Alan Needleman, have nurtured my fondness for books and minutiae since day one. My extended Jewish-Cajun family—Eva and Asher Sapolsky, Daniel and Diana Needleman, Lucille Armintor, and Alice, Floyd, Trip, and Beatrix Walker—has been there for me through it all. My uncle, the historian and activist Steven Sapolsky, taught me never to lose sight of the big things in my pursuit of the little.

This book is dedicated to Marshall, Jonah, and Shulamith "Cowboy" Needleman Armintor, the loves of my life.

THE LITTLE EVERYMAN

one

A VISUAL PREHISTORY

In a metaphorical flourish in Thomas Paine's revolutionary treatise *Rights of Man* (1791), the author describes aristocrats as dwarfs, claiming that "[t]he artificial noble shrinks into a dwarf before the noble of nature," a rhetorical strategy intended to underscore the "natural" superiority of common men.[1] Interestingly, this is not Paine's sole use of dwarf imagery to belittle high class and status. Elsewhere in *Rights of Man*, he extends the metaphor:

> Titles are but nicknames, and every nickname is a title. The thing is perfectly harmless in itself, but it marks a sort of foppery in the human character which degrades it. It renders man diminutive in things which are great, and the counterfeit of woman in things which are little. It talks about its fine blue "riband" like a girl, and shows its new "garter" like a child. A certain writer, of some antiquity, says, "When I

> was a child, I thought as a child; but when I became a man, I put away childish things." It is, properly, from the elevated mind of France that the folly of titles has been abolished. It has outgrown the baby clothes of "count" and "duke," and breeched itself in manhood. France has not leveled, it has exalted. It has put down the dwarf to set up the man.[2]

Besides the unintentional irony that modern readers might observe in the mythical dwarfishness of Paine's one-time hero Napoleon Bonaparte, Paine's words associate the aristocracy, and, in turn, dwarfs, with an infantilizing foppishness, effeminacy, and, above all, obsolescence, a creature whose time, like the childhood of a grown man, has long passed. Aside from the obvious metaphorical equation of pettiness with littleness, why would the most outspoken English advocate of the American Revolution use dwarfs as a metaphor for the outdatedness of the English aristocracy?

The answer would have been apparent to most readers of the time: Paine is invoking the centuries-old association of dwarfs with British and other European royalty and aristocracy, a phenomenon that had become almost obsolete by his time and was already an anachronism by the early 1700s, when the aristocratic dwarf had all but disappeared. As Leslie Fiedler writes in his groundbreaking work on non-normative bodies, *Freaks: Myths and Images of the Secret Self*, although court dwarfs were in fashion from the Renaissance through the seventeenth century ("King Sigismund-Augustus of Poland had nine Dwarfs of his very own, and Catherine de' Medicis six; while a Roman cardinal called Vitelli was able to assemble thirty-nine to serve at a special dinner . . . "), "within a hundred years royal Dwarfs had begun to disappear from Western Europe, the last official Dwarf at the court of France dying in 1662."[3] Dwarfs had not disappeared altogether, however. To the contrary, they actually became more visible, having moved from the elite and increasingly outré world of the private courts to the urban streets, where they displayed themselves in public exhibitions. And yet, while dwarfs were becoming increasingly visible in the real world, they had effectively disappeared in the world of visual art along with court-dwarf portraiture, the long-standing aesthetic tradition with which dwarfs were inseparably linked in the popular imagination.

In laying out a visual prehistory for the following chapters, this chapter demonstrates that, at precisely the moment that the tradition of elaborate court-commissioned paintings of dwarfs began to fade in the early eighteenth century, publicly available illustrations and etchings of *metaphorical* dwarfs and other little men began to flourish in the commonly accessible genre of Hogarthian visual humor and other such satirical engravings. These new kinds of little men were depicted as physically small men who were not dwarfs per se. Instead, such visual representations redeployed the subtle tropes of pre-eighteenth-century court-dwarf portraiture (particularly the classed relation between spectator and dwarf and the hierarchized relation between dwarf man and normal-size woman), but for contrarily antiaristocratic ends.

The Visual Rhetoric of Court-Dwarf Portraiture before 1700

The story of early-modern dwarf representation begins with the history of dwarfs in the courts. As Betty Adelson explains in her recent book on dwarf history (the first and, at this point, only book-length study on that topic), before the eighteenth century, the most reliable way for dwarfs to earn a living was by securing positions as court dwarfs and entertainers for aristocracy and royalty.[4] Although not all dwarfs were court dwarfs, in the alternate reality of the public imagination, the image of the dwarf had become a symbol of nobility, and the dwarf was hereafter thought of as paradigmatically aristocratic. British male dwarfs, as elsewhere in Europe, were often given the title "Sir," especially in the court of Queen Henrietta and Charles I, some of the best-known dwarf "collectors" in all of Europe.[5] A prime example of the paradoxical aristocratic status and subhuman treatment granted dwarfs at this time is Sir Jeffrey Hudson (1619–1682), who was presented to Henrietta and Charles at the tender age of seven when he burst out of a pie at a party; at this point, he measured a mere eighteen inches (a height he maintained until the age of thirty, when he grew to three foot nine). At the same time, Hudson's aristocratic status was confirmed by his regal dress and newfound status as a companion and confidante (rather than a personal servant) of the queen's, a bond commemorated in the 1633 painting *Queen Henrietta Maria with Sir Jeffrey Hudson* (fig. 1), by the renowned Dutch painter Anthony Van Dyck, who has been characterized as the "chief image maker for the [English] ruling class."[6]

In spite of their often degrading treatment in real life, court dwarfs were rarely portrayed as animals or monstrosities in art but were figured instead as human members of the aristocracy—indeed, as *representatives* of the aristocracy functioning as stand-ins for the very aristocratic spectators of court portraiture themselves. As Adelson and others have argued,

FIGURE 1
Sir Anthony Van Dyck (Flemish, 1599–1641), *Queen Henrietta Maria with Sir Jeffrey Hudson,* 1633. Oil on canvas, 86 1/4 × 53 in. Image Courtesy of the Board of Trustees, National Gallery of Art, Washington, D.C., Samuel H. Kress Collection.

before the 1800s, dwarfs were typically seen as deformed human beings rather than as nonhuman monstrosities: "In European art of the fifteenth to eighteenth centuries, dwarfs, ubiquitous in the artwork of that period, were portrayed as realistic rather than symbolic or mythic figures."[7] Fiedler concurs: "[Dwarfs] are categorized, with Giants and Fat Men and Women, as *mirabilia hominum,* human marvels, rather than *mirabilia monstrorum,* monstrous marvels," not to be "lumped with monstrosities" until the nineteenth century.[8]

Although typically taken as an example of the marginal status of court dwarfs, Van Dyck's famous Hudson portrait and others in the same vein are worth examining up close for their invocation and manipulation of the spectator's gaze in order to imply a crucial commonality between the aristocratic spectator and the aristocratic dwarf, an implied commonality that is emblematic of the genre. In an arrangement typical of seventeenth-century European court portraiture, Van Dyck's Hudson is shown posing alongside his royal mistress and her pet monkey. Compared to Queen Henrietta, Hudson is clearly a marginal figure in the mise-en-scène, while Henrietta, with her elaborately depicted gown, its rich folds highlighted by an unidentifiable light source, is the central human subject for the spectator to regard and admire. One might even say that Hudson is so marginal as to be on a par with the monkey atop his shoulder. As one critic has noted, "when an artist painted a dwarf next to a monkey, the message was conveyed that they too somehow belonged together, that although both bore a striking resemblance to normal people they were nevertheless subhuman."[9] And yet Hudson's face, like Henrietta's and unlike the monkey's, is illuminated by the same light source, encouraging the spectator's gaze to shift from the face of one (Queen Henrietta) to the face of the other (Hudson) and back again, suggesting that although the queen is physically and hierarchically above him, they both share a common humanity and noble status. Hudson's gaze, moreover, could be said to be almost identical to the aristocratic spectator's (and spectators of such private portraits were exclusively aristocratic, excepting the servants who attended them, for such paintings were almost never exhibited publicly), focused on the adored queen. Hence, although Hudson is undoubtedly beneath the queen in status, stature, and pictorial composition, his marginality in comparison to her does not imply that he is subhuman, only that he is sub-queen. Indeed, once we take into account the extent to which spectators are also made subjects of the paintings they observe, Hudson's subservience to the queen, together with his spectatorial gaze, makes him a stand-in for the aristocratic spectators whose gaze he shares, like them, in close proximity to the queen, admiring of her, but ultimately deferential. To the aristocratic spectator of court portraits, then, the dwarfs depicted were manifestations of his or her own self: an admiring aristocratic subject of the queen, closer to her than most, but emphatically not equal.

Van Dyck's portrait is also emblematic in its representation of male dwarfs' tendency to appear alongside normal-size ladies, both in art and in life. From the Middle Ages through the late 1600s, female aristocrats were known to make dwarfs their sexual servants, and members of European royalty and aristocracy—such as Catherine de' Medici—actually orchestrated forced matings of dwarfs, "breeding" these rare human beings like animals while still classifying them as human.[10] This troping of male dwarfs as the sexual objects of normal-size women dates back to Classical times. Noting that artistically represented dwarfs have historically been predominantly male ("There are very few women dwarfs among Greek artifacts, an apparent taboo that resulted from respect, modesty, or discomfort with female deformity"), Adelson writes that in ancient Greece, "[c]ountless vase paintings show dwarfs participating in rituals of the Dionysian cult. . . . Dwarfs in these pictures are typically assimilated to satyrs—companions to Dionysos—and are depicted as bald men with exaggeratedly large penises, dancing towards female figures and expressing lascivious desire."[11] Similarly, in ancient Rome, male dwarfs were "mismatched with Amazons" in violent spectacles; in one, "A beautiful Amazon hurled at least one dwarf across the arena for the amusement of onlookers." The famously nymphomaniacal "Julia, the daughter of Augustus," to choose one particularly colorful example, supposedly had "whole troupes" of male dwarfs "to draw from when she wished to satisfy her desires."[12]

By the seventeenth century, nobles had developed a somewhat more "polite" manner of exploiting dwarf bodies, staging marriages between dwarfs as a form of entertainment. As late as 1710, Peter the Great, who kept an entourage of dwarfs, orchestrated an elaborate wedding between two of them.[13] And in 1645, Queen Henrietta arranged a marriage between Richard Gibson and another dwarf, Anne Shephard, a union commemorated by Edmund Waller's poem "At the marriage of the Dwarfs" (1645). In the poem, Waller describes the affair not as an old-fashioned sexual experiment with dwarfs on the part of the queen (which indeed it was) but, idealistically and inaccurately, as an example of a paradigmatically egalitarian match emerging victorious over traditional societal prejudices, proclaiming in the second stanza:

> Thrice happy is that humble pair
> Beneath the level of all care;
> Over whose heads those arrows flie
> Of sad distrust and jealousie:
> Secur'd in as high extream,
> As if the world held none but them[14]

Although their union and wedding ceremony were orchestrated entirely for the amusement of Queen Henrietta, Waller's poem nevertheless depicts the dwarf pair as a modern companionate couple, their size making them quite literally equal to each other and, punningly, "[b]eneath the level of all care."[15] Here, as early as 1645, the figure of the dwarf is becoming a symbol of the middle-class ideologies of companionate marriage and self-sufficiency, no longer a figure of aristocratic dependency. Companionate marriage was at this point still in its infancy; the idea of the little man as paradigmatic companionate husband emerged in the 1730s and returned later in the century in conjunction with the discourse of feeling.

Such depictions were rare in the seventeenth century, however. More typically, dwarfs were seen as naturally dependent, rarely portrayed independently from the aristocrats and royals that they served. Adelson notes that "[b]ecause [dwarfs] were such an integral part of imperial activities—serving, entertaining, and present at royal celebrations—they are almost never depicted as autonomous beings; rather, they are shown as decorative elements situated at the fringes of the lives of others more important than themselves."[16] This view is demonstrated in Giorgio Vasari's court portrait *Marriage of Catherine de' Medici and Henry II of France* (fig. 2) and in Peter Paul Rubens's *Alatheia Talbot with dwarf*, Van Dyck's *Lady Mary Villiers with her Dwarf, Anne Gibson*, and Diego Rodríguez de Silva Velázquez's *Prince Baltasar Carlos with a Dwarf*, to mention several others whose titles alone underscore the dwarf's marginality. On the one hand, such paintings illustrate how dwarfs, paradoxically thought of as both human beings and "decorative elements," "were considered collectibles that, like other rarities, dramatized the royal power to subdue the world," as Barbara Benedict puts it.[17] On the other hand, just as in Van Dyck's painting of Jeffrey Hudson, the dwarfs' humanity and aristocratic social status are emphasized by their positioning in these paintings as the miniature alter egos of their aristocratic spectators, gazing up admiringly, like them, at royal betters to whom they are flatteringly near while still humbly beneath.

In Velázquez's painting *Prince Baltasar Carlos with a Dwarf*, the connection between spectator and dwarf is explored at an even deeper level: although the dwarf might look the part of king, dressed regally and holding the royal scepter, it is Prince Baltasar Carlos whose posture and positioning in the painting are most authentically regal. Like Velázquez's dwarf, the aristocratic spectator may share an intimate moment with a monarch by staring at his likeness while having the privilege of entering his court, but that proximity only emphasizes the humble inferiority of the aristocratic spectator, as represented by the bashful gaze of the dwarf before actual royalty.

FIGURE 2 Giorgio Vasari (Italian, 1511–1574), *Marriage of Catherine de' Medici and Henry II of France*, 1556–59. Fresco. Sala di Clemente VII, Palazzo Vecchio, Florence, Italy. Courtesy of Art Resource. Photo: Scala, Art Resource, New York

Sir Peter Lely's portrait of the court dwarf Richard Gibson (fig. 3), in contrast, invokes the established visual rhetoric of court-dwarf portraiture only to subvert it. Like Hudson, Gibson was another famous, relatively well-respected, seventeenth-century British court dwarf who enjoyed a luxurious life in the court of Henrietta and Charles. Himself a celebrated painter of miniatures who often signed his paintings DG for "Dwarf Gibson," Gibson was depicted in a remarkable 1658 painting by Lely, who, like Van Dyck, was a Dutch émigré and renowned portraitist of British royalty in the court of Charles II.[18] Lely's Gibson portrait, unusual in the court-dwarf painting tradition for its depiction of an autonomous dwarf without the presence of his aristocratic and typically female "owner," speaks volumes about the tenuous position of the seventeenth-century English court dwarf. Leaning on a marble bust of a woman, the Gibson of the portrait can be seen as alternately object and subject of the court and its women: either in possession of the objectified female body on which he rests his hand or on a par with it as just another valuable commodity in a royal still life. And yet here, the standard dynamics of the aristocratic dwarf gaze, by which the dwarf becomes a surrogate for the aristocratic spectator, is subverted in order to elevate the dwarf's social standing even further beyond a mere representation of the typical sub-royal aristocrat. For in Lely's portrait of Gibson, the dwarf looks directly at the spectator, appropriating the gaze of the absent royal personage (the queen or king typically featured alongside the court dwarf) whom, at the level of the mise-en-scène, the dwarf-cum-spectator seems to have supplanted.

On one level, the fact that a dwarf like Gibson could not only be represented solitarily and seemingly without condescension in a royally commissioned painting but also be accepted and respected as a court painter of miniatures can be read as a simple indication of the kind of paradoxical humanity attributed to dwarfs at the same time that they were seen as the property of the aristocracy. On a more subversive level, however, Lely's clever reframing of the dwarf-lady trope of court portraiture, with Gibson's hand on the female bust to his right (the viewer's left), can be seen as standing in direct and self-conscious contrast to that of Van Dyck's Hudson, which has the queen's hand on *him* to *her* right (the viewer's left). Contributing to this reversal of the dwarf-lady dynamic of Van Dyck's portrait is the position of the male dwarf in Lely's portrait, front and center in the mise-en-scène, while the female figure is the one objectified and off to the side. This subversive repositioning of court dwarf and lady visualizes Gibson's power to objectify and even belittle aristocratic women through his production of miniature paintings of them, literally dwarfing the English aristocracy through his visual representations, and supports Susan Stewart's argument that artistic miniatures, because of their size and condensation of context, have the potential to "move away from hierarchy" and "conventions of subordination"[19]—in this particular case, in a direct reversal of the typical manner of objectifying and belittling dwarfs by placing them next to aristocratic women in the European aesthetic tradition. Dressed in impeccably tailored clothing and portrayed as a master of his well-equipped domain, Lely's Gibson not only represents the court dwarf as a kind of stand-in for the aristocratic spectator (as in other court-dwarf portraiture of the period) but also makes the slyly heretical suggestion that the painting's well-heeled aristocratic spectators might even be equal in status to those royal personages compared to whom, like the

FIGURE 3 Sir Peter Lely (Dutch, 1618–1680), *Richard Gibson*, 1658. Oil on canvas, 49½ × 40 in. Image Courtesy of the National Portrait Gallery, London

court dwarf in European art, they were previously considered inferior and dependent.

The striking individual dwarf portraits of Velázquez, *The Dwarf Don Diego de Acedo* and *The Court Jester Don Sebastian de Morra* (fig. 4), are an even more radical exception to the seventeenth-century aesthetic of

FIGURE 4 Diego Rodríguez de Silva Velázquez (Spanish, 1599–1660), *The Court Jester Don Sebastian de Morra*, 1643–44. Oil on canvas, 41¾ × 32 in. Museo del Prado, Madrid, Spain. Courtesy of Art Resource. Photo: Eric Lessing, Art Resource, New York

depicting male dwarfs alongside typically female royalty. At first glance, as a recent critic has said of Velázquez's portrait *The Dwarf Sebastian de Morra*, "With his short legs stuck straight out and his thick hands clenched aggressively at his waist, de Morra looks like a plaything stuck up on a shelf. But one glimpse of his intense face and black, angry eyes is enough to convince the viewer that de Morra detested his role, that he wanted to be regarded as the human being he was, not as the toy the court wanted."[20] If the normal-statured aristocratic spectator is invited to compare himself or herself to the dwarf in this strikingly uncluttered painting (no props or royal personages denote the dwarf's class or status), it is not with the sense of aristocratic class consciousness that typifies other court-dwarf portraiture of the period (including Lely's portrait of Gibson) but with an emboldened sense of independence from class markers of any kind. Like Gibson's gaze in Lely's portrait, de Morra's is directed not humbly up at his superiors but directly at the aristocratic spectator; however, in contrast to Lely's Gibson, the tabula rasa–like brown backdrop that constitutes Velázquez's mise-en-scène is unfettered by the usual markings of aristocratic status. Even de Morra's potentially regal robe is conspicuously unembellished. And thus, the move from Van Dyck to Lely to Velázquez signifies an increasingly radicalized portrayal of court dwarfs and their imagined spectators, from a humble subservience in the face of royalty, to an emboldened supplanting of their social superiors, to an even more radical disregard for the very markers of class privilege that hierarchize one kind of person over another. This artistic movement leading up to Velázquez's individual dwarf portraits (but not the relatively traditional coupling of his *Prince Baltasar Carlos with a Dwarf*) may be seen as a foreshadowing of the new type of ideologically middle-class dwarf to come in the eighteenth century: the dwarf as autonomous, self-made man, earning his own livelihood in the public sphere rather than being defined by the rigid social hierarchies of aristocratic culture.

The Modernization of Dwarf Images in the Eighteenth Century

Indeed, as Adelson has noted, by the eighteenth century, European "court life" in general "was becoming less ostentatious and court dwarfs rare. Many who would previously have served royalty turned instead to exhibiting themselves for money."[21] Much of what we currently know about exhibiting dwarfs in eighteenth-century England comes from Henry Morley's *Memoirs of Bartholomew Fair* (1880) and John Ashton's *Social Life in the Reign of Queen Anne* (1925), which unearthed numerous advertisements from the period such as the 1787 illustration of exhibiting dwarf Keham Whitelamb (fig. 5). Invoking the grandiose "swagger portrait" tradition so popular in seventeenth-century court painting, the advertisement shows Whitelamb strutting autonomously and confidently in front of his "travel-

FIGURE 5
Anonymous, Kelham Whitelamb with traveling closet, 1787. Pen and ink. From Henry Morley, *Memoirs of Bartholomew Fair* (London: Chapman and Hall, 1859), 460. Courtesy of Eliscia Kinder. Photo: Eliscia Kinder

ling closet," appearing more as the owner of his cage than its captive, an apt representation of the new kind of self-sufficiency associated with dwarfs in the eighteenth century; this is in contrast to the aristocratic dependence attributed to their predecessors from just a century before (indeed, one recent catalogue of swagger portraiture lists Van Dyck's portrait of Queen Henrietta and Jeffrey Hudson as a prime example of the genre).[22]

The disappearance of the court-dwarf tradition in favor of the autonomous exhibiting dwarf seems to have accompanied a revival of interest in the pairing of male dwarfs with normal-size women, but with one key difference indicative of the shifting ideology of the times: these normal-size women were no longer exclusively aristocrats but were increasingly of the middle and lower classes. Matthew Buchinger, the best-known exhibiting dwarf in eighteenth-century England, was especially famous for the fruitfulness of his four marriages to (nonaristocratic) normal-size women, who collectively bore him eleven children.[23] Advertised as a man who defied his physical limitations, Buchinger was described as "twenty-nine inches high, born without Hands, Feet, or Thighs," a man who "played on the Hautboy, and on the Strange Flute, in concert with the Bag-Pipe, Dulcimer and Trumpet; wrote in concert and drew with a pen; played cards and dice; performed tricks with cups and balls . . . [and] his playing at Skittles is most admirable."[24] Buchinger's apparent success against all odds and toward relentless self-improvement perfectly epitomized a crucial component of the ideology of the newly emergent middle class: any man can achieve anything as long as he works hard enough.

It might seem from this depiction of Buchinger that by the eighteenth century, the figure of the dwarf had moved from ladies' fetish object and aristocratic spectator surrogate to a sexually potent and autonomous individual middle-class male subject. Other dwarf representations of the time, however, played on the historical rhetoric of dwarf representation to suggest that in spite of changing ideologies, the realities of actual lives had neither changed nor improved all that much since the sixteenth and seventeenth centuries—either for male dwarfs or for normal-size ladies. A bawdy 1732 ballad, "The Lucky Dwarf; or the Marriage of a Young Lady-Lord to a Carbuncle Rich Heiress" (1732), printed in *The Pall Mall Miscellany*, wittily and somewhat cruelly portrays a marriage between an aristocratic dwarf and a wealthy normal-size woman as a comical scenario of a modern companionate marriage gone awry—and a sexually unproductive one at that.[25] The woman in question is rich but ugly (with "a rubicund Face, / Which many Carbuncle, and Pearls did grace") and is described in modern middle-class terms as an experienced female consumer, a heavy drinker who "drank of her Bottle but hated a Glass" (note the pun on "glass," meaning both wine goblet and mirror), and who, in mercantile metaphor, "never would deal / By Way of *Retail*. / The Method she follow'd was always Wholesale."[26] Emboldened and empowered by her choice in husbands, she rejects the numerous suitors who court her for her money. One day, on a drunken whim, she decides to marry a dwarf to belittle them all: "A *Pigmy* was he / In ev'ry Degree, / As vain and conceited as any could be; / Some call'd him a *Man*, and some call'd him a *Boy*, / But the old Women call'd him a *Hobbedy-hoy*." [27] The lustful woman is convinced that this "Hobbedy-hoy," a nickname suggestive of a woman's plaything, will make an excellent lover ("tho' he's a *Dwarf* of a Lord, / Yet Pleasure and Pastime he'll surely afford"),[28] invoking the age-old association of court dwarfs with sexualized female playthings. But in fact she is terribly disappointed by their wedding night:

So wedded they were,
To Bed they repair,
But no Man can tell what it was they did there;
The Proverb, said she, I find nothing avails,
Little Creatures there are, who have not *long T—ls*.
What a Fool have I been to chuse a *Dwarf-Spouse*;
My great Mountain hopes are now turned to a Mouse;
Why did I not chuse for my Husband a Man?
For now I am baulk'd let me do what I can.[29]

Through its invocation of dwarf history as a metaphor for the evolution of modern marriage, the ballad implies that when the new consuming women "chuse" their own husbands, the result is the dwarfing of male Lords and the dissatisfaction of women who wrongly imagine that the new middle-class emphasis on freedom of choice in marriage will inevitably serve them better than the husbands—and the sexually fetishized but reputedly impotent dwarfs—of yore.

A similar representation of the eighteenth-century dwarf as paradoxically embodying both old aristocratic and new middle-class forms of representation is apparent in a mid-eighteenth-century advertisement for an exhibiting dwarf:

> being but 3 Foot high, and 32 Years of Age, strait and proportionable every way, who is distinguished by the Name of the *Black Prince*, and has been shown before most Kings and Princes in *Christendom*. The next being his Wife, the *Little Woman*, NOT 3 Foot high, and 30 Years of Age, strait and proportionable as any Woman in the Land, which is commonly call'd the *Fairy Queen*, she gives a General satisfaction to all that sees her, by Diverting them with Dancing, being big with Child.[30]

Here, the dwarf couple is presented as a prince and a queen, reflecting a kind of nostalgia for the now anachronistic court-dwarf prototype. Yet, in a thoroughly modern form of dwarf representation, the two are advertised for public exhibition and as a sexually productive, happy, modern couple. In other cases, the English male dwarf's ability to overcome the limitations with which he was born served as nationalistic inspiration for the tiny country of England itself, as in an advertisement for an exhibiting dwarf that concludes: "Let others boast of stature, or of birth, / This Glorious Truth shall fill our souls with mirth: / 'That we now are, and hope, for years, to sing / The SMALLEST subjects of the GREATEST King!"[31] Here, the dwarf could be said to represent the paradigmatic early-eighteenth-century English subject: one modern enough no longer to believe that birth determines merit, yet who still considers himself loyal and subordinate to—smaller than—the English monarchy.

Other advertisements for exhibiting male dwarfs tended to promote not only their measurements but their sexual potency as well, à la Matthew Buchinger. One speaks of "a Little Man, Fifty Years of Age, Two Feet Nine

Inches high, and the Father of Eight Children," his reproductive ability presumably being as interesting as his small stature to potential spectators.[32] In a similar vein, a bawdy 1768 ballad, "The Little Man," imagines a biblical legend behind the modern myth of male dwarfs' sexual prowess.[33] According to the poem, after making man out of mold, God had a little extra left over, which he used to make a diminutive man. Dissatisfied with his lowly form, the little man asked God to make him bigger, so God used the remaining bit of mold to fashion him a sizable penis ("Then having scrap'd up all the mould, / That scatter'd lay here and there, Sir, / Like dispalma-plaister roll'd, / He plac'd it you know where, Sir").[34] The mock-happy ending pretends to show once and for all the procreative abilities and sexual powers of male dwarfs when paired with normal-size females:

So now thou art as good, says Jove,
As any, tho' the smallest,
The females see, as well thou'lt move
As those that are the tallest.
In this 'tis plain Jove rightly guessed;
Fore'er since the creation,
Women love little men the best
In acts of procreation.[35]

Indicative of real-life dwarfs' newfound sexual freedom and general independence from the courts, and in place of the arranged dwarf marriages of the courts of England's Henrietta and Charles I and Russia's Peter the Great, the new generation of exhibiting dwarfs was able to pair up on their own, without aristocratic assistance. The exhibiting dwarfs John Hauptman and Nanette Stocker toured together as a romantic couple, and Robert and Judith Skinner, who met while touring, fell in love on the road and married in London, where Judith was exhibiting.[36]

Outside of dwarf exhibitions, the eighteenth century also saw the first examples of well-known self-made dwarf men outside the business of (private or public) entertainment: Hugh MacPherson was a non-exhibiting dwarf known simply for being "a well-dressed dandy," and Thomas Blair "was deputy comptroller of the Stamp Office in Edinburgh."[37] The English dwarf and hunchback William Hay, whose treatise on deformity is discussed in chapter 5 and the concluding chapter, was ultimately elected to Parliament. Over the course of a century, it seems, the dwarf had moved from a symbol of aristocratic values to a thoroughly modern symbol of economic self-sufficiency, urbanity, and middle-class self-improvement—a move foreshadowed by the increasingly radicalized visual dynamics of spectatorship and identification in seventeenth-century court-dwarf portraiture. But, as in the aforementioned eighteenth-century examples, psychosocial holdovers from previous eras, such as the fascination with sexual pairings between dwarf men and normal-size women, and the association of dwarfs with a now anachronistic aristocracy, remained, in spite of all that had changed for dwarfs in both social and visual culture.

The Decline of Dwarf Art and the Emergence of the Eighteenth-Century Little Man

It is true that, as Adelson asserts, the depiction of *real-life* dwarfs in the visual arts had all but disappeared with the waning of the court dwarf tradition,[38] but at precisely the moment that the tradition of elaborate court-commissioned paintings of dwarfs alongside royalty began to fade (in the early eighteenth century), publicly available illustrations and etchings of *metaphorical* little men began to flourish in the commonly accessible genre of Hogarthian visual humor and other such satirical engravings. As Mark Hallet writes, "[f]rom the time of the Civil War onwards, the print entrepreneurs of London had commissioned and published" many such Hogarthian visual satires.[39] In contrast to the "polite" paintings of seventeenth-century court dwarfs, which were accessible only to an elite few,[40] these publicly available engravings, which depended on familiarity with the tropes of their "polite" seventeenth-century predecessors, were "[d]istributed to overflowing print shops and boisterous coffee houses, pinned up in cluttered street windows, scattered across crowded shop counters and coffee tables."[41] Writes Hallet:

> In the later seventeenth century, for instance, print sellers such as Peter Stent and John Overton recognized the particular appeal of such images during periods of urban controversy, and their publications in this line gave London's print buyers the chance to enjoy individual engravings as both works of art and as vehicles of metropolitan commentary. . . . Functioning simultaneously as a specialized commodity within the print market, and as pictorial interventions in the realms of public debate, they constituted an important part of the capital's visual culture.[42]

Just as the visual arts went from private to public in the eighteenth century, and just as the lives of dwarfs went from private to public at roughly the same time, so did artistic renderings of little men, which, like their predecessors, explored the connection between aesthetic mise-en-scène and social status. These publicly available visual representations of little men were able to draw on, and assume a familiarity with, the private court-dwarf portraits that came before them, thanks to the widespread circulation of authorized and unauthorized print reproductions of aristocratic portraits that allowed these works and their creators to enter into the public imagination, even while the original works of art remained accessible only to an elite few. As Louise Lippincott explains, although private portraits themselves "changed hands by gift or inheritance rather than by public sale" and were almost never shown in "public exhibitions," it was common knowledge and practice that commissioned *prints* of these portraits were extensively circulated as an effective means of boosting both the artist's and the subject's reputations (not to mention augmenting the former's opportunities for future work).[43] Eighteenth-century satirical engravings of little men were then able to draw on a visual language established by seventeenth-century portraits of court dwarfs through public familiarity with the most famous portraits of dwarfs, such as those by Van Dyck and Velázquez, whose widely circulated portrait prints made household names of these artists and their works even while the originals remained inaccessible to all but their aristocratic owners and spectators. In eighteenth-century satirical engravings, which, as predecessors of modern-day political cartoons, "fused pictorial representation with religious and political critique,"[44] the figure of the metaphorical little man became a commonly used trope for belittling men in positions of power and denoting differences in class and social status in ways that both mimicked and subverted the visual rhetoric of their court-dwarf portrait predecessors.

In the visual satires of Hogarth, for instance, the figure of the male dwarf is typically portrayed not as a little aristocrat or aristocratic object (as in the century previous) but as a representative "man in the crowd": his deformity, rather than making him stand apart from the crowd, makes him representative of the grotesquery and moral lowness of a London street scene. In *The Stage Coach or Country Inn Yard* (fig. 6), the hunchbacked dwarf postilion is depicted as both an observer and a participant in the competition of class and status that characterizes the boarding of the stagecoach, in which the choice of where, how, and what to ride was, as

FIGURE 6 William Hogarth (English, 1697–1764), *The Stage Coach or Country Inn Yard*, 1747. Engraving, 12 1/4 × 8 2/3 in. Courtesy of Art Resource. Photo: Snark, Art Resource, New York

M. Dorothy George puts it, "governed by the social hierarchy."[45] The object of ridicule here is not the little man himself but the large, central, and illuminated posterior of a female traveler—not an aristocrat, but quite obviously the dwarf postilion's social superior—squeezing and being squeezed (or "assisted") onto the coach. And yet, in spite of the obvious differences between Hogarth's dwarf of the street and the court dwarfs of yore, one constant remains: the dwarf is portrayed as an observer on a par with the spectator, but now the assumed spectator is not a private aristocratic audience but a public middle- and even lower-class one to whom actual street scenes such as these would have been familiar.

Such depictions of seemingly real dwarfs in eighteenth-century illustrations were, however, atypical. Now that the representation of actual dwarfs was seen as an outdated aristocratic art form, more common were representations of regular men turned into metaphorical dwarfs because of their proximity to strikingly larger men or women, a visual phenomenon that one might call "little men by relativity." In Hogarth's *Evening* (fig. 7), for instance, from his *Four Times of the Day* series, the little husband is dwarfed by his domestic servitude to his large (and seemingly pregnant) wife, alongside whom he appears marginal in the composition, just as in court-dwarf paintings of previous centuries. In spite of the dramatic changes in social class and aesthetics from seventeenth-century polite art to eighteenth-century popular satire, this engraving relies on the tradition of court-dwarf painting to make its joke: just as in seventeenth-century court-dwarf art, the woman appears front and center, and the little man is marginalized beside her. Is he a cuckolded object of scorn (as one recent critic has remarked of this print, "it is no coincidence that the horns of the animal have aligned themselves atop the husband's head"), or a good husband to be pitied, or both? [46] Just as in court-dwarf paintings of the seventeenth century, the exact position of the little man with regard to the spectator is not clear. Yet, similar to the empathetic relation between dwarf and spectator in pre-eighteenth-century aristocratic portraiture, the little man in Hogarth's engraving remains somehow the object of the assumed middle-class audience's sympathy: in the eyes of his wife, he may be a mere accessory, but he is not necessarily one in the eyes of the male or female spectator whom the engraving invites to imagine carrying his load of child, spouse, and other related responsibilities.

Especially well suited to the metaphorical potential of little men by relativity were satirical engravings of prime ministers, who embodied a new and potentially threatening kind of political power previously unattainable outside the royal family. In visual satires of Robert Walpole, the portly first prime minister, Walpole was often mockingly depicted as a self-important "colossus," while the people he was supposed to represent were often drawn as indistinguishable little men dwarfed beneath his towering legs, as in the anonymous 1740 engraving *The Stature of a Great Man or the English Colossus* (fig. 8). As in Bosse's famous frontispiece for Hobbes's *Leviathan*, the huge Walpole and the anonymous little people are equally striking in a visual sense, making graphic political satires like this anti-establishment heirs to the elitist, pro-aristocratic tradition of court-dwarf painting.[47] Looking up at their giant opponent like Davids against Walpole's Goliath, the dwarf figures here are observers on a par with the spectator who assumes the perspective of Van Dyck's Jeffrey Hudson; only now, the assumed spectator is not a private aristocratic audience but, like the modern dwarf, a public

FIGURE 7 William Hogarth (English, 1697–1764), *Evening*. Engraving, 25 1/4 × 19 1/4 in. From *The Four Times of the Day* (1738). Courtesy of Corbis. Photo: Philip de Bay

middle- and even lower-class one. The class critique in a satire like this is doubly underscored by its reversal of the court-dwarf painting tradition; it is as if twenty Jeffrey Hudsons were shown taking arms against the queen. Through antiaristocratic spectatorial little-man identifications like these, the idea of the common man as sympathetic "little man" was born.

Showing how extendable such a visual metaphor could be, *The Colossus* (fig. 9), a caricature of Bute, follows a near-identical formula. As

FIGURE 8 George Bickam, *The Stature of a Great Man or the English Colossus*, 1740. Etching and engraving, 12 7/8 × 7 7/8 in. London: Sold at the Black Moors head a Print shop in the Strand. Peel Collection, Pierpont Morgan Library.

Why man he doth bestride this narrow World
Like a Colossus; *and we petty ministers*
Walk under his huge Legs, and peep about
To find ourselves Posts, Peerages, and Pensions.
Shakespeare.

FIGURE 9 Anonymous, *The Colossus*. Etching and engraving, 7⅞ × 4⅞ in. Peel Collection, Pierpont Morgan Library.

Herbert M. Atherton writes of Bute, "If Walpole was the stereotype of 'first minister' during the reigns of the first two Georges, John Stuart, third Earl of Bute, seemed the exemplification of court 'favourite' at the outset of the reign of George III. Bute became, like Walpole, a victim of historical parallels, and he was as readily accepted into that notorious company of favourites and ministers from the past."[48] In such Butean visual satires, as in those of Walpole, the giant who claims to represent the little man is actually a corrupt favorite of the courts; the metaphorical little men, as in Hogarth's street scenes (evocative of the implied empathetic relationship between spectator and dwarf in pre-eighteenth-century court portraiture), represent the inferiors he dwarfs.

Still, this particular engraving is far from sympathetic to those dwarfed inferiors of the self-important prime minister. In the caption, an intentionally butchered quote from Shakespeare's *Julius Caesar*—"Why man he doth bestride this narrow World / Like a COLOSSUS; and we petty ministers / Walk under his huge Legs, and peep about / To find ourselves Posts, Peerages, and Pensions"—substitutes "ministers" for the Bard's "men" and "Posts, Peerages, and Pensions" for "dishonorable graves," suggesting that Bute's inferiors, in this case aristocratic social climbers not equal to his status but aspiring to political positions, are as much to blame for their own dwarfed status as he is. The famous ending to the Shakespearean passage, unquoted in the engraving, provides an invisible punch line, suggesting that in this new age of middle-class self-reliance, such metaphorical dwarfs must take at least partial responsibility for their own debasement: "The fault, dear Brutus, is not in our stars, / But in ourselves, that we are underlings."[49]

Indeed, in other such visual political satires of eighteenth-century public art, the metaphorical dwarfs or little men by relativity are as much the object of ridicule as is the grand prime minister. In a 1740 engraving of Walpole, *Idol Worship or the Way to Preferment* (fig. 10), for instance—which, as David Bindman puts it, is "[a] classic satire on Walpole's system of preferment, by which he used the influence and prerogatives of the court to reward those who supported him"[50]—tiny aristocrats are seen lining up to stand on a pedestal in order to kiss the naked buttocks of the prime minister, who bends over, appearing to moon the spectator. It is impossible to tell who is more shameless here, the self-exposing prime minister or his ass-kissing worshippers. What is indisputable is that this bawdy public image engages in the very same visual discourse as polite court-dwarf paintings of

FIGURE 10
Anonymous, *Idol Worship or the Way to Preferment*, 1740. Etching and engraving, 13¾ × 9⅞ in. Courtesy of the Lewis Walpole Library, Yale University, Connecticut, USA.

the 1600s in having the large figure appear front and center while the little man or men appear off to the side, denoting the paradoxical entitlement and dependency of their social position.

In a 1762 satire of Pitt, titled *Sic Transit Gloria Mundi* (fig. 11), by contrast, the spectator is invited to be sympathetic to the "common" little men in the street, who emanate bubbles of "Poverty," while the enormous prime minister, floating above, like a false god, offers them "Pride, Conceit, Patriotism, Popularity," and, ironically, "Moderation," among other virtues. When seen as an antiaristocratic descendant of the elitist European tradition of court-dwarf painting, this illustration demonstrates that just as the tone of British dwarf art has changed—from private and polite in the seventeenth century to public and largely satirical in the eighteenth—so has its subject, the little man, from an aristocratic object-cum-subject of the courts to a definitively unaristocratic common man. Still, one important element from the tradition of court-dwarf portraiture remains: the

FIGURE 11 Anonymous, *Sic Transit Gloria Mundi*, 1762. Etching, 6 × 7 1/2 in. The British Museum, London. © The Trustees of the British Museum

implicit suggestion that the little man is somehow a stand-in for the spectator. Drawing from the visual discourse established by dwarf art of the 1600s, the large figure here is both physically and socially above the spectator: the little man below him—with whom the spectator is encouraged to empathize—is portrayed not as the spectator's inferior but as his or her equal or proxy. In aligning the sub-aristocratic spectator of little-man art with the sub-aristocratic little man in this way, these engravings provide a slight exception to Benedict's observation in *Curiosity* that in art of the period, "[t]he contrast between an abnormally small and an abnormally large person usually implies the spectator's normality"; here, the spectator's normality is underscored by his association with little men—littleness, in satirical engravings like these, *is* normality.[51]

FIGURE 12 George Cruikshank (English, 1792–1878), *Longitude & Latitude of St. Petersburgh*, 1813. Etching, 10 × 14 in. The British Museum, London. © The Trustees of the British Museum

Occasionally, however, in satirical engravings of the long eighteenth century, the little man still represents the aristocracy (as in the Thomas Paine anecdote that begins this chapter), but in ironic modern restagings of the anachronistic court-dwarf portraiture tradition. Take, for instance, the 1813 engraving by George Cruikshank *Longitude and Latitude of St. Petersburgh* (fig. 12), in which, as one critic explains, "the tall thin woman and the short fat man are Madame de Lieven and Prince Pierre Koslovsky, who called himself '*l'aimable roué*,' waltzing at Almack's. The setting shows the austerity that was a protest against the lavish entertaining of the rich."[52] Here, the little man seemingly fancies himself running the show, becoming—given the illustration's roots in the court-dwarf painting tradition—a sort of court dwarf turned prince, moved from margin to center. In the eyes of the spectator, however (and of the amused observers in the painting), for whom the outmoded figure of the artistically represented court dwarf still resonates with meaning, he is merely a human spectacle, unaware of the metaphorical marginality of his own figure, an otherness underscored by the exaggerated height and plumage of his female dancing partner, Madame de Lieven. Behind the social satire in Cruikshank's illustration lies an understanding that by 1813 the idea of aristocratic entitlement had become, like the court dwarf of seventeenth-century portraiture, a freakish anachronism, while the actual dwarfs (like the unknowing Prince Pierre Koslovsky) worked to entertain the masses.

Whether portraying the little man as a commoner or an aristocrat, as a subhuman Other or as one of "us" (a spectator surrogate, whether the intended viewers were aristocrats, as in pre-eighteenth-century court portraiture, or common men, as in eighteenth-century satirical engravings), such artistic and literary renderings of dwarfs and other kinds of little men assumed and took full rhetorical advantage of a reader's or spectator's cursory understanding of the clichés and changes of the history of dwarf representation. On the one hand, as Adelson and others have noted, by the eighteenth century, both dwarfs and representations of them could be said to have moved from the courts to the London streets, from the world of private entertainment to the world of publicly available commodities. But in spite of this apparent change, the age-old association of dwarfs with aristocracy, and the fascination with the sexual performance of male dwarfs paired with taller women, were often invoked as anachronistic holdovers from earlier eras, now used self-consciously or ironically, and always for satirical effect, giving birth to the new eighteenth-century prototype of the metaphorical dwarf and the non-dwarf little man that pervaded the rest of the century and provides the subject for the remainder of this book. The time was ripe for visual and written public satire to take on the similarly paradoxical—public yet private, quintessentially middle-class yet socially and ideologically aristocratic, thoroughly modern yet strikingly anachronistic—little male body of Alexander Pope.

two

THE DWARFING OF LITTLE-MAN POPE

At the same time that dwarfs were moving from the courts to the public sphere, a similar transformation was taking place for writers who, by the 1700s, no longer depended on aristocratic or royal patronage but were free to earn a living selling their works by subscription or directly to the newly abundant array of London booksellers—or so the popular version of literary history goes. By the 1710s, the writer to have done so most successfully was Alexander Pope, who also happened to be the best-known little man of his time. He was, in Joshua Reynolds's estimate, "about four feet six high"[1] and was labeled in print by his many Grub Street critics with a variety of dwarf epithets: "Little Pope," "Little Man," "The Little Satyrist of Twickenham," "little Creature," "little *Tom Tit*," "little Author," "Little Satyrical Poet," "little Gentleman," "Little Monster," "Elf," and "Pigmy," to name just a few.[2] "Elf" and "Pigmy" were often interchangeable with "dwarf," and "little Man" and "Little Gentleman" were established dwarf nomenclature dating back to the Renaissance.[3]

These writers' "dwarfings" of Pope were more than just gratuitous ad hominem attacks on his appearance. In actuality, his numerous critics were keenly aware that Pope, as both a writer and a little man, had much in common with the new breed of modern dwarf who was now expected to earn a living for himself and entertain the masses and was no longer assumed to be an aristocratic dependent. They also understood that Pope, contradictorily, fit the mold of the dependent and pro-aristocratic court dwarf of yore, through his social and economic dependence on his aristocratic friends and patrons and his pro-aristocratic aversion to the capitalistic maneuverings of Grub Street, of which he, a famously ruthless self-promoter, nonetheless took full advantage. When read collectively and with the history of dwarf representation in mind, Popiana (the term for anti-Pope publications) depicts Pope's body as not only small and deformed but also, specifically, dwarfish. In spite of his middle-class origins (his father, as was commonly known, was a successful textile merchant) and the increasingly antiaristocratic bias of the times, Pope, in the eyes of his critics, and sometimes by admission of his own pen, played the anachronistic court-dwarf role of aristocratic flatterer and entertainer, particularly with aristocratic women, whom he actively courted as his readers, friends, and patrons. Since, as John Barrell has noted, economic dependence for male poets within the new free-market literary culture was so often seen as a sign of cultural irrelevance and emasculation, the paradox of Pope's modern capitalistic business model, by which he prided himself on being a self-made man and a keen manipulator of the new literary marketplace, and his anachronistically aristocratic ideology and social connections thus found a rich and particularly scathing metaphorical counterpart in the figure of the eighteenth-century dwarf, who was in a period of transition from the courts (and their associations with the aristocracy) to the new modern world of public exhibition (and its association with the rising middle class).[4] By likening Pope to old-fashioned court dwarfs, his critics therefore painted him as an aristocratically dependent and emasculated living anachronism, while their emphasis on his resemblances to the modern self-promoting exhibiting dwarf made him out to be an impotent hypocrite, a court dwarf unsuccessfully attempting to penetrate the new commercial marketplace.

This chapter aims to remedy the absence of analyses of dwarf representation in recent Pope criticism by demonstrating how Popiana's dwarf allusions explain many of the metaphors and motives deployed by Pope's critics and, ultimately, his responses to them.[5] Never one to be denied the last word, Pope, who collected and read all of the attacks against him, appropriated his critics' use of dwarf metaphors in order to belittle the writers who were attempting to dwarf him, at times, by characterizing aristocratic dwarf-loving women as even more perverse and anachronistic than the court dwarf (Pope) himself and, at other times, and more effectively, by depicting himself as a part of a larger club of dwarfish writers positioned uncomfortably and comically, like the eighteenth-century dwarf, between contradictory old and new worlds.

Pope's Body and Its Critics

On the subject of Pope's stature, Mack writes that "by the time he began to be known as a successful poet he was already established in his own mind and in the minds of others as a dwarf and cripple."[6] As Marjorie Nicolson and G. S. Rousseau have shown, the cause of Pope's hunched back and small stature was likely tuberculosis.[7] Pope himself was known to have been particularly touchy about the subject of his diminutive figure. Although he supervised numerous artistic renderings of his likeness, he did not permit full-length portraits of himself.[8] He nonetheless still referred to his small stature on occasion, at times confidently and self-mockingly and at other times wearily and self-deprecatingly; often he adopted both attitudes at once. In a letter to his friend John Caryll, Pope reflects: "'Tis certain the greatest magnifying glasses in the world are a man's own eyes, when they look upon his own person; yet even in those, I appear not the great Alexander Mr. Caryll is so civil to, but that little Alexander the women laugh at."[9] In that passage, Pope admits to seeing himself not as a man empowered with magnified vision but as a microscopic object of women's amusement. In another letter, to Judith Cowper, Pope similarly acknowledges his "ugly Body (that stands much in the way of any Friendship, when it is between different Sexes)."[10] Elsewhere in his correspondence, Pope demonstrates what one might call a stereotypically Catholic objectification and rejection of his own body; in an epistle to Swift, for instance, Pope refers to his body as "the wretched carcase I am annexed to."[11]

A similar mixture of wit and self-loathing regarding his shortness is visible in Pope's verse. In "Imitations of Horace," he refers to his small stature with understatement as "Far from a Lynx, and not a Giant quite."[12] And in

"An Epistle to Dr. Arbuthnot," he implies that there might be little difference between the flatterers who praise his poetic talent and the enemies who insult his diminutive body:

> There are, who to my Person pay their court,
> I cough like *Horace*, and tho' lean, am short,
> *Ammon's* great Son one shoulder had too high,
> Such *Ovid's* nose, and 'Sir! You have an Eye—'
> Go on, obliging Creatures, make me see
> All that disgrac'd my Betters, met in me.[13]

Pope was well aware that both his talent and his non-normative body, in their exceptionality and resemblance to the Ancients, could be as easily seen as "disgrac'd" anachronisms as taken for signs of his greatness.

Helen Deutsch makes an important argument about the self-fashioning rhetorical strategy behind Pope's references to his deformity. She contends that, rather than trying to "write himself out of his body,"[14] Pope fashions an approach by which his

> deformity becomes his most powerful weapon in his fight to win authority and authenticity from both the literary marketplace and his literary-canonical predecessors. The body that exposes him to a reader's derision provides Pope with the means to orchestrate that reader's response to his literary performance. The author ultimately comes to champion his deformity as a bridge between life and art, between corrupt deviation and moral example, between homely virtue and beautiful hypocrisy, between the classical tradition and the contemporary reading public.[15]

Building on Deutsch's argument for what Judith Butler would call Pope's "resignification" of his own stature,[16] the rhetorical possibilities of Pope's stature become even richer when we consider how such allusions to his height on the part of both Pope and his critics extend beyond Pope's body to the history of dwarf representation and its stereotypes and, in turn, to the metaphorical dwarfishness of early-eighteenth-century writing culture itself, the same culture that spawned both Pope and his harshest critics.

With the patronage system in decline by the early 1700s, and sale by subscription replacing it as a more commercial but by no means antithetical alternative,[17] Pope, as Colin Nicholson and others have noted, paradoxically "surveyed and profited from this rapidly-evolving capitalism" in his business dealings, while in his poetry and social life, he "simultaneously adopted political attitudes and promoted associations that were reactionary and backward looking."[18] The decidedly anticapitalist and anti–Grub Street ethos behind much of Pope's verse, such as the *Dunciad* and his Epistles to Bathurst and Arbuthnot, which explicitly favor "aristocratic generosity over middle-class commerce," competes with his ruthlessly capitalistic marketing of these anticapitalistic poems as well as his ingenious and lucrative "payment by installment scheme" for his six-volume translation of the *Iliad*.[19] As Catherine Ingrassia observes in her study of the interconnected literary and commercial worlds of Grub Street and Exchange Alley, Pope's work is an attempt to reflect an opposition between art and the marketplace, with "the frantic and mercenary hacks with their ephemeral devalued products stand[ing] in stark contrast to the privileged and 'classical' gentleman-author who writes for a place in literary history."[20] His desire to position himself as the latter while surpassing the self-marketing strategies of the former led him, inexorably and schizophrenically, to embody that very opposition. Moreover, as both Nicholson and Flavio Gregori have pointed out, Pope's aristocratic posturing appears even more self-contradictory in light of the fact that his Catholicism systematically and prejudicially barred him from joining the very group of landowners whom he identified with and championed in his writings.[21]

In its contradictory amalgamation of old (aristocratic, dependent) and new (middle-class) dwarf prototypes, Pope's abnormally small writer's body reminded his critics of the unsettling truth that modern middle-class English culture, with its ideology of self-sufficient capitalism and disdain for the patronage system, was still linked to its hierarchical aristocratic past and its potentially demoralizing culture of aristocratic dependence. The still widespread assumption that eighteenth-century print culture delivered a final and revolutionary blow to the old patronage system is a myth that postmodern criticism has only recently begun to expose as false. This recent turning of the tides in print history can be found in critiques of Elizabeth L. Eisenstein's influential 1979 book *The Printing Press as an Agent of Change*, which itself supplanted the once widely accepted elitist assumption that the popularization of literature via the printing press and the commercialization of the printed book represented an aesthetic devolution away from an idealized oral culture. Eisenstein's well-intentioned rejection of misguided efforts to demonize the eighteenth century's commodification of literature led her mistakenly to idealize the reach and democratizing potential of the new literary marketplace, promoting, in the words of Nicholas Hudson, a utopian "Whiggish" version of print history in which the tony aristocratic literary world gets swept away by a democratized flood of new writing from the emerging middle class, with women as major beneficiaries.[22] According to Margaret J. M. Ezell, the more complicated truth was that traditional "manuscript culture" was far longer lived than Eisenstein and her followers have suggested, and that "rather than being a nostalgic clinging to an outdated technology representing a fading aristocratic possession of the world of letters . . . manuscript culture permitted and encouraged participation in literary life of groups of people [such as women] whom print technology effectively isolated and alienated."[23] As Dustin H. Griffin argues in his book-length study of the English patronage system, rather than disappearing in the face of new forms of print reproduction and distribution, the patronage system simply continued in different forms, taking shape through the regular bestowal of monetary gifts, pensions, and plum appointments at court, the parsonage, or academia.[24] In the midst of all this, Pope nurtured his connections with his patrons, though he no longer explicitly referred to them as such; Griffin writes of how Pope embraced this anachronism by "[choosing] to present himself in letters and poems not as a painstaking craftsman or a brilliant entrepreneur but as a gentleman who wrote for his leisure and for the pleasure of a few noble friends, to whom he addressed many of his poetic epistles both early and late."[25] In Griffin's analysis, Pope maintained a near-perfect balance between these old and new literary worlds, never spurning his long-standing patrons in exchange for writerly credibility; that his constellation of friends "extended from patrons to booksellers" indicates the range of his achievement in cementing his unique position.[26] In portraying him as an aristocratic court dwarf, then, Pope's critics not only expose their resentment of what J. V. Guerinot calls Pope's class betrayal but also reveal their subconscious aversion to Pope's dwarflike existence as proof that the old system still exists, that their era was not as thoroughly modern as they would like to think, that they themselves might be metaphorical dwarfs, too. And thus, although the unsympathetic cruelty of their attacks on Pope's dwarfish body might seem to contradict the spirit of spectatorial empathy or self-identification directed toward the dwarf and little-men subjects of European court portraiture and eighteenth-century satirical engravings, the authors of Popiana reveal a kind of subconscious understanding that they themselves are not unlike the dwarfish little man they resent.

But who were these critics for whom the comparison between Pope and the early-eighteenth-century dwarf carried so much meaning, and what were their motives? For the most part, they were fellow professional writers who either were or imagined themselves to be the target "dunces" of Pope's *Dunciad* and retorted by cruelly and venomously putting Pope's small frame on display for ridicule and public consumption in pamphlet form. Their fundamental motives, according to Guerinot, were various, but most were rooted in the class-based ideological differences between Pope and themselves. Contrary to Pope's presentation of himself as a gentleman writer, these real-life "dunces" were, as Guerinot points out, the inhabitants of Grub Street. A writer of this breed who attacked Pope in pamphlet form was one who, in Guerinot's words, "was not writing a masterpiece for the happy few. . . . He was seeking commercial success. He was, in other words, the antithesis of the romantic 'Artist'—a hack writer . . . a man whose pen was for sale."[27] These writers thereby were not entirely misrepresented as such in Pope's *Dunciad* and Epistles to Bathurst and Arbuthnot, in which writers turn literary tricks for "half a crown" (a sum, as other critics have noted, that was the customary fee of a contemporaneous prostitute).[28] "Above all," writes Guerinot, "they did not share the aristocratic ethos. Their spirit was lower middle-class, capitalist, commercial. . . . They are concerned with profit, not with the transmission of a cultural tradition." As Guerinot posits in a passage worth quoting at length:

> In their hatred of Pope, therefore, one detects a powerful infusion of pure class-antagonism. Nothing offends them so much as the thought of Pope's wealth. Far more important to them even than his satire against them is the fact that he has made a fortune by literature and is thus free of the captivity they are enslaved to. That he has done this, at least in part, through a passionate concern for values which simply do not exist in their own world picture, a concern that has made him the spokesman, as Dryden was before him, of order in art, society, and man, simply compounds their antagonism. To the dunces, for these reasons, Pope appears a betrayer of his own class. Who was this Alexander Pope anyway? The son of a farmer or a hatter at best, they said, in an attempt to cut this man down socially. What right had he to a villa at Twickenham, to a comfortable income, and visiting acquain-

tance with half the peerage? Why should he be accepted on equal terms in households where their own acquaintanceship was among the footmen—and he a Catholic, a Jacobite, legally a pariah, to boot?[29]

Guerinot's contention that class antagonism—even at a time in which new conceptions of class difference were just coming into being—accounts for much, if not all, of the hostility directed against Pope in the many pamphlet attacks on him may be extended to suggest that Pope's critics, in depicting Pope as a "little gentleman" dwarf dependent on aristocratic patrons (aristocratic women in particular), implicitly invoke the classed and gendered history of the early-modern dwarf. Not only is Pope, in his critics' eyes, a perverse and despicable anachronism (like the outdated court dwarf, part aristocratic pet, part little gentleman); he is also a reminder that the modern economy and writing culture (what Ingrassia describes as the interconnected and parallel worlds of Exchange Alley and Grub Street) have not evolved as much in their favor as they would like to think. Dependent court dwarfs and their aristocratic patrons, and their counterparts in the eighteenth-century literary marketplace (the patronage system and its dependence on aristocratic favor and benevolence), are not dead and gone but instead flaunt their anachronistic presence in these "free-market" writers' faces.

Popiana

Throughout Popiana, such writerly class antagonism is combined with historically resonant references to dwarfishness. Thomas Bentley's *Letter to Mr. Pope, Occasioned by Sober Advice from Horace* (1735), for instance, combines insults about Pope's stature and business practices to accuse him of ruthless capitalism and shameless self-promotion. In denouncing Pope's promotion and sale of his *Imitations of Horace*, Bentley charges: "You sold those Imitations already published for 40 or 50 Pounds each. Fifty Pounds for 150, or 200 lines! . . . How dare you impose upon the Public at this rate?" And just several lines later, he accuses Pope of making a ridiculous spectacle of his tiny performing body: "'Tis very amazing, to see a little Creature, scarce four Foot high, whose very Sight makes one laugh, strutting and swelling like the Frog in Horace, and demanding the Adoration of all Mankind, because it can make fine Verses."[30] By combining the seemingly unrelated accusations of capitalistic greed and publicly performative littleness,

Bentley creates a caricature of Pope as a modern-day exhibiting dwarf who overcharges the "Public" by putting his ridiculously small body on display.

Similarly, a 1728 pamphlet accuses Pope of being a dwarfish creature ("A little scurvy, purblind-Elf; / Scarce like a Toad, much less himself. / Deform'd in Shape, of Pigmy Stature: / a proud, conceited, peevish Creature") whose pride and conceitedness are undermined not only by his small body but also by his lowly status as the son of a mere "Husbandman on *Windsor-Forest*"—only his physical limitations have caused his working-class parents to "excus[e] [him] from the laboring Work of the Field."[31] Here and elsewhere in Popiana, Pope's embodiment of both early and modern dwarf stereotypes is used to expose his aristocratic posturing as the false conceit of a mere laborer—in reality, he is a hungry scribbler like the rest of the dunces he deigns to look down upon.

This trend, here called the "dwarfing" of Pope, began with John Dennis's *Reflections Critical and Satyrical, Upon a Late Rhapsody Call'd an Essay Upon Criticism* (1711), a disproportionately cruel response to Pope's relatively minor slight of Dennis in his "Essay on Criticism." Repeatedly referring to Pope as "little author" and "little Gentleman"—the latter being a term traditionally used to denote court dwarfs—Dennis uses dwarf terminology to expose the hypocrisy and audacity of a writer of middle-class origins who poses as a nobleman. Writes Dennis: "While this little Author struts and affects the Dictatorian Air, he plainly shews that at the same time he is under the Rod; and the while he pretends to give Laws to others, he is himself a pedantic Slave to Authority and Opinion."[32] Pope, as Dennis sees him, is but a servile court dwarf who, ridiculously, fancies himself the king. Similarly, in a satirical mock heroic poem printed in pamphlet form in 1714 and purported to be written by an ancestor of Pope's, the author John Lacy takes another jab at Pope's littleness and his false and anachronistic presumptions to noble status, comparing "little P-pe" to Alexander the Great: "P-pe's name being *Alexander*, a *Little Man*, my Ancestor has describ'd him as a Second *Little Alexander the Great*."[33]

Pope's critics used other distinctly classed and gendered dwarf stereotypes against him as well, citing his erudition as further proof of his aristocratic dwarfishness. As Barbara Benedict has noted, the equating of big learning with small stature is typical of eighteenth-century depictions of dwarfs: "It was not merely that dwarfs were physically feeble but mentally powerful, but rather *because* their bodies were weak that their minds were strong. Popular discourse also implied that it was because dwarfs wasted their time on culture that their bodies shrank."[34] Giles Jacob, for instance, wrote of Pope in a one-shilling 1733 pamphlet titled "A legal Conviction of Mr. Alexander Pope of Dulness and Scandal, in the high Court of Parnassus": "So that it is from his Mind alone, whence this Source of Vanity essentially springs; and as his Body is so very unpromising a Figure, his Mind should be rare and excellent to lift him to that Pitch of Pride which he hath lately so eminently display'd."[35] Just as in earlier and contemporaneous depictions of overly cultivated dwarfs, the size of Pope's body is portrayed here as inversely proportional to his mind, implying that his erudition is reprehensibly dwarfish and, by association, a sign of aristocratic vanity. As with Dennis's 1711 attack, the reader is meant to laugh at Pope as a court dwarf who, because of his noble bearings and associations with royalty, imagines himself a monarch, as if in direct imitation of the court dwarf's gradual supplanting of royalty in seventeenth-century portraiture.

Pope's critics repeatedly invoked the outdated though still resonant stereotype of dwarfs as aristocratic women's playthings in their attacks on Pope for his cultivation of female readers, patrons, and subscribers—a self-promotional strategy of Pope's that is well documented by Claudia N. Thomas in her book on Pope and his female readers.[36] In one bawdy pamphlet satire printed in 1721, the author describes Pope as the erotic object of aristocratic women for whom his small stature is not a deterrent but the very source of their attraction: "his Person is as amiable as his *Muse*, and certainly not to be seen by *any of the Sex* without some fatal Effect." Likewise, in Edward Ward's *Apollo's Maggot in his Cups: Or, The Whimsical Creation of a Little Satyrical Poet. A Lyrick Ode* (1729), Pope is a "little satirical poet" fawned over by "Ladies" who love him not for his mind but for the amusement his puny body gives them: "Nor do the Ladies that frequent / The Wells, for Health and Merriment, / Tho' to thy Merits over kind, / Admire the Beauties of thy Mind, / But like them, as they do their Apes, Not for thy Wit, but Monkey-shapes"; these lines hark back to the implicit comparisons between ladies' pet monkeys and dwarfs made by pre-1700 court portraiture.[37] Relating Pope's small stature to his popularity among women readers, Aaron Hill's *The Progress of Wit: A Caveat* (1730) calls Pope "The Ladies Play-thing, and the Muses Pride," implying that in spite of his poetic talent, he, like a court dwarf of yore, is to aristocratic women a mere (sex) toy, a comparison that works only because of Pope's well-known appeal to aristocratic women and patrons.[38]

Pope's critics did not miss the opportunity to seize on one particularly potent example of his court dwarfishness with regard to women: his well-known friendship turned courtship turned rivalry with Lady Mary Wortley Montagu, who, early in their relationship, functioned as a sort of "patron of the arts" to her artistically celebrated but socially and physically lower friend. In one 1732 anti-Pope pamphlet, written as a mock Restoration-era comedy, the Pope stand-in, Alexander Taste, is described as a farmer's son and "Poet who, in spite of deformity, imagines every Woman he sees in love with him, and imprudently makes Addresses to Lady Airy," an obvious proxy for Lady Mary. Like an aristocratic woman's favorite dwarf, he is granted by Lady Airy "the Liberty of hopping about my Rooms sometimes, because the Folly and Vanity of the Creature diverted me." Lady Mary herself famously joined the fray after resisting Pope's romantic overtures, publicly insulting in verse Pope's "wretched little Carcass."[39] Pope, rather than refusing to be dwarfed by his associations with Lady Mary and other aristocratic ladies, embraced such depictions of himself as a dwarflike fetish object of female aristocrats in order to use them against Lady Mary, labeling her a sexually perverse aristocratic fetishizer of dwarfs, and therefore perhaps even more perverse than he. In the following rondeau, for instance, a variation of one by Voiture, Pope writes:

> You know where you did despise
> (T'other day) my little Eyes,
> Little Legs, and little Thighs,
> And some things, of little Size,
> You know where.
> You, 'tis true, have fine black eyes,
> Taper Legs, and tempting Thighs,
> Yet what more than all we prize
> Is a Thing of little Size,
> You know where.[40]

Pope's dwarfish body, the poem implies, might indeed be a sexually impotent fetish object, but that only makes Lady Mary his equally reprehensible counterpart, an oversexed female aristocrat with a correspondingly oversize (and therefore undesirable) vagina.

Even in his courtship of Lady Mary before their falling out, Pope seems to have taken a perverse pleasure in playing the court dwarf to her female aristocrat, fantasizing in one of his many love letters to her about his desire to "meet you in Lombardy, the Scene of those celebrated Amours between the fair Princess and her Dwarf."[41] As the editors of Pope's correspondence point out, Pope's reference to "the fair Princess and her Dwarf" alludes to the poem "Woman" in the Dryden-Tonson *Poetical Miscellanies* of 1709, a short piece of comic erotica that tells the story of a queen who carries on an affair with "the King's ugly Dwarf" and is spied on through a peephole having sex with her diminutive paramour, thereby "slight[ing] the King, / For such an ugly, little thing."[42] By invoking that poem in his letter to Lady Mary, Pope appropriates the classed and sexualized court-dwarf metaphors used by his critics and turns their insults into a self-aggrandizing sexual fantasy in which his body is fetishized not for its reprehensible deformity but for its admirable uniqueness.[43]

Keenly aware of the hindrance his stature posed to any attempt at courtship, especially in the case of a woman as comely and brilliant as Lady Mary, Pope may very likely have penned the anonymously published sonnet, "Of a Dwarf Courting a Bright Lady," that appeared in the very same sixth part of the Dryden-Tonson *Poetical Miscellanies*:

> Giants, that durst invade the Sky
> By wrathful Pow'rs were doom'd to Die;
> Shall better Fate this Pygmy share,
> Who dares attempt a Heav'nly fair? . . .
> Strike this absurd Assailant Dead,
> And make his Grave his Bridal Bed.
> This Lofty Tree to Heaven Aspires
> And who can blame his Bold Desires?
> 'Tis for that End he seems so grown,
> And therefore's wondered at by none.
> But if some humble shrub would soar,
> Meant for the ground, and nothing more,
> All this pretending Folly chide
> And laugh at its prepost'rous Pride.[44]

Here, a dwarf's desire for a normal-size "Lady" is depicted as both fatally futile ("strike this absurd Assailant Dead, / And make his Grave his Bridal Bed") and laughably hubristic, his desires making him a "humble shrub" attempting to "soar," in a full body erection of sorts, like a "Lofty Tree." In the world of the poem and its metaphorical conflation of social and physical stature, the dwarf's attempt to circumvent both the height disparity and the hierarchical social differences separating himself and his "Lady" will always be seen as a ridiculous spectacle of "prepost'rous Pride." Formally speaking, the poem's use of Pope's signature heroic couplets underscores a dwarfism of its own: the writer is using short rhymed couplets with a heroic grandiosity more befitting the ancient world than the modern, underscoring the anachronistic nature of the protagonist's own particular brand of dwarfishness.

Not all portrayals of Pope as an aristocratically identified court dwarf sexualized alongside female superiors depict the seraglio in question as aristocratic. Colley Cibber's 1742 pamphlet *A Letter From Mr. Cibber, To Mr. Pope*, for instance, depicts him instead as an aristocratic court-dwarf type hubristically attempting to penetrate both a normal-size woman and the modern world of (sexual and literary) public commerce represented here by a venereal-disease-ridden whorehouse. Using physical stature as an inversely proportional indication of social stature, Cibber accuses "our little Gentleman," Pope, of entering a brothel and proposing "to slip his little *Homer*, as he call'd him, at a Girl of the Game, that he might see what sort of Figure a Man of his Size . . . would make." The little poet's penis is referred to as "the little-tiny Manhood of Mr. Pope," and his pathetic attempt at sexual intercourse is described as a perverse and physically ridiculous scenario: Cibber claims to have thrown "open the Door upon him, where I found this little hasty Hero, like a terrible *Tom Tit*, pertly perching upon the Mount of Love."[45] In another Cibber pamphlet on the same subject, "my little Tom Tit" is "shewn a *ridiculous Lover*," whom Cibber finds "crawling on the Boson of thy dear Damself, he gently, with a Finger and a Thumb, picked off thy small round Body, by thy long Legs, like a Spider, making Love in a Cobweb."[46] Eighteenth-century readers would have been familiar with Tom Tit, the miniature trickster of the English folktale "Tom Tit Tot," about a tiny man who saves a woman and demands her hand in marriage as a reward unless she guesses his name—a variation on the Rumpelstiltskin myth. Indeed, the very mythological status of the "Tom Tit Tot" parable (its precise origins are unknown, but it long predates the eighteenth century) constitutes another jab at the anachronistic nature of Pope's unique embodiment of dwarfism. Through their invocation of dwarf stereotypes both old and new, Cibber's Tom Tit pieces make Pope out to be an old-fashioned aristocratic dwarf, a "Little Gentleman" who belongs neither in his present place (the whorehouse, simultaneously embodying the worlds of both sex and commerce) nor time (modernity). Both displacements expose his impotence as a social actor in the sexual and commercial worlds. Here, "Little Gentleman" Pope's small physical stature is inversely proportionate to his high social stature, a fact that, far from putting him at an advantage over his social inferiors, only emphasizes his inability to produce sexually or commercially within the metaphorically conflated sexual and literary marketplaces. In this anecdote, Cibber portrays himself as Pope's "savior" in the literary/sexual marketplace where both sex and literature are for sale, a world that Cibber claims to know far better than Pope. Pope, a horny and out-of-place aristocratic court dwarf pathetically trying to mount a modern prostitute in a public brothel, literally cannot fit into the modern literary marketplace, the inner workings of which (like the mechanics of the female body) his literary rival, Cibber, pretends to know far better.

In portraying Pope as a sexualized yet sexually impotent dwarf, Cibber and the other critics who portray Pope as a court dwarf in relation to women all draw from an old stereotype of dwarfs, according to which penetrative sexual intercourse between male dwarfs and normal-size women and actual sexual reproduction are physically impossible, however much aristocratic women may sexually fetishize dwarfs.[47] This stereotype had been debunked by the time of the eighteenth century but was still invoked occasionally, in spite of several highly publicized sexually reproductive marriages between male dwarfs and normal-size women. It plays out in Waller's poem on the marriage of two dwarfs (discussed in chapter 1) and is also invoked in a *Gentleman's Magazine* article on the dwarf Jeffrey Hudson's renown among aristocratic women: "The ladies were fond of him. He could make married men cuckolds without making them jealous, and Mothers of the Maids, without letting the World know they had any Gallants."[48] Like the false eunuch Horner in Wycherley's *Country Wife*, dwarfs like Hudson could associate freely with normal-size women without being suspected of penetrating them in any traditional sense of the term. In a 1711 *Spectator* essay on the social value of female chastity, for instance, Joseph Addison remarks on how in "Books of Chivalry," the female protagonist "must have a Dwarf for her Page" in order to avoid a sexual scandal.[49] As one critic points out, even classical representations of dwarfs as large-phallused Dionysian icons of lust show that they were seen as sexually impotent, for "despite their association with virility," they were typically "viewed as disappointed lovers—better known for desire than for its fulfillment."[50] It is this long-standing stereotype of male dwarf sexuality that Popiana employs in its portrayal of Pope as a lustful and sexually fetishized object of his aristocratic female acquaintances and patrons, who is nonetheless incapable of successfully penetrating the literary marketplace or producing commercially viable literary output. Pope's relation to women, Popiana implies, is not a normative reproductive one but a queerly masochistic one, in which male sexual masochism is equated with the commercially unproductive literary masochism involved in Pope's court-dwarfish affiliation with the aristocracy and his submission to (female) patrons and other social (and physical) superiors. Male sexual potency and productivity, by contrast, is associated with largeness both in physical stature and in literary productivity. Like the anticommercial Thomas Gray half a century later, who feared that his resistance to the commercial marketplace's emphasis on quantity over quality in literary production might result in his modestly numbered "works . . . be[ing] mistaken for the works of a flea" and himself being mistaken for "a shrimp of an author," Pope, in Cibber's eyes, is a pathetic "shrimp" of an author—the insufficiency of his bodily and literary corpus underscored by his court-dwarfishness and his self-contradictory attempts to penetrate and master the commercial marketplace.[51]

Popiana's use of the long-established connection between dwarfs and aristocrats to make physical shortness a metaphor for commercial ineptitude is symptomatic of an era in which many imagined an inverse relationship between writers' commercial popularity and their aesthetic greatness, and in which male physical stature was often used as a metaphor for social stature. This idea that the commercialization of a work of literature makes it aesthetically "little" is expressed in John Brown's 1757 *An Estimate of the Manners and Principles of the Times*, in which he reflects that "The Laurel Wreath, once aspired after as the highest Object of Ambition, would now be rated at the Market-price of its Materials, and derided as a *Three-penny Crown*."[52] Although for more liberal thinkers such as David Hume, commercial appeal and aesthetic value went hand in hand (Hume professed that "arts and commerce [are] the necessary attendants of liberty and equality"), even Hume, as James Noggle points out, manifests an awareness that in order to claim literary refinement, one must sometimes embrace the elitist and anticommercial view that the relationship between aesthetic merit and commercialism are often inversely proportional, admitting that "[s]ometimes arts flourish when commerce languishes or liberty flounders."[53] In this self-contradiction of Hume's, and throughout the eighteenth century, writes Noggle, "a gap appears between . . . Britain's liberal, commercial pieties and its [aristocratic and elitist] sense of its own cultural refinement."[54] For Pope and his critics, this conceptual gap between the liberal commercial values of the eighteenth century and its lingering belief in an aristocratic and elitist brand of aesthetics brought about the possibility that if Pope's shortness could signify low utility, commercial ineptitude, and aristocratic identification all at once, then the very physical and metaphorical markers of his high aesthetic talent could also be used to signify his social irrelevance within the new literary marketplace. And thus, in Popiana's pseudo-populist attack on its "highbrow" dwarfish nemesis, the difference between highbrow and lowbrow—a difference that, as Martha Woodmansee writes, was invented in the eighteenth century—is perceived as inversely relational to physical stature.[55] Pope's art may be great, his critics suggest, but his relevance to the modern world, like his dwarfish body, is small.

The publication of Swift's *Gulliver's Travels* in 1726 made possible another genre of sexualized anti-Pope satire that also played on the parallels between the history of dwarf representation and the prejudices of and about the new literary marketplace: the portrayal of Pope as the patronized Gulliverian toy of Brobdingnagian noblewomen. In one, *Memoirs of the Court of Lilliput. Written by Captain Gulliver*, once thought to have been authored by Eliza Haywood (whom Pope ridiculed in the *Dunciad*), Gulliver tells a Lilliputian maid of honor that

> the inequality of our Stature rightly consider'd ought to be for us as full a Security from Slander, as that between Mr. *P-pe*, and those *great* Ladies who do nothing without him; admit him to their Closets, their Bed-sides, consult him in the choice of their Servants, their Garments, and make no scruple of putting them on or off before him: Every body knows they are Women of strict Virtue, and he a harmless Creature, who has neither the Will, nor Power of doing any farther Mischief than with his Pen.[56]

Capable of doing mischief to women only with his pen as opposed to his penis, Pope in this Gulliverian satire appears as an aristocratic court dwarf of Lady Mary's and the other aristocratic women in his circle of patronage and friendship—characterizing the author as sexually fetishized by his female patrons but commercially impotent himself.

At around the same time that Pope was being satirized as a miniature masochistic sexual prop for Brobdingnagian lady-patrons, he penned "The Lamentation of Glumdalclitch, for the Loss of Grildrig. A Pastoral," Glumdalclitch being the Brobdingnagian farm girl who first owns Gulliver, calls him by the pet name Grildrig, and moves with him into the Brobdingnagian court when he is bought by the queen. As Pope's Glumdalclitch says of those "filthy Sluts" in searching for her precious Grildrig, she failed to look in the one place he was sure to be found, in perverse double entendre, in a giantess's vagina: "Why did I not suspect Hippina's Muff, / And search the shag of Thighatira's Ruff."[57] Similar to his responses to Lady Mary's attempts to dwarf him in print, Pope appropriates his female critics' metaphor here in order to portray the women concerned with his small body as more perverse than he, and himself as miniature victim of their insatiable sexual and literary appetites.

Pope as Pygmy-Dwarf Hybrid

Another noteworthy trend in dwarf-related Popiana is the tendency to combine portrayals of Pope as a ladies' dwarf with characterizations of the author in primate metaphors as a ladies' "Ape" and "monkey." Sometimes, as in Dennis's "A True Character of Mr. Pope and his Writings" (1716), the author simply refers to Pope as a "monkey" or "Baboon,"[58] but elsewhere others play on his initials, renaming him "AP-E."[59] The connection between monkeys and court dwarfs was a pervasive one, not only in court painting (as, for example, with Van Dyck's portrait of Queen Henrietta with Jeffrey Hudson, discussed in chapter 1) but also in the cultural imagination at large. Monkeys, like dwarfs, had been the exotic playthings of aristocratic women since the Middle Ages and were linked to the sexuality of female aristocrats and nobility. According to Andrew Wilton, primates were occasionally used in European portraiture to represent lust, and, as Fiedler remarks, they often "functioned as court pets side by side with Dwarfs," one explicitly animalistic, the other definitively human.[60] In a manner typical of what Deutsch identifies as Pope's tendency to resignify his attackers' insults against his physical deformities as a means of self-empowerment, Pope plays on the metaphor of himself as a woman's pet monkey in a letter to John Caryll: "But if you know one particular Nymph that can carry herself and me, whom you can give upon [your] word, pray acquaint me, that I may wear her Chain forthwith; I fancy my Size and Abilities may qualify me to match her Monkey very well."[61] Here, Pope humorously reconfigures his critics' occasional dehumanization of his small body as a sign of his enviably animalistic sexual prowess.

Although separated by their relative embodiment of or lack of humanity, the figures of the dwarf and monkey come together in Popiana through the image of the pygmy, that small-statured cultural Other who, in the eighteenth century, was imagined to be part man and part monkey. A 1729 pamphlet, *Pope Alexander's Supremacy and Infallibility examin'd* (a title that belittles the Catholic poet's ostensibly lofty reputational stature by comparing it to the unpopular idea of papal infallibility), which includes an oft-duplicated frontispiece depicting Pope as a crowned monkey perched on a pedestal and hunched over a pile of books, describes the poet as:

> Half Man, half Monkey, own'd by neither Race.
> Be his Crown Picked, to One Side reclin'd,
> Be to his Neck his Buttocks closely join'd;
> With Breast protuberant, and Belly thin,
> Bones all distorted, and a shrivell'd Skin.
> This his Misshapen Form: But say, what Art
> Can frame the monst'rous Image of his Heart.
> Compos'd of *Malice, Envy, Discontent,*
> Like his Limbs crooked, like them impotent.[62]

In addition to the accompanying illustration's allusion to stereotypes of dwarfs as royal and overly cultivated, the detailed anatomical description "Half Man, half Monkey" fits the well-known illustration of a pygmy in Edward Tyson's influential though error-laden tract on the subject, *The Anatomy of a Pygmy* (London, 1699). In Tyson's illustration (fig. 13), by Flemish engraver Michael van der Gucht, as in the frontispiece to *Pope Alexander's Supremacy and Infallibility examin'd*, the pygmy is depicted with large chest (in the aforementioned poem, "Breast protuberant"), small abdomen ("Belly thin"), overlong arms ("Bones all distorted"), and cocked head ("his Crown Picked, to One Side reclin'd").[63] Tyson's main point in this pseudoscientific tract (the author is presented as a "Fellow of the College of Physicians, and the Royal Society") is to make the scientific case that African pygmy skeletons resemble monkeys more than men, supposedly proving that pygmies, both ancient and modern, are "all either APES or MONKEYS, and not MEN, as formerly pretended," thereby placing the pygmy on the inferior side of the *Homo nocturnus* (primate) / *Homo diurnus*

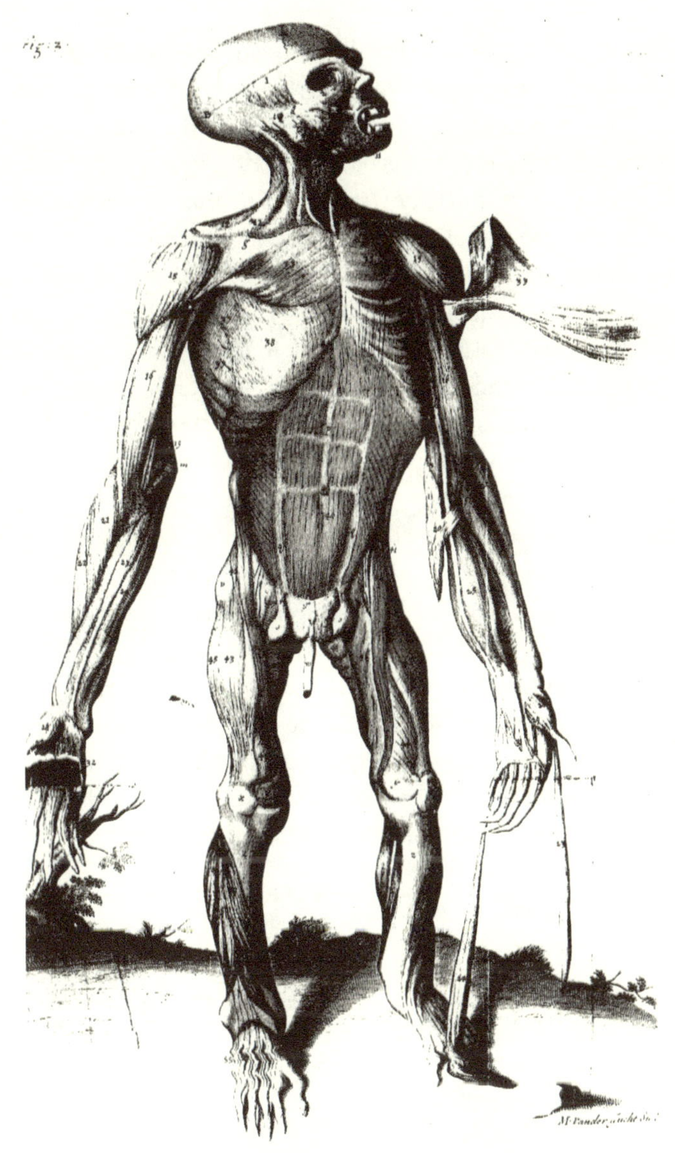

FIGURE 13 Michael van der Gucht (Flemish, 1660–1725), Frontal view of pygmy musculature. Engraving. Unpaginated plate from Edward Tyson, *Orang-outang, sive, Homo sylvestris, or, The anatomy of a pygmie compared with that of a monkey, an ape, and a man to which is added, A philological essay concerning the pygmies, the cynocephali, the satyrs and sphinges of the ancients : wherein it will appear that they are all either apes or monkeys, and not men, as formerly pretended* (London, 1699). Courtesy of ProQuest and Rare Books and Special Collections Division of the Library of Congress.

(human) binarism that would eventually be drawn by Linnaeus in 1758.[64] By invoking the man-monkey figure of Tyson's pygmy for the purpose of supplementing their portrayals of Pope as an antiquated court dwarf caught between old and new literary and economic worlds, Pope's critics were able both to dehumanize him *and* to portray him as an anachronism, the primitiveness of the modern pygmy representing an anachronism as powerful as (although antithetical in social status to) that of the displaced aristocratic court dwarf. Such pygmy imagery in Popiana also underscored his association with the Ancients, dating pygmies back to the mythical Homeric battle between the cranes and the pygmies. Since eighteenth-century popular opinion considered dwarfs to be miniature humans (they were not thought of as monsters until the nineteenth century, as noted in chapter 1),[65] Pope's attackers occasionally implemented such dubious conflations of dwarf and pygmy imagery in order to depict their rival writer as a living anachronism and aristocratic female plaything (through their invocation of the historically resonant rhetoric of dwarf representation) and at the same time as another species.

Another verse pamphlet, *A Poetical Dialogue: Occasioned by A Late Letter from the Laureat of St. James's, To the Homer of Twickenham*, dated August 31, 1742, alleges that Pope's pygmy status with women (who despise him as somewhere between "Man" and "Monkey") is the reason for his poetic misogyny in poems such as "Of the Characters of Women":

> For who, except a venal *Punkey*,
> That car'd not whether Man or *Monkey*,
> But set to Sale her *Titillation*,
> For Bread, not carnal Recreation,
> Would suffer Thee, *small* Friend, to come
> Within ten Foot of her *Fore-bum*?[66]

Only a prostitute or patroness would allow herself to be penetrated by this revolting hybrid of man, monkey, pygmy, and dwarf, who in the same piece draws his "*pigmy Oar*," a "*Quill*" "so *very, very small*, / I trust, it holds but little *Gall*."[67] This physically ridiculous creature, paradoxically both primitive like a monkey and overly cultivated like a court dwarf, the author implies, is simultaneously dwarf, pygmy, monkey, and human, although his human side is belittled such that his penis, if not his pen—which still gains the favor of whorish female patrons—is imagined to be as impotent with regard to the ladies as the stereotypical sexualized but neutered aristocratic court dwarfs of yore. Popiana's occasional conflation of disparate dwarf and pygmy imagery, then, took the form of a self-contradictorily, sloppily mixed metaphor (how could Pope be both subhuman like a pygmy and an overly cultivated aristocrat like a court dwarf?), but it did its job of invoking the potent dwarf stereotypes used to characterize him elsewhere in Popiana as an anachronistically aristocratic writer out of place in the modern commercial world he attempts to penetrate, while at the same time dehumanizing him as a premodern literary primate both sexually and aesthetically displaced within modern civilization.

The Short Club

What did Pope stand to gain by affirming his critics' problematic use of such diverse and often contradictory dwarf and little-man stereotypes? In addition to suggesting that the aristocratic women in his dwarf-fetishizing circle of female friends and patrons were even more perverse than he (Lady Mary in particular), Pope's redirection of his critics' dwarf metaphors also indicated that the figure of the emasculated male dwarf characterized not only Pope himself but all other modern writers as well, including and especially his attackers. A case in point is Pope's "To Quinbus Flestrin the Man Mountain. An Ode. By Titty Tit, Esq; Poet Laureate to his Majesty of Lilliput. Translated into English," composed in 1726 upon his first reading of *Gulliver's Travels* and printed in 1727. Written in satirically short rhymed couplets ("In Amaze / Lost, I gaze! / Can our Eyes / Reach thy Size?"), the poem is narrated by the Lilliputian poet Titty Tit, who flatters the patron-like Gulliver, requesting to stand on his hand so that he might reach loftier aesthetic heights ("On thy Hand / Let me stand, / So shall I, / Lofty Poet! Touch the Sky"). Depicting the poet as a dependent Lilliputian flattering a potential patron ("May my Lays / Swell with Praise / Worthy thee! / Worthy me!"), the poem is as much a portrayal of his hypocritically dependent court-dwarfish critics and fellow writers as it is the autobiographical commentary of a real-life Lilliputian poet attempting to succeed within a print market that was not fully modernized.[68] If the sycophantic and sexually masochistic court dwarf seems to embody the flattery of one's betters still required in the literary marketplace, the poem suggests, then Pope himself may be the most obvious and successful example but by no means the sole practitioner. Indeed, as Abigail Williams argues, some of Pope's most antiaristocratic Grub Street critics were themselves the beneficiaries not of the new free market but of a system of "aristocratic patronage that supported many Whig writers" in the early eighteenth century, including the Whiggish Kit-Kat Club. Ironically, Williams observes, "[t]he evidence of such a well-developed patronage system suggests that many Whig poets . . . were far from being the penniless Grub Street hacks lampooned by Alexander Pope or Jonathan Swift, and they benefited—unlike these Tory writers—from unprecedented levels of financial support from the Whig aristocracy," a point made by Pope himself in this short verse satire of a representatively dwarfish modern writer praising an enormous benefactor.[69]

Nowhere, however, does Pope more effectively deflect such loaded dwarf metaphors from himself and onto modern literary culture at large than in his three humorous *Guardian* pieces on the subject of male stature, published in June 1713. About a fictitious Short Club and a rival Tall Club, they describe an organization of men under five feet tall, and another organization formed to counteract this trend-setting group that has set a new, belittling, and undesirable standard of masculinity that others feel pressured to follow. The first of these, Pope's two Short Club pieces, are written in the form of letters addressed to the journal by Bob Short, the club's secretary and a man "half as tall as an ordinary man," who has established a club "by which he hopes to bring those of his own size into a little reputation."[70] The motto of the club, states Bob Short, is "Dare to be short," and the aim of its members is to "boldly bear out the dignity of littleness under the noses of those enormous engrossers of manhood, those hyperbolical monsters of the species, the tall fellows that overlook us."[71] Since these pieces have yet to be analyzed beyond their autobiographical significance,[72] it is important to understand how they function as self-defensive satires of the dwarflike status and aspirations of Pope's Grub Street critics. In "dar[ing] to be short," Pope's critics embrace their lowbrow aesthetic and commercial stature against the critiques of their highbrow superiors.

Like the often cliquish Grub Street writing culture to which many of Pope's critics belonged, this Short Club is, after all, a club of writers whose president, Dick Distick, is identified primarily as a writer, a "little poet," elected "not only as he is the shortest of us all, but because he has entertained so just a sense of the stature, as to go generally in black, that he may appear yet less. Nay, to that perfection is he arrived, that he stoops as he walks. . . . But indeed what principally moved us in his favour was his talent in poetry, for he hath promised to undertake a long work in short verse to celebrate the heroes of our size."[73] Critics have tended to see Dick Distick as Pope's "self portrait,"[74] but it is more precise to say that as a reputationally insignificant poet whose every action emphasizes his smallness, he is a paradigmatic modern writer, much like Pope's critics or the imagined writer of this piece, who is also identified as a minor male writer of a socially and aesthetically even lesser kind, "Bob Short, Secretary."[75] In fact, writing is at the center of the Short and Tall Clubs' agendas. Toward the end of the Tall Club piece, the Tall Club representative compares the writing skills of his club's members to those of his small-statured rivals:

> I know the short club value themselves very much upon Mr. Distick, the poet, who may possibly play some of his Pentameters upon us, but if he does he shall certainly be answered in Alexandrines. For we have a poet among us of a genius as exalted as his stature, and who is very well read in Longinus his treatise concerning the sublime. Besides, I would have Mr. Distick consider, that if Horace was a short man, Museus, who makes such a noble figure in Virgil's sixth Aeneid, was taller by the head and shoulders than all the people of Elysium.[76]

In this light, Pope's Short Club may be said to function as a satire of the clubbish and paranoid tendencies of the very same "lowbrow" Grub Street writing culture that has attacked Pope so frequently in print:

> We have spies appointed in every quarter of the town, to give us informations of the misbehavior of such refractory persons as refuse to be subject to our statutes. Whatsoever aspiring practices any of these our people shall be guilty of in their amours, single combats, or any indirect means to manhood, we shall certainly be acquainted with, and *publish to the world* for their punishment and reformation. For the president has granted me the sole property of exposing and shewing to the town all such intractable dwarfs, whose circumstances exempt them from being carried about in boxes: Reserving only to himself, as the right of a poet, those smart characters that will shine in epigrams.[77]

Here, the staturally and aesthetically insignificant writers of the Short Club are shown to police their members just as Pope's lesser critics policed him, accusing him in writing and in the public arena (in their published attacks) of being a dwarf hypocritically guilty of "aspiring practices."

Demonstrating the flexibility of the dwarf-writer analogy, Pope also uses it to suggest that if he himself is a court-dwarfish flatterer of his aristocratic female patrons and admirers, then he is no different from his lesser peers, who include, for instance, the "little lover," Tom Tiptoe, "the most gallant lover of the age" and a lover exclusively of tall women who, in one case indicative of the dwarf writer's dependence on socially superior women readers and patrons, ties himself to a tall woman's toe.[78] The biggest threat to the Tall Club is the possibility that women should actually come to prefer dwarf writers like Pope: "If the ladies should once take a liking to such a diminutive race of lovers, we should, in a little time, see mankind epitomized, and the whole species in miniature."[79] Here, Pope gets to the heart of his attackers' transferential anxieties, their worry that Pope's court-dwarfish status among his female readers and patrons only highlights their own need to flatter a female readership whom they are incapable—because of their artistic, reputational, and socially low stature—of attracting or satisfying with either their physical or their literary bodies (of work).

In contrast to Popiana's depiction of male littleness as a court-dwarfish anachronism, Pope's Short Club pieces envision these little male writers as distinctly modern, a sentiment indicated by the Tall Club representative's statement that "we serve our country by discouraging this little breed, and hindering it from coming into fashion. If the fair sex look upon us with an eye of favor, we shall make some attempts to lengthen out the human figure, and restore it to its ancient procerity."[80] The letter writer's invocation of "serv[ing] our country" emphasizes that the problem of little men is a national problem, and to correct it is an act of patriotism. At the same time, his use of the phrase "coming into fashion" equates this trend with the advent of modern consumerism, while his suggestion of restoring the male body "to its ancient procerity" invokes the Moderns versus Ancients debates of the late seventeenth and early eighteenth centuries, in which modern Englishmen were often described as "dwarfs standing on the shoulders of [ancient] giants."[81] The implication then is that those "lowbrow" modern writers who are not naturally dwarfish like Pope (a socially elevated and "highbrow" modern author) struggle to measure up to the contradictory expectations of the modern literary marketplace by unsuccessfully attempting to become dwarfs themselves. As the unnamed representative of the Tall Club complains, modern Englishmen actually strive to be short and go to extreme means to do so, including one "overgrown runt" who "has struck off his heels, lowered his fore top, and contracted his figure, that he might be looked upon as a member of this new erected society."[82] And thus, in Pope's clever reframing of his critics' dwarf and little-men metaphors, all writers are either successful and self-aware modern little men like Pope or paranoid and socially/artistically inferior want-to-be dwarfs like his critics. Such writers hate Pope only because they strive to be self-contradictorily dwarfish and little-mannish like him: a bridger of the old and new worlds of aristocratic patronized dependence and independent "free market" middle-class modernity; a high-class and highbrow courter and pet of comparatively big women (and therefore a financially successful flatterer within the still thriving patronage system); and a popular commercial entertainer of the public "at large."

three

THE LITTLE MAN–MICROSCOPE IN BROBDINGNAG

After the publication of Jonathan Swift's *Gulliver's Travels* in 1726, the notion of the little man no longer necessarily conjured up images of old and new kinds of real and metaphorical dwarfs in the imaginations of the expanding male and female English reading public. Given the enormous success of Swift's book and its widely available imitations and offshoots, the Gulliver-mad reading public was more likely to have in mind the even smaller six-inch Lilliputians from that book's first section or, just as likely, the equally fantastical reversal of circumstances in the second section, in which the normal-size English hero becomes a little man himself in a world that seems initially to consist of predominantly female giants. As Jonathan Lamb has noted, Lemuel Gulliver's adventures in Brobdingnag, where "the hero is treated by turns as an animal, automaton, and insect," place that section of *Gulliver's Travels* within the genre of the eighteenth-century "it-narrative," in which circulating objects (typically small objects like corkscrews and banknotes) become the little (and typically male-gendered) protagonists of these cynical send-ups of modern consumerism.[1] This chapter explores the connection between Swift's portrayal of Gulliver as a circulating little man–thing alongside enormous women in Brobdingnag and the curiously gendered and sexualized eighteenth-century culture of microscopy by which the little is made large and, although less obviously, the large (specifically, the paradigmatic Enlightened man of science as well as the actual thing, the microscope, itself) is made little.

The Microscope in Brobdingnag

Marjorie Nicolson's well-known analysis of the microscopical subtext of the first two sections of Jonathan Swift's *Gulliver's Travels* has remained the standard reading on the subject since the publication of her 1955 essay "The Microscope and the English Imagination." Nicolson argues that Gulliver becomes a metaphorical microscopist in Lilliput, where he is an elevated observer of small creatures and objects, and even more so in Brobdingnag, where his scientific curiosity is complemented by a perspective that makes everyday objects appear to him in magnified detail, as if seen through a microscope.[2] As evidence, she cites Gulliver's dissection of giant Brobdingnagian wasps and his preservation of their stingers as a gift to Gresham College (the Royal Society) as well as the famous passages in which he observes Brobdingnagian anatomy in hideously magnified detail: witness Gulliver's recollection of one of "the most horrible spectacles that ever an European eye beheld . . . a woman with a cancer in her breast, swelled to a monstrous size, full of holes, in two or three of which I could have easily crept, and covered my whole body."[3] For Nicolson, "A Voyage to Brobdingnag" serves as one of many examples of covertly and overtly microscope-oriented fiction, drama, and periodical literature of the time. When read together as a genre, she argues, these texts demonstrate how the figure of the microscopist and his fascination with little worlds made large was a popular object of both satire and awe in the age of Enlightenment.

Nicolson's broader argument about *Gulliver's Travels*—that its Brobdingnag section is indicative of microscopy's appeal to writers outside the scientific community—is undeniably sound, but her sweeping thesis on Gulliver's role as microscopist in Brobdingnag demands some careful rethinking. For if Gulliver does play the part of microscopist in Brobdingnag, then he is a most unusual kind: an accidental microscopist who views things he would rather not see and then curses his magnified vision, an unwanted perspective used as often to observe or accompany women's bodies as to study insects and objects. Moreover, it is not Gulliver's "enlightened" mind but his puny body that endows him with microscope-like sight and compels him, helplessly and aversely, to observe not his *own* skin and specimens but a Brobdingnagian woman's breast, "so varified with spots, pimples and freckles, that nothing could appear more nauseous," as well as insects' "loathsome excrement or spawn . . . which to me was very visible, though not to the natives of that country, whose large optics were not so acute as mine in viewing smaller objects."[4] Gulliver's role in these passages and in others like them is that of a miniature "seeing-object," whose singular function is to view everything in magnified detail but without the power to pick and choose the objects of his magnified gaze—a power that belongs not to Gulliver but to his gigantic and predominantly female owners and manipulators. All of this makes the Brobdingnagian Gulliver far less of an eighteenth-century micro*scopist* than an eighteenth-century micro*scope*, particularly when we consider that Swift's writing of the fictitious Gulliver's reduction to a small woman-manipulated object with magnified vision coincided with the actual microscope's historical "decline" from a sizable and relatively inaccessible tool of male-dominated science for most of the seventeenth century to the portable commodity popular with middle- and upper-class women by the early eighteenth century.

A closer look at the wasp-stinger incident cited by Nicolson, for example, reveals that Gulliver is in a position to observe these enormous specimens in magnified detail only because he happens to have been placed on a windowsill by his gigantic female owner, who carries him about in a specially made box or "traveling closet," just like the popular pocket microscopes of the day.[5] As if to underscore Gulliver's status as a miniature woman-owned seeing-object, Swift begins the anecdote not with Gulliver's search for wasp stingers to dissect and donate to the Royal Society but with his recollecting that "I remember one morning when Glumdalclitch had set me in my box upon a window."[6] In fact, Gulliver holds the position of microscopist for only a very short time—if at all—in Brobdingnag before he embarks on a three-stage devolution from (1) microscopist to miniature microscope, to (2) a woman-owned miniature microscope, and finally to (3) a woman-owned miniature microscope cum sexual prop in the hands of the queen's maids of honor (other critics have commented upon the maids' use of Gulliver as sexual prop but without noting its microscopical subtext).[7] Gulliver's role as a miniature microscope and his cumulative devolution to a freakish hybrid of pocket microscope and sex toy expose a heretofore unexplored satirical element of "A Voyage to Brobdingnag": Swift's joke at the expense of "enlightened" male scientists who imagine themselves to be far removed from the world of women and commodities, but who are themselves, like Gulliver in the land of the giants, as affected by the whims of female consumption as are the newly commodified microscope and what might be called the ultimate object of female "consumption," the dildo.

The Microscope in the Eighteenth Century

This reading of the microscopical subtext of Brobdingnag demands a reconsideration of a rarely examined chapter in the history of science, on which Nicolson herself is one of the few commentators: the microscope's shift from rare scientific instrument to popular female commodity.[8] Although the microscope's precise date of origin and the identity of its inventor are up for debate, it is safe to say that the microscope was invented in the early 1600s and quickly became the much-used instrument of European scientists such as Antony van Leeuwenhoek, Marcello Malpighi, and Royal Society member Robert Hooke, all of whom made their own microscopes. These men and their fellow natural philosophers were fascinated to see the inner workings of small insects under the microscope and to witness tiny creatures moving about in magnified mold, their own semen (as exemplified in Leeuwenhoek's observations of human spermatozoa under the microscope, both the sperm and microscope presumably of his own making), and other organic matter. As Robert Boyle effused of the microscope's newfound capacity to ennoble—indeed, almost to deify—seemingly trivial matter, "though the Thing itself, which sets a mans thoughts a-work . . . may be but Mean in Other regards, yet that which the Reflector pitches upon to consider, may be of another Nature . . . though the Glo-worm . . . be but a small and contemptible Insect, yet the Light which shines in his Tail, and which makes the chief Theme of the Meditation, is a noble and heavenly Quality."[9] In this sense, Boyle and the microscope's other chief proponents in the Royal Society, particularly Hooke, firmly believed that this scientific instrument had the power to advance the cause of scientific observation in particular and also, more generally, to change how people saw and experienced the mundane (and small) world around them. Wrote Hooke, "it is my hope, as well as belief, that these my Labours will be no more comparable to the Productions of many other Natural Philosophers, who are now every where busie about greater things; then my little Objects are to be compar'd to the greater and more beautiful Works of Nature, A Flea, a Mite, a Gnat, to an Horse, an Elephant, or a Lyon."[10]

In 1665, Hooke published a hugely influential book, *Micrographia*, a beautifully illustrated collection of microscopical observations. *Micrographia*, as Joseph Roach has noted, is a largely aesthetic celebration of "the microscopic sublime," the phenomenon in which "[t]he micrographic image presents a paradox of scale. To appreciate it the beholder must alternate in wonder between a perception of its actual smallness and commonplace familiarity, on the one hand, and its gigantic appearance, on the other."[11] Rather than espousing any particular discovery achieved by the microscope, *Micrographia* was in many ways an advertisement for the instrument itself (Hooke's self-designed compound microscope, specifically) and for Hooke's self-consciously Baconian method of scientific observation, unprejudiced by any religious, economic, gendered, or other obstruction to the finding of "pure" visual truth.[12] A commercial success as well as a big hit within the Royal Society, *Micrographia* also met with high acclaim from the close-knit English scientific community and seemed to signal the ever-growing prominence of the microscope in modern scientific thought and publication.

All this changed in the 1680s, however, when the microscope began its alleged century-long decline within the scientific community, during which comparatively little was written on microscopical observation outside the world of fiction. Hypotheses for this deterioration in the microscope's standing range from the Royal Society's collective disappointment over its inability to observe atoms to the irresolvability of theological debates over whether the microscope reveals the orderliness of God's Universe or the godlessness of a chaotic Universe.[13] In recent histories of science, the microscope's decline is most commonly ascribed to its failure to live up to Hooke's claim in the preface to *Micrographia* that "by the help of Microscopes, there is nothing so small, as to escape our inquiry";[14] unfortunately for Hooke, that noble aspiration would be technologically impossible until the mid-nineteenth century, when major advancements in optical glass technology facilitated the groundbreaking microbiological work of Louis Pasteur.

When considered from a purely cultural perspective, however, the century-long lapse in microscope-oriented scientific innovation and publication in the late 1600s appears to be less a decline than a lateral change of hands, for at precisely the same time that the microscope seemed to have lost its high standing in the scientific community, it caught hold of the English popular imagination (partly as a result of the unexpected commercial success of Hooke's *Micrographia*) and began to be produced in multiple English workshops for the consumption of middle- and upper-class men and women. As James B. McCormick notes, "the predominance of the English workshops may also be explained by the lack of guild restrictions on the industry, especially in comparison with France. . . . Makers of optical instruments could belong to such guilds as the Clockmakers Company or the Spectaclemakers Company, but the rules on apprenticeship and admission were not strictly enforced. The advantages of greater freedom may have helped to stimulate the creativity of the English craftsman." This shift in the microscope's status could be said to parallel the contemporaneous popularization of previously elitist visual representations of *human* "minute bodies" (Hooke's term for microscopic specimens), as discussed in chapter 1. This populist episode within the history of the microscope also recalls the simultaneous transition from private to public experienced by writers negotiating the complex and contradictory new literary marketplace, which both Pope and his critics characterized as a world of real and metaphorical little men.[15] No longer the exclusive property of the male elite of the Royal Society, the microscope became a recreational tool for laypersons of both sexes who could now purchase affordable and easy-to-use microscopes in conveniently portable small shapes and sizes, produced in greater quantities for the amusement of the English public. And thus, although the 1690s was a bad time for both the Royal Society and the role of the microscope within it, the decade was a good time for producers of microscopes outside of this elite "gentlemen's club."[16] As Michael Hunter has noted, the Royal Society's changing fortunes in the 1690s—a decline in its wealth, membership, and ability to recruit new members—created "alarmist" fears of its demise within the Society.[17] At the same time, as Hunter has mentioned elsewhere, in the larger world beyond this small group of men, the 1690s marked a time of growing public acceptance and consumption of scientific theory and instruments, specifically microscopes, and saw the birth of the concept of science as "leisure activity."[18] Although the transition of Enlightenment scientific practice from "private laboratories to public spaces" was one of the original democratizing principles of post-Newtonian natural philosophy (as Larry Stewart has pointed out), the Royal Society saw the popularization and commodification of microscopes not as an achievement but as an embarrassing failure.[19]

Women and the Pocket Microscope

Evidence of women's use of these newly commodified microscopes has only recently come to light. Ignored by prefeminist histories of the microscope, the microscope's accessibility and appeal to eighteenth-century women have been taken up by two historians of microscopy, Catherine Wilson, who writes of the eighteenth century's "feminization of the microscope,"[20] and Marian Fournier, who observes "the opportunities this instrument proffered young—and not so young—ladies to participate, however far removed, in the adventure of scientific discovery."[21] The earliest critic on record to acknowledge this cultural footnote is Nicolson herself, who traces the advent of female microscope use in Susannah Centlivre's *The Basset Table* and elsewhere in eighteenth-century drama and fiction. When Centlivre's female virtuoso, Valeria, is asked to elope, her response—"What, and leave my Microscope?", —shows that she prefers this useful instrument to a man.[22] Indeed, the only way for her suitor to win her hand is to reduce himself to the level of what her father derides as the "Baubles" (her microscope and its accompanying minute specimens) in her collection and, ultimately, to become an accessory in her microscopical investigations.[23]

The most popular and most commonly produced of this new breed of scientific instrument was the appropriately named "pocket microscope" (fig. 14), which belonged as much, if not more, to the world of fashion as to that of science. Measuring a mere three to six inches in length and sold in elegant snuffbox-size containers, brass, silver, and ivory models such as "Mr. Wilson's Pocket Microscope" and Wilson's screw-barrel model were not only far more user-friendly and elegant-looking than the big and bulky compound model built by Hooke (fig. 15); they were also technologically superior, generating much clearer images at greater magnification.[24] And yet, in spite of this, the author of a recent sourcebook on eighteenth-century microscopes says of the popular pocket model, "Little or no serious study was undertaken with these instruments."[25]

In light of their newly commodified, miniaturized, and technologically improved status, the eighteenth-century pocket microscope had much in common with another commodity, the "small timepiece," which, in Maxine

FIGURE 14 Pocket microscope and accessories. Courtesy of Science Heritage Limited.

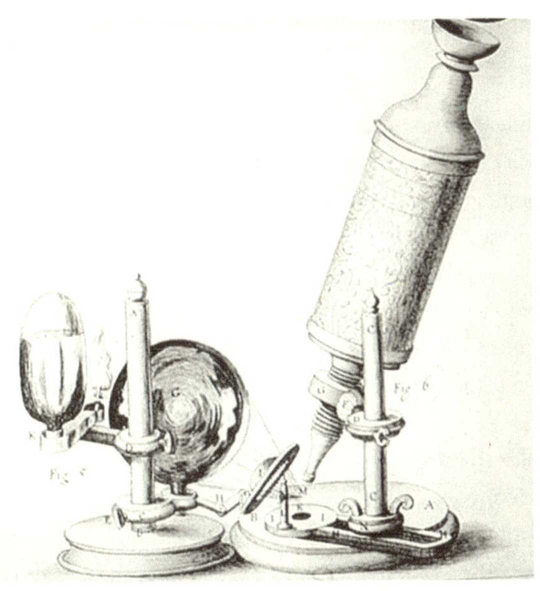

FIGURE 15 Robert Hooke (English, 1635–1703), Hooke's compound microscope. Etching. From Robert Hooke, *Micrographia* (London, 1665). Courtesy of Science Heritage Limited.

Berg's analysis, afforded "the pleasures of miniaturization" together with "the comparison of performance." In the case of the eighteenth-century small timepiece, as with the pocket microscope, "[t]he sources of pleasure were also the sources of technological progress."[26] As Adam Smith wrote of such simultaneously fashionable and practical miniature commodities in his *Theory of Moral Sentiments*, "What pleases these lovers of toys is not so much the utility, as the aptness of the machines which are fitted to promote it. All their pockets are stuffed with little conveniences."[27] The efficiency of small timepieces and pocket microscopes was evidence that the divide between the worlds of science and commodities was not as vast as many in the Royal Society (Hooke included) would have liked to believe; Berg points out, for instance, that new luxury goods such as "lightweight cottons instead of silks, earthenwares instead of porcelain . . . and veneers instead of exotic woods" were as much about the technological innovation and invention behind them as about pleasure and utility for their middle- and upper-class consumers.[28] Moreover, writes Berg, the relatively new practice called "shopping" was, like the new science, "a practice based in knowledge":

> While "useful knowledge" conveyed across networks of artisans, inventors and producers contributed to the production of an "industrial Enlightenment," the resulting newly invented products conveyed these attributes to the shopper. Precision tooling, accurate timekeeping, or clever mechanics were not needed by many of the buyers of watches, clocks, scientific instruments, automata, toys, and hardware. But they were attractive, desirable, and a connection with "modern" useful knowledge. Shopping for such items was a participation in performance, spectacle, and scenes of laboratory and workshop life.[29]

The relation between the two eighteenth-century female prototypes of female shopper and female virtuoso is captured by Harriet Guest, who writes that "Feminine learning is perceived with increasing insistence in the mid- to late century in a parallel relation to fashionable elegance."[30] To anticommercial and phallocentric advocates of Enlightenment science, like Hooke, the pocket microscope was an unwelcome symbol of this feminizing connection between shopping and natural philosophy.

Thanks to their affordability, portability, and ease of use, these dainty yet powerful seeing instruments became fashionable among middle- and upper-class women who could purchase the microscopes with their pocket money, such that the pocket microscope became "very popular among the ladies" as well as the "gentlemen of the wealthier classes."[31] Swift himself, as Nicolson has noted, toyed with the idea of buying one for his lover, Esther ("Stella") Johnson. He wrote to her: "I doubt it will cost me thirty shillings for a microscope, but not without Stella's permission; for I remember she is a virtuoso. Shall I buy it or no? 'Tis not the great bulky ones, nor the common little ones, to impale a louse (saving your presence) upon a needle's point; but of a more exact sort, and clearer to the sight, with all its equipage in a little trunk that you may carry in your pocket. Tell me, sirrah, shall I buy it or not for you?"[32] Swift's charmed description exemplifies the fact that by 1710, these trendy little microscopes were almost as accessible and portable as the common lice they were often used to observe.

But not everyone was amused by this new development. Hooke, for one, saw a direct relation between the fashionable new pocket microscope and the contemporaneous decrease in microscope-oriented Royal Society publication. As early as 1691, he delivered a pessimistic address to the Royal Society about "the Fate of Microscopes, as to their Invention, Improvements, Use, Neglect, and Slighting." Addressing this recent "Change of Humour in Men of Learning, in so short a Time," Hooke decries the microscope's devolution from a productive tool of male scientists into a miniaturized plaything in the hands of frivolous amateurs. Proper use of the microscope, Hooke complains, has been "reduced almost to a single Votary, which is Mr. Leeuwenhoek; besides whom, I hear of none that make any other Use of that Instrument, but for Diversion and Pastime, and by that reason it is become a portable Instrument, and easy to be carried in one's pocket."[33] The once prestigious microscope had in Hooke's eyes been reduced to a mere toy, a literal and metaphorical shrinkage that was for him a symbolic castration of the worst kind. This must have been especially vexing for a man who, in his preface to *Micrographia*, characterized his own compound microscope as no less than a man-made solution to Original Sin (which of course was brought about, as Hooke surely understood but does not mention, by the joined forces of Woman and Satan): "By the addition of such artificial Instruments and methods, there may be, in some manner, a reparation made for the mischiefs, and imperfection, mankind has drawn upon itself, by negligence, and intemperance, and a willful and superstitious deserting of the Prescripts and Rules of Nature, whereby every man, both from a deriv'd corruption, innate and born with him, and from his breeding and converse with men, is very subject to slip into all sorts of errors."[34] The fact that these fashionable little women's toys could actually magnify better than Hooke's model—a detail notably absent from his 1691 complaint—must only have increased his fear that these contemptible commodities would emasculate the already endangered species of "enlightened" Englishman (it is no coincidence, then, that the one man named by Hooke as an exemplary microscope user, Leeuwenhoek, is not English). And it is this emasculation anxiety at the heart of Hooke's lament that Swift seizes upon in his portrayal of the scientifically minded Gulliver as a helpless woman-manipulated miniature microscope in Brobdingnag.

Gulliver in Brobdingnag

Like Hooke, Gulliver goes out of his way to distinguish his enlightened sensibility from the materialism of the new consumer culture. In the beginning of "A Voyage to Lilliput," for example, Gulliver describes his travels as motivated by the pursuit of knowledge rather than wealth:

> I was surgeon successively in two ships, and made several voyages, for six years, to the East and West Indies, [by which I got some addition to my fortune]. My hours of leisure I spent in reading the best authors ancient and modern, being always provided with a good number of books; and when I was ashore, in observing the manners and dispositions of the people, as well as learning their language, wherein I had a great facility by the strength of my memory.[35]

And yet, Gulliver's account of his enlightened motives for travel suppresses the actual conditions of his voyages to the East and West Indies, the purpose of which is not to read books and scientifically observe foreign cultures but to import foreign goods for English consumption.

By the time Gulliver reaches Brobdingnag and actually becomes a small imported commodity himself, his resemblance to an eighteenth-century pocket microscope undermines Hooke's presumption that masculine Enlightenment ideals were ever immune to the new and markedly feminine world of commodities—this, in a nutshell, is Swift's joke at Gulliver's expense. Just as in the history of microscopy itself, the role of women becomes apparent in the microscopical subtext of Brobdingnag only after the object in question has been first claimed by men, who later mark

Gulliver's role as "instrument" by imagining him to be a "piece of clockwork . . . contrived by some ingenious artist." Early on, Gulliver is picked up by an elderly male giant who "was old and dim-sighted [and] put on his spectacles to behold me better, at which I could not forbear laughing very heartily for his eyes appeared like the full moon shining into a chamber at two windows."[36] Gulliver's laughter at the sight of the bespectacled giant calls to mind not a natural philosopher (or even a microscopic specimen) but, more accurately, a microscope staring back up into the eyes of its enormous user and mocking him for his optical inadequacies.

As if in mimicry of the microscope's historical change of hands, Swift has Gulliver's philosophically curious adult male handlers retreat to the background once our small microscope-like hero finds himself in the more corporeal sphere of women and children, where he is snatched up by a breastfeeding baby who tries, "after the usual oratory of infants, to get me for a Plaything." From this vantage point, Gulliver is forced to observe a magnified scene of mundane domestic consumption that he finds grotesque:

> I must confess no object ever disgusted me so much as the sight of her monstrous breast, which I cannot tell what to compare with, so as to give the curious reader an idea of its bulk, shape and colour. It stood prominent six foot, and could not be less than sixteen in circumference. The nipple was about half the bigness of my head, and the hue both of that and the dug so varified with spots, pimples, and freckles, that nothing could appear more nauseous: for I had a near sight of her, she sitting down the more conveniently to give suck, and I standing on the table. This made me reflect upon the fair skins of our English ladies, who appear so beautiful to us only because they are of our own size, and their defects not to be seen but through a magnifying glass, where we find by experiment that the smoothest and whitest skins look rough and coarse, and ill coloured.[37]

Whereas an actual male microscopist would not have observed the magnified "fair skins of our English ladies" unless he specifically chose to do so, Gulliver is forced to observe hideously magnified body parts, specifically female body parts, even and especially when he does not want to. And in contrast to the female virtuosos of Swift's day who took pleasure in viewing their own skin and hairs magnified under pocket microscopes, for Gulliver, in the position of a pocket microscope relegated to the status of domestic plaything, that sight is highly undesirable. Given Gulliver's microscopical point of view, the excessive gastronomic consumption in this scene—the baby's attempt to consume Gulliver, followed by the breastfeeding episode—further satirizes the microscope's and male microscopist's devolution from participants in the elite masculine world of the Royal Society to consumable objects in the world of women and children.

The misogyny in these descriptions of such magnified female body parts is obvious and has been remarked upon by numerous critics.[38] Gulliver's disgust with enormous female bodies is more interesting in terms of the connection Swift makes between this neurosis (Gulliver's phobic and microscope-like gaze as a human plaything in the hands of the new female virtuoso cum consumer) and Gulliver's scientific pretensions. The following passage shows this particular pathology, or microscopical masculinity crisis, at work. When Gulliver's forty-foot-tall, nine-year-old mistress Glumdalclitch (the farmer's daughter) takes him to visit the chief temple in Brobdingnag, Gulliver tries to play the part of scientific observer by assessing and measuring his minute discoveries: "I measured a little finger which had fallen down from one of these statues, and lay unperceived among some rubbish, and found it exactly four foot and an inch in length. Glumdalclitch wrapped it up in a handkerchief, and carried it home in her pocket to keep among other trinkets, of which the girl was very fond." The passage shows Gulliver initially trying to play the part of the virtuoso by detecting, observing, and measuring the finger. Very quickly, however, we find that he has merely served as the observing apparatus of his enormous mistress: first by his calling this "unperceived" treasure to her attention after finding it in a pile of trash with his magnified gaze, and second by assessing it as only he can, with his unique magnified vision. In spite of Gulliver's attempts to portray himself as a scientific observer in a strange land, by the end of the sentence, he cannot keep from unwittingly revealing his true standing: Gulliver as miniature microscope, like the phallic "little finger," is just a "trinket"—a commodity—in the collection of this young female virtuoso and collector. Gulliver's puzzlingly inaccurate early note to the reader that he is to become the "unhappy instrument" of Glumdalclitch's disgrace (when no palpable disgrace actually befalls Glumdalclitch) appears in this light as a Swiftian pun on the word "instrument" that speaks more to this scientific man's own disgrace as an "unhappy instrument" in the hands of Brobdingnagian women.[39] And thus, Gulliver begins his travels presuming himself to be a scientific observer, but female ownership makes him akin to the new plaything microscopes, the small instrument rather than the willing observer of new discoveries.

After the queen buys Glumdalclitch's "instrument" for one thousand pieces of gold "for the diversion of the Queen and her ladies"—underscoring once more Gulliver's newly commodified and feminized status—Glumdalclitch is adopted as Gulliver's caretaker in the royal palace. There, her new access to wealth adds to her virtuoso-collector persona a related eighteenth-century prototype, the female "shopper," with Gulliver as a magnifying seeing-object playing a key role as her shopping accessory, carried in his own special box like the pocket microscope Swift imagines purchasing for Stella: "A coach was allowed to Glumdalclitch and me, wherein her governess frequently took her out to see the town, or go among the shops; and I was always of the party, carried in my box."[40] As Hoh-Cheung Mui and Lorna H. Mui explain in their study of shops and shopkeeping in eighteenth-century England, by the 1700s, the indoor "shop" had all but replaced the open-air market as the hub of urban consumer activity.[41] Individual consumers, rather than merging with a larger group in an outdoor space, would travel conspicuously by coach from shop to shop, accumulating commodities as they went. Regarding one such shopping trip of Glumdalclitch's, Gulliver recalls:

> Whenever I had a mind to see the town, it was always in my traveling-closet which Glumdalclitch held in her lap in a kind of open sedan, after the fashion of the country, borne by four men, and attended by two others in the Queen's livery. The people, who had often heard of me, were very curious to crowd about the sedan, and the girl was complaisant enough to make the bearers stop, and to take me in her hand that I might be more conveniently seen.[42]

Gulliver would *like* to explore the town as a curious and enlightened English traveler, but his will to observe and investigate is thwarted by his role as a commodified object with microscope-like vision—a pocket microscope—in the hands of a young woman gone shopping. As such, he sees not the attractions of the town but its enormous magnified inhabitants looking down at him. As Elizabeth Kowaleski-Wallace notes, in the eighteenth century, the framed spectacle of the coach window not only enabled female shoppers to display their latest commodities en route to buying more but also helped them display themselves to the urban public, as if their own bodies were the latest fashions on display.[43] The disparity between this reality and Gulliver's is quite telling. In Brobdingnag, the shoplike display of Glumdalclitch's coach window makes a commodity not of the female shopper but of her miniature male accessory, the boxed-up Gulliver, Swift's enlightened man of science, who has become both observing object and object observed. In his new role, the miniature Gulliver, like the fashionable new pocket microscope, is as much a small spectacle as an instrument used to produce magnified spectacles.

While Gulliver's magnified gaze makes him literally incapable of seeing "the larger picture," his status as a woman's shopping accessory and thing that sees makes him unable to reflect philosophically on the new economy that subjects him to this treatment and subjects others to worse. As Gulliver recalls of another of Glumdalclitch's shopping trips:

> the governess ordered our coachman to stop at several shops, where the beggars, watching their opportunity, crowded to the sides of the coach, and gave me the most horrible spectacles that ever a European eye beheld. . . . But, the most hateful sight of all was the lice crawling on their clothes. I could see distinctly the limbs of these vermin with my naked eye, much better than those of an European louse through a microscope, and their snouts which they rooted like swine. They were the first I had ever beheld, and I should have been curious enough to dissect one of them, if I had proper instruments (which I unluckily left behind me in the ship) although indeed the sight was so nauseous, that it perfectly turned my stomach.[44]

On this excursion of Glumdalclitch's, Swift has Gulliver vacillating between one state of scientific emasculation, as an eager virtuoso deprived of his tools ("I should have been curious enough to dissect one of them, if I had proper instruments"), and another, as a former man of science shrunk to the stature of a portable object with a magnified gaze, like that of the pocket microscope, more intense than that of most European microscopes ("I could see distinctly the limbs of these vermin with my naked eye, much better than those of an European louse through a microscope"). Overwhelmed by the magnified image before his eyes and reduced to a woman-owned seeing-object with magnified vision, Gulliver is incapable of going beyond his purely sensory response (describing the sight as "nauseous") and responding to that visual image on an enlightened philosophical level as well: by, for example, reflecting not only upon the particulars of the lice themselves (as a natural philosopher would do) but also upon the socioeconomic condition of the people on whom these enormous insects live (as an economic philosopher would do). In the philosophical terms of the English Enlightenment, Gulliver's reduction to an objectified thing that sees makes him incapable of doing more than seeing, unable to take the crucial step that John Locke calls the transition from "perception" (which is purely sensory) to "reflection" (which is intellectual), and therefore unable to see the larger visual and philosophical picture.[45] And thus, this oblivious seeing-object, in the hands of an enormous modern-day female consumer and incapable of philosophical reflection, is so busy unreflectively perceiving small items of scientific interest that he cannot even realize that he is one himself: not a microscopic specimen per se, but a pocket microscope as miniature spectacle.[46] This, Swift jokes, is the imagined philosophical and cultural predicament of the "serious" eighteenth-century male microscopist, overcome and seemingly objectified by the emasculating and feminine consumer culture in which he and his instrument have become helplessly immersed.

The enlightened Englishman's metaphorical reduction to the position of a pocket microscope—a hyperperceptive but astonishingly unreflective female commodity—is apparent not only in Gulliver's microscope-like gaze and status but also in Swift's use of imagery of gastronomic female consumption for characterizing Gulliver's plight.[47] Thus, while Swift makes Glumdalclitch a female virtuoso and a specimen collector turned shopper, he makes the queen, in the eyes of Gulliver as seeing-object, a voracious eater magnified to misogynistically grotesque proportions who almost consumes Gulliver orally after consuming him economically (having recently purchased him for those one thousand pieces of gold). As Gulliver recalls during his first meal at the royal palace, the queen "took up at one mouthful as much as a dozen English farmers could eat at a meal, which to me was for some time a very nauseous sight. She would craunch the wing of a lark, bones and all, between her teeth, although it were nine times as large as that of a full-grown turkey; and put a bit of bread in her mouth, as big as two twelve-penny loaves."[48] Swift has Gulliver frequently invoke the sensory (as opposed to reflective) word "nauseous" to describe this and other magnified images in Brobdingnag, not only to reveal the neurotic depths of Gulliver's misogyny, but also to show that male nausea can be used as a pathetic countermeasure against the perceived threat of female consumption. Swift has Gulliver associate these magnified acts of female consumption with the act of "throwing up"—the opposite of and antidote to the act of gastronomic consumption—characterizing Gulliver's own misogyny-induced nausea as a comically futile defense mechanism against the female consumption that reduces scientific instruments as well as enlightened Englishmen to mere playthings with extreme magnified vision.

Swift completes Gulliver's devolution from ostensibly enlightened Englishman to a pocket-microscope-like object of female consumption by placing him in the hands of the queen's maids of honor, who employ him as a sexual prop. As Gulliver recalls, the maids of honor "would often strip me naked from top to toe, and lay me at full length in their bosoms; wherewith I was much disgusted; because, to say the truth, a very offensive smell came from their skins; which I do not mention or intend to the disadvantage of those excellent ladies, for whom I have all manner of respect; but I conceive that my sense was more acute in proportion to my littleness." Horrified by the magnified image before him, Gulliver observes the maids' "naked bodies, which, I am sure, to me was very far from being a tempting sight, or from giving me any other emotions than those of horror and disgust . . . when I saw them near, with a mole here and there as broad as a trencher, and hairs hanging from it thicker than pack-threads; to say nothing further concerning the rest of their persons." The "prettiest" giantess, adds Gulliver, "would sometimes set me astride upon one of her nipples, with many other tricks, [wherein the reader will excuse me for not being over particular. But, I was so much displeased, that I entreated Glumdalclitch to contrive some excuse for not seeing that young lady any more]."[49] Although Gulliver censors out of his narrative the particular "tricks" that displease him so much, Swift allows the reader to imagine that this enormous woman uses Gulliver—in what might be the ultimate act of female consumption—as a human dildo, rendering Gulliver's own genitalia both physically and symbolically insignificant.[50]

Swift's humorous conflation of the dildo's-eye view and the pocket microscope in this Brobdingnagian sex scene is not as preposterous as it might seem. Functioning as both a pocket microscope and a phallic prop in the hands of consuming women, Gulliver's body and gaze in Brobdingnag indicate the precise point of intersection between anxieties over the popularization of the microscope and contemporaneous anxieties over the dildo. Following Locke's belief that, in Wilson's words, "all true knowledge is acquired through ordinary unassisted sensory experience,"[51] the microscope was scorned by Joseph Addison and Alexander Pope as an unproductive "toy of the age" and a reprehensibly unnatural "microscopic eye."[52] At the same time, the dildo was perceived, on similar grounds, by its detractors in the late seventeenth and early eighteenth centuries as a reprehensibly artificial penis and un(re)productive female plaything (and as contributing to what many wrongly perceived as a nationwide depopulation crisis).[53] While woman's appropriation of the male member (in dildo form) was seen as a threat to man's claim to his own genitalia, Hooke feared that her appropriation and belittlement of the scientific instrument that served as an "artificial eye" was a threat to the enlightened Englishman's claim to the scientific gaze, and others saw it as a threat to God's.[54]

As the final stage in Gulliver's devolution from ostensibly enlightened observer to woman-owned pocket microscope to sexual prop, his role as a combined human dildo cum pocket microscope also adds a new scientific dimension to an established late-seventeenth- and eighteenth-century erotic tradition featuring sexual props as male protagonists, as in the comic-erotic poems "Signior Dildo" (commonly attributed to John Wilmot, Earl of Rochester) and the anonymous "Monsieur Thing's Origin," in which male heroes, like Gulliver in Brobdingnag, are bought, sold, exchanged, and forced by their enormous female users to observe the unimaginable.[55] While others have hypothesized the incident's origins in *The Arabian Nights*,[56] it is certainly possible that Swift had read "Monsieur Thing's Origin," about an émigré dildo from France who—like Gulliver in Brobdingnag, a little man in a strange land—ends up in the hands of an English queen's maid:

> From hence *Monsieur* took moving to the Court,
> To see what Pastime there was, or what Sport:
> So came he to the Hand of Lady's Maid,
> With whom some little time our *Monsieur* stay'd
> She like Cade Lamb was pleas'd with *Monsieur* play'd.
> No sooner had she tasted of his Favour,
> But she embrac'd the Sweetness of his Savour;
> To him alone she shew'd her good Behaviour.
> By this time *Monsieur* having thus infus'd
> His Friendship in the Maid, she introduc'd
> Him to her kind Mistress's first Acquaintance,
> As a fine Thing of noted Worth and Sense:

So that the Lady was to make a Tryal
Of *Monsieur*'s Skill, which was without denyal
The best, most pleasing thing as e'er she felt,
Ever since she near to the Court had dwelt.[57]

The scientific side of female sexual experimentation with newly purchased instruments is also apparent in the following passage from the comic-erotic poem "The Bauble: A Tale" (1721), in which a newly dildo-wielding female protagonist is characterized as a virtuoso of sorts who conducts "experiments" with her enlightening new scientific/sexual instrument:

Ten Thousand Methods [she] does explore,
Experiments not known before.
Invention racks, in hopes to find
A Thing more pleasing to her Mind.
No Philomath e'er pump'd so hard,
To gain the Longitude-Reward.
UNHAPPY CLOE! Fruitless Brain!
I think, says she, but think in vain.[58]

Describing Chloe as a "Philomath," the poem equates sexual curiosity with scientific curiosity, satirically portraying female dildo users as scientifically minded virtuosos. When the talented Chloe is finally successful, she instructs other women in the art of using this "Instrument for *Titillation*" and "Teaches young Virgins, pale and wan, (without th'Assistance of a Man),"[59] as if this new breed of sexually insatiable, scientifically minded female consumer—as Hooke seems to have feared of the new generation of microscope user—will eventually make Englishmen irrelevant.

Indeed, the actual *Philosophical Transactions of the Royal Society*, in contrast to "The Bauble: A Tale" and the sexualized satire of microscopy in "A Voyage to Brobdingnag," prided itself on "present[ing] science as masculine," chaste, and disconnected from the world of commodities.[60] As one critic has noted, Thomas Sprat's *History of the Royal Society* (1667) characterized "good scientific writing as 'masculine' and chaste' . . . [associating] chastity . . . with fertile intellectual activity because the 'passions' are simultaneously cultivated and constrained rather than driving the male reader into a vain search for empty pleasure."[61] The Royal Society's cool response to Margaret Cavendish's famous visit in 1667 indicates just how hostile it was to the threat of feminization. As Richard Nate explains, in spite of Cavendish's serious scientific intentions, "the visit, which took place at her own request, was a social rather than a scientific event. Entertaining the Duchess with the usual visitors' programme for members of the nobility, the Royal Society performed a number of experiments that were, above all, visually attractive" (Cavendish, miffed by the Royal Society's refusal to ever take her seriously, already had her revenge by sketching a scathing satire of it in *The Blazing World* [1666]).[62]

And yet, as satirists such as Swift and the anonymous author of "The Bauble, A Tale" were apparently aware, neither science nor the Royal Society was as far removed from the world of commerce as some of its members would have liked to think. The very location of many Royal Society meetings, the coffeehouse, was, as Steven Shapin notes, as well known for its commercial dealings as for its exclusion of women.[63] As Svetlana Alpers writes, the Royal Society's "commercial connections were well known; and even Hooke, in spite of his anticommercial Baconianism, acknowledges in the preface to *Micrographia* the interests of 'Merchants' and 'Money'—if not women—in the new science."[64] (Hooke, incidentally, remained unmarried his entire life in spite of a number of well-recorded affairs with women, including his housekeeper and niece.) The Royal Society, after all, was far from adequately funded by the government and had to turn to the private sector, and to its members' private commercial connections, for money. Boyle, for one, was very involved in trade, and in "1660, he was commissioned by the king to membership on the Council for Foreign Plantations," whose purpose was, among other things, trade, the buying and selling of foreign goods, and "the encouragement of shipping."[65] Even the raison d'être of the *Philosophical Transactions*, as expressed by its main advocate, Henry Oldenburg (who also, like Hooke, carried on a torrid undercover affair with *his* young niece), was to extend scientific observation beyond the elite Royal Society for the consumption of the world outside its limited borders: "these philosophical commonplace books are published in the English tongue because they are intended to be for the benefit of such Englishmen as are drawn to curious things, yet perhaps do not know Latin"—people "drawn to curious things" and ignorant of Latin being stereotypically profiled as women.[66]

Gulliver's status in Brobdingnag as a pocket microscope cum sexual prop places "A Voyage to Brobdingnag" within the eighteenth-century genre of the it-narrative, or speaking-object story, in which, as Christopher Flint elaborates, the "speaking object is almost always a product of manufacture rather than a part of nature, and its satiric vision of the world arises from its particular experience of human commerce." [67] As with "A Voyage to Brobdingnag," eighteenth-century it-narratives were similarly concerned about the status of human subjectivity within a new commodity culture and, paralleling the narrative transfer of the male pocket microscope–dildo from woman to woman in "A Voyage to Brobdingnag," were "invariably picaresque: shifts in plot, subject, and locale emphasize the indiscriminate changes of ownership that dictate the object's [in this case, Gulliver's] market value."[68] On a theoretical level, this analysis of the specific scientific and sexual forms taken by the anthropomorphic object protagonist of "A Voyage to Brobdingnag" resonates with the field of Thing Theory, in which the concept of "thing," as one of its founders, Bill Brown, puts it, "names less an object than a particular subject-object relation."[69] The same could be said of "A Voyage to Brobdingnag," in which the little man's thing-ness is marked less by his physical body than by its scientific and sexual usage in the hands of giant women.

In this sense, Swift's it-narrative satire of the parallel emasculation anxieties concerning subject-object relations between modern women and their pocket microscopes and sexual props could be said to be realized in thing-Gulliver's complaint of his body's paradoxical irrelevance in such scenarios, specifically his admission that what "gave me most uneasiness among these Maids of Honor . . . was to see them use me without any matter of ceremony, like a creature who had no sort of consequence."[70] The key to this passage is the illogic of the word "see," since the miniaturized Gulliver—with his extreme magnifying gaze—could not possibly view the scenario from a vantage point that would enable him to observe the women in the act of using him. Rather, his field of vision must be limited to a magnified image of the *vagina dentata* that consumes him, blown up to abstraction and at the expense of the bigger picture. It takes no stretch of the imagination to envision that such a sight would be much like one of Hooke's illustrations of organisms and objects magnified to abstraction on the pages of *Micrographia*. Indeed, it is not unlikely that Swift was keenly aware of how Hooke's Rorschachian depiction of a fly's eyes (fig. 16) could take on an almost obscene new meaning when considered alongside the preceding passages from "A Voyage to Brobdingnag"—bringing the like-minded reader full circle to Gulliver's early magnified observation of Brob-

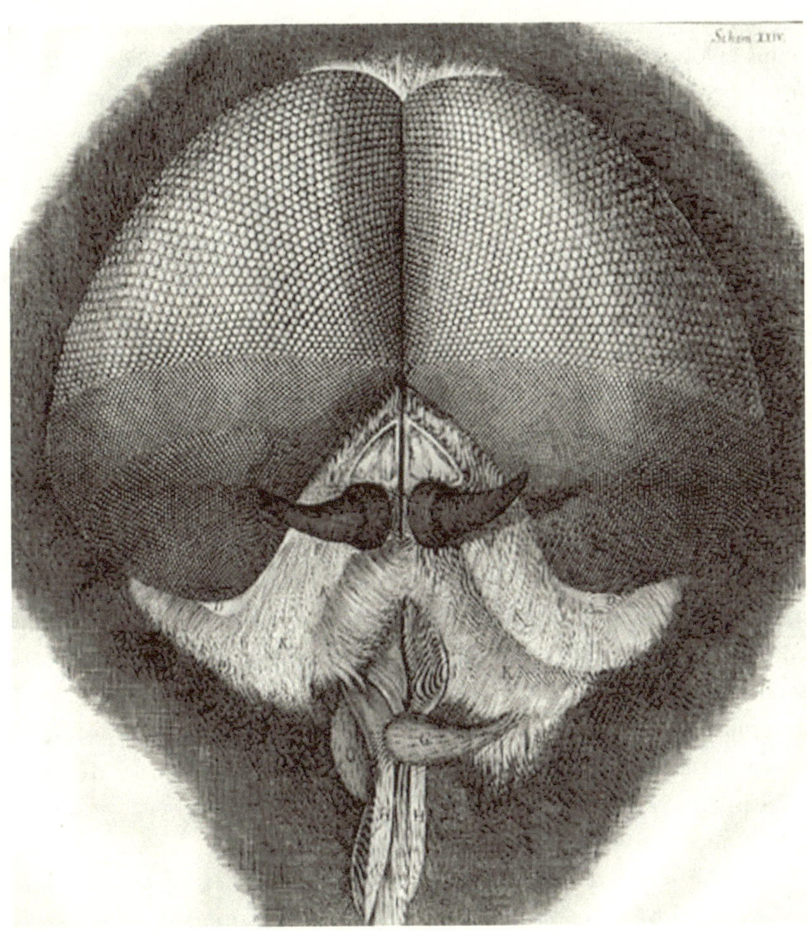

FIGURE 16 Robert Hooke (English, 1635–1703), A fly's eyes. Etching. From Robert Hooke, *Micrographia* (London, 1665). Courtesy of Science Heritage Limited.

dingnagian flies. Swift's joke is on the enlightened male scientist of his day for whom, Swift suggests, the commodification, shrinkage, and "feminization" of the microscope have, metaphorically speaking, made both magnified views one and the same. And thus, by planting such a simultaneously pornographic and microscopical image in the mind of the pornographically or gynophobically inclined or aware male or female reader, Swift allows us to deduce that Gulliver suppresses this magnified spectacle not just out of some generic male fear of the vagina but specifically because his position and gaze in this scene represent the climax of his devolution—and that of his fellow "enlightened" Englishmen in the age of pocket microscopy—from a male giant among dwarfs to a thing that, on its own, is of "no sort of consequence": a miniature, objectified pocket-microscope-like commodity in the hands of the scientifically and sexually curious female consumers who give it meaning only by using it.

Not incidentally, Swift's ideal reader of this particular perverse sexual/scientific scenario was female; he considered Stella not only the ideal recipient of a pocket microscope but also the "perfect audience" for his writing.[71] As Stephen Colclough and others have pointed out, women's reading in Swift's time was associated with both "erotic pleasure" and "conspicuous consumption," even though, as Naomi Tadmor has demonstrated, the actual reading practices of women were less matters of consumption and leisure than matters of work and industry.[72] Indeed, the relation among consuming women, women readers, and even miniaturization at this time was a profound one. Women were some of the most avid book buyers of the new age of print culture, and, as Susan Stewart has noted, the miniature book, especially popular with women as both reading and fashion accessory, "easily held and worn," is symbolic both of the book's progress toward becoming a portable commodity and accessory and of the new world in miniature exposed by the newly accessible (and similarly miniaturized and increasingly portable) microscope, that "mechanical eye that can detect significance in a world the human eye is blind to."[73]

For the remainder of his stay in Brobdingnag, Gulliver finds himself returned to the company of men, but the woman-oriented, censored human-dildo incident and its microscopical subtext remain that section's primal scene. "A Voyage to Brobdingnag" ends, after all, with Gulliver's suppression of that scene and all it represents, with his return home as patriarch to his wife and daughter, whose disconcerting smallness ("My wife ran out to embrace me, but I stooped lower than her knees, thinking she could otherwise never be able to reach my mouth. My daughter kneeled to ask my blessing, but I could not see her till she arose, having been so long used to stand with my head and eyes erect to above sixty foot"), physical manipulability ("I went to take her up with one hand, by the waist"), ostensible aversion to economic and gastronomic consumption ("I told my wife she had been too thrifty, for I found she had starved herself and her daughter to nothing"), and apparent lack of curiosity (significantly, they appear to have no interest in what he saw in his travels) counteract the fantastical "Hooke's worst nightmare" that precedes it.[74]

By reducing an Englishman of enlightened pretensions to a virtual microscope-dildo in women's hands, "A Voyage to Brobdingnag" satirizes the misogyny behind "enlightened" English masculinity and the castration threat it projects onto the new female consumer who is imagined to have abused and belittled both the microscope and the phallus by wresting them from their original and rightful (male) owners. In this light, the Swift of "A Voyage to Brobdingnag" appears as neither misogynist nor antimisogynist per se but as a sexual satirist exposing the latent gynophobia behind Enlightenment science's aversion toward the new consumerism. And thus, Gulliver's eventual use as a sexual prop in the hands of the Brobdingnagian queen's maids of honor must ultimately be understood as an act of consumption *inextricable* from the microscopical subtext in "A Voyage to Brobdingnag." For as we have seen, Gulliver ends up as both pocket microscope and dildo in a cultural satire in which Swift has shown how these two seemingly disparate objects and subject positions have become, metaphorically speaking, and to the imagined horror of Enlightenment purists like Hooke, virtually interchangeable.

four

THE LABOR OF LITTLE MEN

> "In Tasks so bold, can Little Men engage"
> Alexander Pope, "The Rape of the Lock"

> "my Grand-mamma hath often said, /
> *Tom Thumb*, beware of Marriage"
> Henry Fielding, *Tom Thumb*

In 1730, Henry Fielding wrote a series of love poems addressed to "Celia," otherwise known as Charlotte Cradock, whom he married in 1734.[1] In one of these poems, "To the Same. On Her Wishing to Have a Lilliputian to Play With," the author muses: "May I, to please my lovely dame, / Be five foot shorter than I am; / And, to be greater in her eyes, / Be sunk to Lilliputian size."[2] Reduced to Lilliputian size—just under six inches, according to Swift's *Gulliver's Travels*—Fielding imagines himself dancing on his beloved's hand and carted along in her gown, hat, and pocket, in order to "be, / My Celia, what is prized by thee."[3] The poem's conclusion finds the miniature Fielding positioned on the sleeping Celia's pillow "[w]hile I survey her bosom rise," a voyeuristic scenario permissible only because, as he admits in a parenthetical phrase, "afraid she could not be / Of such a little thing as me"—his body and genitals, and their proximity to Celia's body and genitals, no longer posing a sexual threat to her, even in bed.[4] And yet therein lies the catch in Fielding's Lilliputian fantasy: the extraordinary circumstances that grant him unprecedented access to Celia's body and bed leave him physically unable to do anything about it. Becoming what Celia desires, "a Lilliputian to Play with," reduces his entire body to penis size and thereby makes his own genitalia both physically and symbolically irrelevant. Hence, Fielding states, "Here would begin my former pain / And wish to be myself again."[5]

Read alongside Fielding's better-known works of little-man literature—the popular two-act comedy *Tom Thumb* (1730) and the three-act *Tragedy of Tragedies* (1731)—the author's 1730 Lilliputian love poem to his future wife underscores a prominent comical theme in the plays that has yet to be critically explored: the question of how the thumb-size protagonist and his beloved fiancée, the statuesque Princess Huncamunca, will consummate their impending marriage.[6] Whereas in the poem Fielding precludes sexual intercourse between a Lilliputian man and the woman he desires, in the Tom Thumb plays he goes so far as to suggest that Tom Thumb's size actually makes him a superlative sexual partner for the "real-life" modern Englishwoman. Tom Thumb makes the argument himself when, in the last lines of the epilogue to *Tom Thumb*, he propositions the women in the audience who might regard him as sexually incompatible because of his "inferior Size." If they put him to the test, he proposes, they might find him to be a superior lover:

> But, for the Ladies, they, I know despise
> The little Things of my inferior Size
> Their mighty Souls are all of them too large
> To take so small a Heroe to their Charge.
> Take Pity, Ladies, on a young Beginner;
> Faith! I may prove, in time, a thumping Sinner.[7]

The double meaning of the word "thumping" in "thumping Sinner" underscores the sexual joke by linking Tom Thumb's "thumping" (and thumbing) stature—"thumping" meaning "of striking size"—with his ability to "thump," meaning to pound as does a "fist, a club, or any blunt instrument," as defined in the *Oxford English Dictionary*.[8]

"Thumb," like "thump," has a double meaning of its own, being a symbol of female masturbation, and, like the word "Thomas," a common early-modern colloquialism for the penis. Through these and other double entendres, the plays reiterate in act after act the joke that marital consummation is possible for Tom Thumb and his normal-size bride-to-be only if she uses his entire body as a phallic sexual prop—that is to say, as a human dildo. This method of conjugal intercourse, Fielding makes clear, would provide great pleasure for Huncamunca but great danger for Tom Thumb, who risks not only physical discomfort but also the possibility of being literally swallowed up in the act. This brings us to the most surreal and satirical dimension of this comical pornographic scenario: its appearance throughout the plays in the economic and gastronomic terms of male labor and female appetite, with Huncamunca as a cannibalistic consumer and Tom Thumb as both devoured object and abused worker.

When we consider that Fielding's fantastical presentation of spousal intimacy was conceived at a time marked by a dramatic rise in female consumption of the economic variety, the plays' central dirty joke reveals itself to be as socioeconomically relevant as it is bawdy.[9] Starting in the 1720s (as discussed in chapter 3), goods in England were greater in quantity and quality and more available to a wider range of consumers than ever before, and the consumption of goods came to play an increasingly prominent role in eighteenth-century social life.[10] As Swift's depiction of gigantic female consumers of a miniaturized and objectified Gulliver testifies, it was not uncommon in the early 1700s for those skeptical about the new consumerism to project their anxieties over this socioeconomic development onto the bodies of Englishwomen, portraying them as all-consuming, ravenous devourers of goods. "Although women's voracity has long been asserted," writes Elizabeth Kowaleski-Wallace, "history awaited the proliferation of consumer commodities to make the specific connection between female appetite and the world of goods. With the birth of a consumer culture, women were assumed to be hungry for *things*—for dresses and furniture, for tea cups and carriages, for all commodities that indulged the body and enhanced physical life."[11]

By portraying one such woman-consumed *thing* as a pocket-size man, Fielding's Tom Thumb plays combine these anxieties over female consumption with anxieties over contemporaneous changes in the cultural arenas of courtship and marriage. When women become insatiable consumers of goods, the plays suggest, what is to stop those women from extending their behavior in the marketplace into the realms of courtship and marriage and becoming, cannibalistically, insatiable consumers of men? Or, to put it another way, what is to stop men from becoming the consumed objects of this new breed of woman? In Fielding's hands, the husband-to-be is portrayed as more automaton than human being, and this little man–consuming woman sexual scenario does not resemble what we would today call heterosexuality; instead, it recalls the autoerotic female perpetrators in the anonymous anti-masturbation tract *Onania*, the dildo-wielding embodiment of female masculinity in Fielding's *Female Husband*, and, most tellingly, the female employers of the miniature automaton sex workers depicted in the underexamined comic-erotic genre of eighteenth-century anthropomorphic dildo poems.

Companionate Marriage and Fielding's Tom Thumb Plays

The paranoiac reasoning behind the sexual humor of Fielding's Tom Thumb plays (the suggestion that men might get swallowed up by these new object-erotic—as opposed to heteroerotic—consuming women), though comical, is directly connected to the cultural reality of Fielding's time. By the 1730s, the new culture of middle-class consumerism and attendant fears regarding female consumption redrew gender and marital roles to conform to the new rules of the new middle-class cult of companionate marriage, in which women were thought of no longer as merely goods exchanged between two families—or, more specifically, between two men, the father of the bride and the groom—but as discerning buyers in a marriage market.[12] This "enlightened" and quintessentially bourgeois re-visioning of the marriage bond as a romantic partnership of free choice, instead of an economic arrangement between families, reconceived of marriage as a Rousseauian social contract between two equal and consenting individuals.

As many social historians have recently noted, none more famously than Lawrence Stone, the emergence of companionate marriage in the early eighteenth century "equaliz[ed] relationships between husband and wife" not only on an ideological level but also on more concrete economic grounds, since, under the new rules, "the portion [or dowry] was normally invested in land to be settled on the young couple, whereas in earlier centuries it had gone straight into the pocket of the groom's father."[13] The connection Stone makes between companionate marriage and the insertion of a guarantee of the wife's "pin money" into the marriage clause underscores the irony of this new marital ideology pretending to value love over money while both the ideology itself and the reality it tried to police remained intrinsically economic in function.[14] It is not surprising, then, that, as Susan Staves has argued, a vocal antifeminist backlash against pin money emerged in the eighteenth century, attacking the new conflation of wife and consumer that the clause seemed to produce.[15] Indeed, as the pin-money clause seems to illustrate, the consumer in the new marriage market was envisioned specifically as female, thereby forging a direct connection between women who shopped and women who married, that is, shopped for husbands. As if in response to Lady Chudleigh's famous 1703 lament that "Wife and servant are the same, / But differ only in the name,"[16] companionate marriage not only promised to rectify the long-standing socio-economic inequity between husbands and wives but also threatened, in the eyes of its critics, to reverse it, making husbands the commodified and objectified workers for the newly empowered wives who had chosen them.

Perhaps the best cultural example of the connection between female consumerism and companionate marriage in the eighteenth century is the contemporaneous emergence of the dating service, which seemed to empower its female participants with free choice by positioning them as discerning consumers of men. As Katherine Sobba Green has observed, "[b]eneath the surface objectifications of the dating service (which, granted, resemble the calculations of arranged marriage) lie the very real advantages of choice—a prerogative that patriarchal exchange largely denied women of the nobility and gentry but which was generally fostered by capitalism and, more specifically, by the ideology of companionate marriage." However, as Green notes, "as in today's cryptic personal advertisements, while registration insures choice, it also requires self-commodification, an attempt to measure one's own exchange value."[17] Fielding's fantastical presentation of modern marriage in his Tom Thumb plays, by contrast, contains no such self-commodification on the part of the empowered female consumer of little men. Instead, the gynophobic imagination of these comedies envisions a new marriage market that consists only of the enormous female buyers who benefit from their new freedom of choice and the commodified diminutive male laborers who are unwittingly victimized by it.

Providing an explanation for such gynophobia within the context of companionate marriage, Niklas Luhmann argues that behind the new companionate ideology and its apparent empowerment of women's choice in sexual object is a pathological fear of female sexual desire, a fear of that very same affective choice to which it seems, paradoxically, to give license. As Luhmann observes, English companionate ideology contains a certain prudishness that belies its emphasis on romantic love, in contrast to the unapologetically licentious French concept of *amour passion*. Writes Luhmann, "[t]he connection between love and marriage, first proclaimed in England . . . had one crucial, fatal weakness: the woman had to be chaste in order to marry." Beginning in England in the early eighteenth century, and then spreading across the continent, as Luhmann observes, "[t]he woman was discovered to be a human being, the hierarchy in marriage was accordingly dispensed with, and at the same time it was judicious to conform to society. Everyone was meant to be happy—with the aid of his or her partner,"[18] and yet,

> the differences between the *amour passion* complex of the French and the Puritans' notion of marriage based on "companionship" created different preconditions for their respective adaptability, specifically in the following context: only the semantics of *amour passion* was sufficiently complex . . . to absorb the revaluation of sexuality that occurred in the eighteenth century. Despite having provided a preliminary basis for the integration of love and marriage, and under the same conditions as the French, the English were only able to come up with the Victorian malformation of sexual morality.[19]

And thus, in eighteenth-century England, in contrast to France, sex panic (particularly regarding female sexuality) and the belief in companionate marriage went hand in hand.

Coupled with the fear inherent in English companionate marriage of the very female desire that it might otherwise enable were contemporaneous fears of any female sexual activity that defied the companionate ideal by being neither conjugal nor procreative in function, such as same-sex desire and masturbation. According to the influential anti-masturbation tract *Onania* (1718), for instance, which saw itself as a defender of companionate marriage, female masturbation ("self pollution") of any kind can lead to "the End of Marriage in all Countries and in all Societies, and the manner after which God has ordain'd that our Species should be continu'd" and is seen as the ultimate threat to the institution of companionate marriage: "It [masturbation] destroys conjugal Affection, perverts natural Inclination, and tends to extinguish the Hopes of Posterity."[20] In this sense, Fielding's depiction of female sexual desire within companionate marriage as a wish to employ a diminutive husband as an autoerotic prop draws from both what Luhman describes as the fear of female desire intrinsic to English companionate marriage and *Onania*'s view of the anti-conjugal dangers of female masturbation.

It is in this cultural climate that Fielding portrays Huncamunca as an insatiable female consumer who might literally devour her husband-to-be on or before their wedding night. By depicting the little man not only as the object of the female consumer (as both her commodity fetish and sexual fetish) but also as her menial laborer (referring to Tom Thumb as Huncamunca's "Chimney-Sweeper" and her "commissioner to discharge"),[21] Fielding suggests that in a culture in which women are the consumers and men the consumed, women relinquish their roles as producers (of children and breast milk) in marriage and as consumed objects (as wives and prostitutes) in the marital and sexual marketplace, while men become society's new sexual laborers and the objects of the new female consumption. Extending "On Her Wishing to Have a Lilliputian to Play With" into a full-fledged narrative, Fielding's Tom Thumb plays transform the personal poem's subtle sexual humor into a bawdy social satire on the hazards of modern courtship for men in an age in which women have the power to consume anything—and anybody—they choose.

Anthropomorphic Dildo Poetry

Such a reading of Fielding's Tom Thumb plays requires an investigation into two other little men of the period: Monsieur Thing and Signior Dildo, the protagonists of an underanalyzed late-seventeenth- and eighteenth-century comical pornographic genre best described as anthropomorphic dildo poetry. Representing sexual props as miniature menial laborers, these poems not only illuminate the sexual and socioeconomic satire behind Fielding's Tom Thumb plays but also qualify as the plays' unacknowledged forebears. Based on actual single-legged anthropomorphic phallic sexual props sold in English "toy shops" in the seventeenth and eighteenth centuries,[22] these poems depict their dildo protagonists as French or Italian male workers in the hands of enormous Englishwomen who subject them to a form of sexual intercourse characterized in both the poems and in Fielding's plays as an oppressive and emasculating form of abuse.[23] In each of these poems, the foreignness of the anthropomorphic male dildo only highlights the Englishness of the women who abuse him.[24]

In contrast to non-anthropomorphic early-modern dildo literature, a genre that typically portrays the sexual prop as a gender-neutral symbol of female autoerotic or homoerotic sexual pleasure independent of men, anthropomorphic dildo literature provides sexual scenarios in which the key players are paired up as women (the users) and men (the anthropomorphic sexual props themselves).[25] And yet, the men and women in these poems are not depicted as sexual *partners* but are portrayed instead as perpetrator and victim in sexually exploitative arrangements between (male) workers/commodities and (female) self-interested employers/consumers. These satirical characterizations of modern relations between men and women thus sexualize the economic exploitation of the menial laborer in the new capitalist economy while characterizing the new consuming Englishwoman as a sexually "queer" cannibalizer of miniature male automata.

One such poem, "Dildoides" (1722), commonly attributed to Samuel Butler, opens by characterizing the titular props as both inanimate commodities and oppressed foreign workers.[26] Based on a real-life event in which a London mob burned a shipment of imported French dildos, the poem begins with one objecting member of the crowd defending the dildos by appealing to the self-interested capitalist instincts of the other men in the group. Characterizing the dildo as an asset to female consumers, but above all to the male capitalists in the audience, he claims:

If Ladyes rather choose to handle
Our Wax in Dildo, than in Candle,
Much good may't do 'em, so they Pay for't
And that the merchant never stay for't.
For neighbours is't not all one whether
They wear in Shoes, or P—cks our Leather?

This mercantile speaker goes on to claim that although he shares his compatriots' hatred of foreigners, he intends to put his self-interest before his xenophobia (or, rather, to combine the two) by putting "Monsieur Dildo" to work for his own benefit:

Like you, I Monsieur Dildo hate,
But your intentions let's Translate;
You treat 'em may like Turks, or Jews,
But I'le have two for my own use.[27]

The social and economic hierarchy in these passages is clear: at the bottom of the ladder is the exploited foreign worker, Monsieur Dildo; in the middle is the female consumer who consumes him; and at the top is the male capitalist who profits from both the labor of Monsieur Dildo and the buying habits of the female consumer.

Predating Karl Marx's description of the "mystical" quality of the commodity fetish in capitalist culture, "Dildoides" characterizes the props as priapic gods worshipped by the female consumer: commenting upon the actions of the members of the all-male mob who, "[f]orgetting each his Wife and Daughter, / Condemn'd these Dildoes to the Slaughter," the narrator sarcastically exclaims, "Oh! Barbarous Tymes, when Deitys / Become themselves a Sacrifice!" [28] However, rather than confirming their wives' and daughters' idolatry by turning these little men into martyrs, the pyromaniacal mob ultimately defeats the seeming immortality of the dildos' always-erect condition, negating the mystical status of these props once and for all: *"Priapus thus in Box opprest, / Burnt like a Phoenix in his Nest, / But with this fatall difference dyes, / We find no Dildoes from his Ashes Rise."*[29] Leaving the dildo burners victorious over the female commodities that challenge their authority as husbands and fathers, the poem uses the figure of the little man to satirize the misogynistic emasculation anxieties behind the condemnation of female consumerism while at the same time casting doubt on the dildo defenders' belief that men are the beneficiaries, rather than the victims, of female consumption.

The poem "Signior Dildo" (1673, first printed in 1703), commonly attributed to John Wilmot, Earl of Rochester,[30] also depicts female dildo consumption as a metaphor for what Marx calls consumer culture's idolatry of the commodity fetish. Addressing female readers as shoppers, the narrator explains:

At the Sign of the Cross in St. James Street,
When next you go thither to make yourselves sweet
By buying of powder, gloves, essence, or so,
You may chance t'get a sight of Signior Dildo.
You'll take him at first for no person of note
Because he appears in a plain leather coat,
But when you his virtuous abilities know,
You'll fall down and worship Signior Dildo.[31]

Here, in spite of Signior Dildo's unremarkable aesthetic value ("You'll take him at first for no person of note / Because he appears in a plain leather coat"), it is his indefatigable use-value (his "virtuous abilities") that determines his high exchange-value and makes him an object of "worship" on the part of the female consumer.

In contrast to "Dildoides," however, "Signior Dildo" introduces its protagonist not as a foreign worker but as a foreign gentleman, a "Noble Italian call'd Signior Dildo." And yet, "Signior Dildo" asserts its protagonist's alleged gentlemanly status only in order to expose it as a false pretense: "Were this signior but known to the citizen fops, / He'd keep their fine wives from the foremen of shops," the narrator remarks, suggesting that in spite of his pretensions to class privilege, Signior Dildo is in fact a mere consumer commodity. Although Signior Dildo enjoys the access to high society that his gentlemanly status provides him, that status and access serve only to make him the abused commodity of the aristocratic English female consumer, who "stifled him almost beneath her pillow, / So closely sh'embraced Signior Dildo," rather than the abused commodity of the bourgeois female consumer.[32] The titular little man's "tragic flaw," the poem reveals, is his false consciousness of his own commercial status. Like the pro-capitalist dildo defenders of "Dildoides," the little-man protagonist of "Signior Dildo" disavows female consumerism's emasculating effects upon the male body.

The anonymous "Monsieur Thing's Origin: Or Seignior D___'s Adventures in Britain" (1722), the most narratively complex of these poems, introduces its protagonist as a multinational anthropomorphic dildo of French birth and Italian citizenship (interchangeably referred to as "Monsieur" and "Seignior") who emigrates to England and finds work performing grueling sexual labor for Englishwomen. Although the majority of the poem characterizes Monsieur Thing as an oppressed foreign menial laborer made to "slave and toil" for insatiable English female consumers and supervisors, the poem begins by suggesting that upon moving to England and turning his unique talents into a profitable career, Monsieur Thing has ascended the socioeconomic ladder and become a mercantile capitalist and bourgeois English husband. In the beginning of the poem, Monsieur Thing arrives in England with his family, in search of work and lodging:

> When SEIGNIOR first at *London* did arrive,
> Was put to shifts to know how to contrive,

Or find a Place where's Family shou'd live.
At length all day after they had been trudging,
Tire'd with Fatigue, in seeking of Lodging,
Were shew'd a TOY-SHOP, nigh to *Covent-Garden.*[33]

In the lines that immediately follow, Monsieur Thing seems to have become a social-climbing mercantile capitalist whose "Qualities" and "Capacity" have earned him success, renown, and, above all, the status of Englishman.

Where for some time they liv'd in private Room,
But soon became unto the Publick known,
Because his Qualities were really such,
Cou'd with small Help *do Little* or *do Much*:
For his Capacity, made Denizen,
'Twas thus *Monsieur* became an *Englishman.*[34]

As evidence of Monsieur's ostensible climb up the social ladder, the preceding lines characterize an increase in the shop's dildo inventory as a testament to Monsieur's success as a potent paterfamilias who, having added to his family (of dildos), and having acquired the bourgeois pretensions befitting a successful Englishman, moves his growing family from the toy shop in Covent Garden to a larger and better one in the Fleet:

Before 'twas long, the Number did increase,
So the last Brood were to chuse a new Place,
That he should not be taken for a Clown,
A Station chose, in Middle of the Town,
In TOY-SHOP Large, and nigh unto a Church,
In Fleetstreet did this Lovely Creature perch.[35]

However, Monsieur Thing soon discovers that he is not a socially mobile English capitalist after all but is instead an abused immigrant slave laborer whose "Drudge" is to "slave and toil" for the benefit of Englishwomen. What the beginning of the poem praises as his "Qualities" and "Capacity" turn out to refer not to any special talents but to his objectified body's utility to female consumers as an inexhaustible working machine that produces female sexual pleasure. The women

forc'd him in the Summit of their *Bliss*;
And after they had tasted, made a Drudge
Worse than a Waterman, who wears a Badge,
Or Ticket-Porter in the Street that plies,
Burthen'd with Loads, is in no worse Disguise,
Than to their Lust he is a Sacrifice.[36]

Capable of infinitely producing female sexual pleasure because of his eternally erect state, able to withstand incredible abuse, and, like the Marxian worker in a capitalist economy, unable to stake any claim to the product he makes (female sexual pleasure), this self-made "Englishman" turns out to be the paradigmatic objectified, inexhaustible, slave laborer.[37] In its depiction of an orgy of female masturbators unfairly dominating a diminutive male automaton, the poem satirizes the new capitalistic economy as giving license to the very kind of oppressive sexual hierarchy that its new bourgeois ideals (including the new cult of companionate marriage) were meant to eradicate and equalize.

In being even "[*w*]*orse* than a Waterman" or "Ticket-Porter" (my italics)—and other free wage laborers in that Marxian category of "individuals" who sell "the particular expenditure of force to a particular capitalist, whom he confronts as an independent individual"—Monsieur falls under the Marxian category of the slave laborer who "belongs to the individual, particular owner, and functions as his laboring machine."[38] The unfortunate reality of this little man's status as a laboring machine becomes painfully apparent to him when—after posturing as an upwardly mobile bourgeois Englishman—he is snatched up by a merchant's wife who

boldly work'd him up unto an Oil,
So did she make the Creature slave and toil;
She wrought him till he was just out of breath,
And harrast SEIGNIOR almost unto Death;
Until he was forc'd to chuse a new Place,
To alter somewhat of his Slavish Case.[39]

Prior to this pivotal moment in which Monsieur Thing is slavishly abused by the merchant's wife, he has been comically oblivious to the fact that whatever the illusory distinctions might be between the slave laborer and the mercantile individual who is supposedly "free" as a real or honorary

"Englishman" to ascend the social ladder, all working people are mere instruments of production in the eyes of the consumers who benefit from their labor. Fancying himself a bourgeois Englishman, Monsieur Thing has mistaken what he sees as his success as an upwardly mobile mercantile capitalist for what are really the signs of his own commodification (being sold in various stores alongside other identical commodities). It is no coincidence that the abuser who brings Monsieur Thing to this tragicomic realization is the wife of a merchant: in the poem's reality, men only imagine themselves to be at the helm of the capitalist system. English female consumers, the poem suggests, are the ones who truly reap the rewards of capitalism, at the expense of little men.

In spite of Monsieur Thing's self-fashioning as an affective bourgeois individual and self-made Englishman, his entry into the workforce makes his own labor-power—and, in turn, his own body—a mere exchangeable commodity. In Marx's words, "labour-power can appear on the market as a commodity only if, and in so far as, its possessor, the individual whose labour-power it is, offers it for sale or sells it as a commodity."[40] Monsieur Thing, like the Marxian worker who signs a Faustian pact by entering into the capitalistic social contract, is an individual who willingly offers up his own labor-power for sale as a commodity. Ironically and self-defeatingly, only by giving his labor-power to the buyer "for him to consume" (however temporarily) can the worker/commodity establish his ownership of his own body.[41]

In this quasi-Marxian sense, both the anthropomorphic dildo and Fielding's Tom Thumb recall the Enlightenment fascination with automata, defined by Simon Schaffer as "machines in the form of humans and as humans who perform like machines." Schaffer cites the popularity of traveling automaton shows, especially in London, where automatic flutists, chess players, and ducks were put on display for gawkers to observe and compare favorably with their lesser living counterparts. Writes Schaffer, "[l]aborers were . . . judged too secretive, incapable of fully expressing the true principles on which labor processes relied. By making techniques perfectly visible" (as with automata), "they could apparently be reproduced anywhere and everywhere."[42] As Adam Ferguson wrote in 1767:

> Many mechanical arts require no capacity. They succeed best under a total suppression of sentiment and reason, and ignorance is the mother of industry as well as of superstition. Reflection and fancy are

> subject to err, but a habit of moving the hand, or the foot, is independent of either. Manufactures, accordingly, prosper most where the mind is least consulted, and where the workshop may, without any great effort of imagination, be considered as an engine, the parts of which are men.[43]

Unlike human workers, automata were thought to be unstoppable and incapable of error, much like the anthropomorphic dildos of the aforementioned poems who improve upon their male human counterparts through their constitutional inability to sexually expire.

The diminutive male subjects of anthropomorphic dildo narratives and Fielding's Tom Thumb plays are also rooted in the contemporaneous genre of it-narratives or thing-poems, which narrate the adventures of inanimate objects such as rupees, corkscrews, and banknotes (discussed in chapter 3). Although most recent criticism on the genre focuses on its economic implications, these narratives, like the anthropomorphic dildo poems and Fielding's Tom Thumb plays, are not without erotic subtext. Barbara Benedict, for instance, writes of how in thing-poems, objects "rival lovers ontologically: they present a way of existence in specific opposition to that of the lover, who is defined precisely by feeling," in some cases "mak[ing] lovers into objects themselves."[44] As in the anthropomorphic dildo poems, in thing-poems, "the durability of objects throws human vulnerability into relief: beset by time, feeling, and the permeable borders of the flesh, humans are shouldered aside by the parade of commodities that are capturing the center of culture."[45]

"One properer for a Play-thing than a Husband"

Fielding's Tom Thumb plays—invoking anthropomorphic dildo poetry's discourse of sex as menial labor, and with their thematic roots spread wide throughout the eighteenth-century discourses of automata, it-narratives, female consumption, companionate marriage, and sex panic—depict the modern Englishman, specifically the husband or husband-to-be, as an abused, menially laboring phallic toy in the hands of the new consuming woman. The likely influence of these poems on Fielding's Tom Thumb plays is apparent in an early conversation between Huncamunca and her attendant, Mustacha, in which the latter criticizes her mistress's desire for a man of Tom Thumb's size. Proclaims Mustacha: "I am surprised that your Highness can give your / self a Moments Uneasiness about that little insignificant Fellow, / *Tom Thumb*. One properer for a Play-thing than a Husband.— / Were he my Husband, his Horns should be as long as his Body." To any members of an eighteenth-century audience aware that the term "plaything" could refer not only to a child's toy but also to a sexual prop, the joke that the thumb-size protagonist is better suited to be a dildo than a husband would have been hard to miss.[46] Indeed, even audiences who had never encountered "Monsieur Thing's Origin" and "Dildoides" might still have heard of the minor scandal reported in the *Daily Journal* of June 9, 1722, eight years before Fielding's *Tom Thumb*: "Just publish'd, Monsieur Thing; or Seignior D___do's Adventures in Great-Britain, at the Pamphlet Shops of London and Westminster, excepting the French Hugonets, who were so unnatural as to refuse their Countryman a Place in their Shop at the Royal-Exchange, which prevented others from being sold, as the Author supposes, she had the Original by her and would not suffer herself to be tantaliz'd with the Picture. She sent Constables to suppress the Hawkers."[47] Huncamunca's rejoinder—"*Tom Thumb*'s a Creature of that charming Form, / That no one can abuse, unless they love him"[48]—not only accuses Mustacha of desiring him but also hints at Tom Thumb's physical discomfort when used in a sexual scenario in which his "charming Form" makes physically loving him the same as physically abusing him, as in the "Slavish Case" of "Monsieur Thing."

In *The Tragedy of Tragedies*, Tom Thumb's romantic rival, Lord Grizzle, similarly characterizes Huncamunca's diminutive fiancé as "properer for a Play-thing than a Husband":

> And can my Princess such a Durgen wed,
> One fitter for your Pocket than your Bed!
> Advis'd by me, the worthless Baby shun,
> Or you will ne'er be brought to bed of one.
> Oh take me to thy Arms and never flinch,
> Who am a Man by *Jupiter* ev'ry Inch.[49]

And yet, as the play continually reminds us, while Tom Thumb's size might indeed make him unable to cause his to *wife* to go into labor, it makes him perfectly fit for another sexual labor of his own.

Tom Thumb's status as the laboring sexual prop of his wife-to-be is brought to the fore by the ludicrous metaphors and analogies that Tom

Thumb and Huncamunca use in anticipation of their marriage and its consummation. Peter Lewis and J. Paul Hunter have each noted Fielding's use of "completely fatuous" and "ludicrously extended" metaphor and simile in the Tom Thumb plays; Lewis claims that Fielding uses it to mock the overly metaphorical language of Restoration tragedy, and Hunter writes that its effect is to reveal that "metaphor has gone mad, and the artist is shown to have totally lost control of his words."[50] Here, however, Fielding use of ridiculous metaphors is viewed as intended not to suggest an artistic lapse but to indicate lack of control on the part of the characters who utter them. These absurd metaphors, in other words, function as proto-Freudian slips uttered by Tom Thumb and Huncamunca, revealing their subconscious awareness of the sexually and economically "perverse" subtext of their mismatched union. In the following speech, for instance, Tom Thumb expresses his delight that he is now able to throw aside his bloody war garments (having successfully fought off the giants who had been threatening the kingdom) and enter the bed of his beloved. Now that "[t]he dreadful Bus'ness of the War is over," he proclaims,

> I've thrown the bloody Garment now aside,
> And Hymeneal Sweets invite my Bride.
> So when some Chimney-Sweeper, all the Day,
> Has through dark Paths pursu'd the Sooty Way,
> At Night, to was his Face and Hands he flies,
> And in his t'other Shirt with his *Brickdusta* lies.[51]

In the first two lines of the passage, Tom Thumb's clumsy effort to contrast his bloody garment of war with the promise of "Hymeneal Sweets" actually makes an inadvertent and rather gory comparison between the blood of war and the hymeneal blood of conjugal sex. And yet the truly "perverse" subtext of those lines does not fully reveal itself until the remaining lines, in which Tom Thumb goes on to compare himself to a chimney sweep who washes himself of the soot he has acquired, having "through dark Paths pursu'd the Sooty Way," and then lies in bed with his *Brickdusta* (a term that affectionately describes the hypothetical chimney sweep's wife as the rosy color of "brickdust").[52] Although Tom Thumb obviously intends to contrast the dirty work of the chimney sweep with the clean and pure love of a companionate spousal couple, his continued imagery of dirtiness (from the blood of war to the soot of a chimney sweep) indirectly compares the soot that covers a chimney sweep to the mess that will cover Tom Thumb's body on his wedding night; in doing so, he links the chimney sweep's labor in a chimney to the work of his body in coitus, while comparing Huncamunca's vagina to a chimney's "dark Paths" and equating himself, as his fiancée's miniature menial laborer, to the dildo-esque automaton chimney sweep who laboriously, and self-destructively, pursues them.

Tom Thumb's Origins

Significantly, Fielding's emphasis on marriage is the narrative feature that most distinguishes these plays from the anthropomorphic dildo poems and the plays' other literary precursors, the seventeenth-century ballads "The History of Tom Thumb" (n.d.) and "Tom Thumbe His Life and Death" (1630).[53] The narrative of the plays begins in medias res, with Tom Thumb's return to King Arthur's kingdom after having heroically slain the giant that had been threatening the kingdom. When King Arthur asks the little hero to name his reward, Tom Thumb asks to marry the king's daughter, Princess Huncamunca, who is fortunately already in love with him. King Arthur grants Tom Thumb's wish, but Queen Dollallolla, who secretly desires Tom Thumb, is outraged. Meanwhile, Lord Grizzle, Tom Thumb's romantic rival, conspires to do away with his little enemy.[54] All this sets the stage for the outrageous final scene, in which an enormous cow prevents the much-anticipated wedding between Tom Thumb and his physically mismatched fiancée by swallowing Tom Thumb offstage. Not to be upstaged by this bovine intruder, Tom Thumb returns in the form of a ghost, only to have his ghost "murdered" by Grizzle. The absurd murder of Tom Thumb's ghost prompts a parodically Hamlet-esque finale in which the entire cast kills one another off one by one until the only one left standing, King Arthur, takes his own life so as not to be the odd one out.[55] Whereas the early ballads narrate the death-defying adventures and mishaps of the miniature hero while testifying ironically to his virile masculinity, the plays shift the focus of the Tom Thumb narrative from a series of life-threatening adventures to a single danger that hovers over him throughout the plays: his impending marriage and its consummation. The ballads lack any marriage plot whatsoever, but in Fielding's plays, the marriage plot is the narrative's driving force.

By the same token, the ballads have Tom Thumb swallowed by a male giant, while Fielding's plays feature a woman, his future bride—who threatens to swallow him up with love on their wedding night—and another female consumer, the enormous cow, who ultimately does. In this sense, Fielding's depiction of a milk-producing cow as a consumer of men functions as the plays' most overt symbol of the detrimental effects for the English husband of the female producer turned consumer. This is especially telling given the prevalence of contemporary concerns that Englishwomen's consumption of tea would make them incapable of producing breast milk. As Kowaleski-Wallace explains, the new female-oriented tea-drinking culture caused middle- and upper-class women to be thought of as consumers rather than producers of children and of the breast milk to sustain them;[56] this culminated in what Ruth Perry describes as the late-eighteenth-century disassociation of female desire and motherhood, which insisted that desiring women could not produce breast milk, while breast-feeding women, in turn, were thought to be incapable of sexual desire.[57] As Mary Peace explains, the popularity of D. T. de Bienville's influential 1775 antisex treatise *Nymphomania* is proof that by the end of the century, female sexual desire had become fully disconnected from the concept of motherhood. In Bienville's text, the imagined relation between the decline of motherhood and the rise of female desire is attributed to women's "consumption of luxury products," thereby establishing desiring women as detrimental consumers (of men and commodities) as opposed to beneficial maternal producers (of children and breast milk).[58]

A Queer Sort of Cannibalism

Even before Tom Thumb's death by cow, Fielding's excessive use of oral imagery in scenes featuring Huncamunca satirically suggests that the enormous appetites of the new female consumer threaten the life and dignity of any Englishman who desires her. In one exchange between Huncamunca and her father, the king finds his daughter in a state of despair and asks, "What is the Cause? / Say, have you not enough of Meat and Drink? / We've giv'n strict Orders not to have you stinted." "Alas! My Lord," Huncamunca complains, "a tender Maid may want / What she can neither Eat nor Drink—" "What's that?" inquires the King. And Huncamunca replies, "Oh! Spare my Blushes, but I mean a Husband."[59] In *The Tragedy of Tragedies*, Fielding extends the joke by having the king console his desirous daughter, "Oh! thou shalt gnaw thy tender Sheets no more, / A Husband thou shalt have to mumble now" ("mumble" meaning "to eat in a slow, ineffective manner, as if without gums").[60] In both plays, when Tom Thumb says of his bride-to-be that "she shall be mine; / I'll hug, caress, I'll eat her up with Love, Whole Days, and Nights, and Years shall be too short / For our Enjoyment; ev'ry Sun shall rise / Blushing, to see us in our Bed together," the audience is perfectly aware that the opposite is true: it is Huncamunca, of course, the female consumer par excellence, who is apt to "eat [him] up with Love" "in [their] Bed together."[61]

Fielding's invocation of female cannibalism as a metaphor for modern marriage is highly appropriate considering the cultural resonance of the trope of cannibalism at the time and the fears it expressed about consumption, sexual appetite, and the threat of being devoured by some unrestrained cultural Other, personified, in Fielding's case, not by a racist and xenophobic stereotype of a foreign "savage" but by a civilized Englishwoman. As Carol Houlihan Flynn has explained, in travel literature, fiction, and other eighteenth-century prose (particularly Daniel Defoe's *Robinson Crusoe* and Swift's *A Modest Proposal*), the cannibal functions as a metaphor for "the savage 'other' that becomes incorporated into the civilized being, that part that exists 'by necessity' in a consuming society grown complex and interdependent."[62]

Few critics have commented on the sexual implications of cannibalism, particularly female cannibalism, and yet, as Fielding writes in the chapter "Of Love" in *Tom Jones*, love is "namely the Desire of satisfying a voracious Appetite with a certain Quantity of delicate white human Flesh"; love is "Hunger; and as no Glutton is ashamed to apply the Word Love to his Appetite, and to say he LOVES such and such Dishes; so may the Lover of this Kind, with equal Propriety say, he HUNGERS after such and such Women."[63] Quoting that same passage in Fielding, Dagmar Burkhart has noted that the love-as-cannibalism metaphor is typically expressed in Western literature as the male consumption of female victims, as in the passage from *Tom Jones*. "In accordance with the subordinate social standing of the woman," writes Burkhart, "it is predominately female creatures, who, as 'tasty morsels' or 'delicious sips,' arouse the sexual appetite of male literary heroes and whose bodies serve male desire."[64] As far back as Michel de Montaigne's "Of Cannibals" (1580), male consumption of other men and unrestrained male desire for women beyond the confines of conjugal monogamy were seen as connected, linking cannibalism and polygamy as the two "social practices which most radically seem to differentiate the 'cannibals' from 'civilized' and Christianized Europe."[65] In Fielding's Tom

Thumb plays, the relation between female consumption and sexual appetite is depicted similarly as evidence of the uncivilized nature of companionate marriage and the threat it poses to ordinary Englishmen. And yet in Fielding, just as in Montaigne, the male victim of cannibalism is complicit in his own undoing. Just as Tom Thumb and the diminutive male protagonists of anthropomorphic dildo poems consent to their roles as consumed female objects, Montaigne goes out of his way to define cannibalism as requiring acceptance on the part of the eaten.[66] By depicting his devourer of consenting men as a modern bride-to-be, Fielding puts a new anti-companionate and gynophobic spin on this age-old European theme. In the Tom Thumb plays, in contrast to Montaigne's essay, cannibalism is not an aspect of some ancient, foreign, and uncivilized culture but a symptom of the new sexual and economic politics of modern English civilization.

To perpetrate his cannibalistic sexual and economic satire of modern female consumption, Fielding makes use of consumptive anal imagery in addition to imagery of the vaginal and oral variety. Consider the following speech of Huncamunca's in *The Tragedy of Tragedies*, in which Fielding underscores the modern suitor's or husband's status as the anal-erotic sexual prop of an insatiable female consumer. Engaged to her beloved Tom Thumb, but having previously promised to marry Grizzle, Huncamunca laments:

> I, who this Morn, of two chose which to wed,
> May go again this Night alone to Bed;
> So have I seen some wild unsettled Fool,
> Who had her Choice of this, and that Joint Stool;
> To give the Preference to either, loath
> And fondly coveting to sit on both:
> While the two Stools her Sitting Part confound,
> Between 'em both fall Squat upon the Ground.[67]

Characterizing both the tiny Tom Thumb and his normal-size rival as inanimate objects on which to position her "sitting part," Huncamunca reveals that she sees all of her male suitors, regardless of height, as virtually indistinguishable commodities, mere pieces of furniture that fulfill her own queerly nonreproductive anal-erotic desires. Simply by wanting to be the husband of this desirous female consumer, Fielding implies, a normal-size man can shrink to the size and sexual status of a mere Tom Thumb.

Vaginal and phallic imagery function similarly in another speech of Huncamunca's, which occurs immediately before the wedding is scheduled to take place. After being eagerly encouraged by the king to impregnate his new bride (a task that, as Grizzle points out, Tom Thumb will have a hard time achieving), an overexcited Tom Thumb exclaims, "I'm so transported, I have lost my self," to which Huncamunca responds:

> Forbid it, all the Stars; for you're so small,
> That were you lost, you'd find your self no more.
> So the unhappy Sempstress, once, they say,
> Her Needle in a Pottle, lost, of Hay.
> In vain she look'd, and look'd, and made her Moan;
> For ah! The Needle was for ever gone.[68]

Given the bawdy dildo jokes leading up to this moment, Huncamunca's comparison of Tom Thumb's small body to a seamstress's needle lost in a stack of hay underscores his status as a phallic female commodity and instrument of production that her genitals might literally and permanently devour in the act of conjugal intercourse. Although Huncamunca characterizes the needle's disappearance as a grave misfortune, the implicit joke is that the modern English husband, like the proverbial needle that gets tragically and irrecoverably lost in the haystack, is a common and easily replaceable commodity in the eyes of the new queer, defiantly unreproductive, and autoerotically self-interested female consumer.

Playing on contemporaneous associations between the "savage" practices of cannibalism and polygamy, Fielding has the queen in *The Tragedy of Tragedies* characterize the husband as a devourable morsel while praising a polygamous giantess named Glumdalca (an obvious reference to Glumdalclitch, Gulliver's first, young giant mistress in Brobdingnag): "Oh happy state of Giantism—where Husbands / Like Mushrooms grow, whilst hapless we are forc'd / to be content, nay happy thought with one."[69] While Fielding's thumb-size protagonist is warned to "beware of Marriage" to this new breed of woman, his cannibalistically consuming woman laments that the new marriage marketplace is not consumer-friendly *enough* to suit her appetite for vast quantities of goods. Just as the multiplicity of goods is what most distinguishes the new consumer culture from the old economy, so does the multiplicity of consumable little husbands signify polygamy as the most advanced and desirable form of marriage for Fielding's caricatured modern woman.

Both the anthropomorphic dildo poems and their better-known dramatic successors reveal an aspect of eighteenth-century anxieties over female consumption unacknowledged by recent criticism on the literature of nascent consumer culture: in these texts, misogynistic anxieties over female consumption are projected not only onto the female body but onto the male body as well. In the Tom Thumb plays, the most striking example of the little man as a symbol of this reversal comes in *The Tragedy of Tragedies* when Tom Thumb compares himself to a female prostitute while describing his relation to Huncamunca and Glumdalca:

> In the Balcony that o'er-hangs the Stage,
> I've seen a Whore two 'Prentices engage;
> One half a Crown does in his Fingers hold,
> The other shews a little Piece of Gold;
> She the Half Guinea wisely doth purloin,
> And leaves the larger and the baser Coin.[70]

Counterintuitively, the commodified and sexually objectified body here belongs not to a female prostitute but to the future husband of a princess. By extension, the sexual consumers of this little man are in turn the women, Huncamunca and Glumdalca, with the coins of different sizes and values signifying their relative charms. The labor of little men, Fielding suggests, is the vocation of every modern husband and male suitor of the new consuming woman, no matter what his class or stature may be.

> As Grizzle says in *The Tragedy of Tragedies*:
> Think'st thou that I will share thy Husband's place,
> Since to that Office one cannot suffice,
> And since you scorn to dine one single Dish on,
> Go, get your Husband put into Commission,
> Commissioners to discharge, (ye Gods) it fine is,
> The duty of a Husband to your Highness.[71]

Employing conspicuously mixed metaphors of cannibalistic consumption and menial labor, Grizzle complains that as one among the "Commissioners to discharge" in the delegated "Office" of husband, as one "put into Commission" to do his "duty," and as a "Dish" on which she dines, any husband or suitor of the new consuming woman is but a mere Tom Thumb.

For Fielding in the early 1730s, as for Grizzle, the answer to the question "What does the modern woman want in a husband?" seems to have been "A Lilliputian to play with." Even in the case of Fielding's later and even more famous Tom narrative *Tom Jones*, one can see the same dynamics at work in the passage in which the normal-size Tom gives his beloved Sophia a bird, which she names "little Tommy." "Little Tommy," the narrator explains, "for so the bird was called, was become so tame, that it would feed out of the hand of its mistress, would perch upon the finger, and lie contented in her bosom, where it seemed almost sensible of its own happiness; though she always kept a small string about its leg, nor would ever trust it with the liberty of flying away."[72] As a not-so-distant relative of the Tom Thumb plays, the "little Tommy" anecdote (together with the novel's unflattering depictions of Tom's Amazonian first lover, Molly Seagrim, and his six-foot-tall nemesis, Sophia's aunt Mrs. Western) shows that for Fielding, the figure of the little man never quite lost its relevance as a metaphor for the modern husband's dubious role in a commodity-oriented culture that engenders a new kind of female desire.

Tom Thumb and The Female Husband

Similarly, analysis of the plays suggests that Fielding's *Female Husband* (his infamous tale of female cross-dressing and dildo use) is not the author's only flirtation with the dildo as a symbol for the tenuousness of modern masculinity in an age in which women have the freedom to choose and consume both spouses and things. In *The Female Husband*, Fielding provides a fictionalized account of the true story of Mary Hamilton, who disguised herself as a man in order to marry women and deceived them on their wedding night by using a concealed dildo. Although the story is most obviously a phobic parable about the perils of counternormative female desire, it is also, more subtly, a warning about the sexual license given to women by the cult of companionate marriage. In Fielding's account, before Mary embarks on her dildo-wielding cross-dressing adventures, her first female lover jilts her for a man, and Mary receives a letter from the new Mrs. Rogers encouraging her to "enter as soon as you can into that holy state into which I was yesterday called. In which, tho' I am yet but a novice, believe me, there are delights infinitely surpassing the faint endearments we have experience'd together."[73] Although it would seem as if Mary's subsequent behavior—running away to pursue numerous affairs with women—constitutes an unambiguous rejection of Mrs. Rogers's pro-companionate marriage advice, she actually follows Mrs. Rogers's prescription to the letter by casting aside premarital dalliances in favor of serially monogamous marriages arrived at through the free choice of consenting male (Mary in drag) and female participants.

Indeed, in her new disguise, after several unsuccessful attempts at marriage to other women for all the wrong reasons (specifically, money and lust, motives derided by Defoe in his influential pro-companionate marriage treatise as the most reprehensible kinds of "matrimonial whoredom," second only to polygamy, in which the desirous Mary Hamilton, like Fielding's giantess Glumdalca, could also be said to have participated), Mary finally finds companionate conjugal bliss with her one true love, the naive and virginal Mary Price, with whom she "was really much in love, as it was possible for a man ever to be with one of her own sex."[74] The narrative trajectory of the story suggests that it was Mrs. Rogers's advice that gave Mary Hamilton the idea that companionate marriage, in which there were "delights infinitely surpassing the faint endearments we have experience'd together," could in fact be the most pleasurable means of fulfilling her desires for other women. Indeed, Mary Hamilton, disguised as a male doctor, courts Mary Price in the traditional bourgeois manner, and when Mary Price's sister mocks her choice of a lover, Mary Price responds in stereotypical pro-companionate marriage fashion that "she had chosen for herself only, and that if she was pleased, it did not become people to trouble their heads with what was none of their business."[75] In turn, "[t]he newly married couple not only continued, but greatly increased the fondness which they had conceived for each other"; this is not surprising, since Mary Hamilton's dildo, like the automaton bodies of Tom Thumb and Monsieur Thing, bests the penises of more traditional husbands by never expiring (that is, as long as the object in question remains on hand and is never lost, like Huncamunca's metaphorical needle in the haystack, or like the female husband's dildo, which is misplaced on one occasion, leaving her unable to perform with an elderly widow).[76] At the end of the story, Fielding disposes of his happily married husband as violently as he does Tom Thumb (Mary Hamilton is brutally whipped and imprisoned, while her wife, like Huncamunca up until the very end, gets off scot-free); however, the true object of the story's scorn is companionate marriage, which empowers women with so much free choice that they and their self-destructive spouses are blind to the justifiable misgivings of their families (embodied by the chastisements and warnings of Mary Price's sister, Huncamunca's attendant, and Tom Thumb's "Grand-mamma"). In this light, the female husband, like Tom Thumb, gets disciplined by Fielding's narrative not so much for desiring women as for taking Mrs. Rogers's advice to enter into a companionate marriage, just as Fielding's masochistic thumb-size husband is punished for making the fatal mistake of ignoring his elder's sage instruction to "beware of Marriage." Like the dildo-wielding serial monogamist of *The Female Husband*, the little man–anthropomorphic dildo protagonist of Fielding's Tom Thumb plays—when considered in light of their lesser-known verse precursors—reveals that there is something either dangerously (for husbands) or pleasurably and empoweringly (for wives) "queer" about companionate marriage.

five

THE LITTLE MAN OF FEELING

In 1750, a poem titled "The Author Apologizes to a Lady, for His Being a Little Man" appeared in *The Student*, under the name "Mr. Lun," a pseudonym for the poet Christopher Smart. The poem's self-mocking characterization was typical of Smart's references to his own small physical stature, which, like Pope before him, he represented as inversely proportionate to his fame and highbrow poetic stature. As Smart wrote elsewhere, in spite of the greatness of his literary reputation, "my stature is so very low . . . [that] In the rest of my person there is nothing very singular, saving that when I take the air, having neither horse nor vehicle, I am obliged to do it on a pair of bandy legs."[1] In the poem, Smart's narrator pleads with the woman he desires, and his reader, to hear him out before casting him aside on account of his size:

Yes, contumelious fair, you scorn
The amorous dwarf, that courts you to his arms,

But ere you leave him quite forlorn,
And to some youth gigantic yield your charms.[2]

Smart begins his "apology" with the argument that stature (physical or reputational) should be irrelevant in affairs of the heart, insisting that it is unwise for this woman to measure "Your lover's worth by quantity, or weight" as if he were a mere vegetable or piece of meat at a market. Yet he contradicts this assertion in the remaining stanzas by advertising himself to the addressee as a small person, claiming that both his low physical stature and its inversely proportionate relation to poetical stature actually make him more useful to her as a sexual object.[3] Constructing his female addressee as a physically fragile creature who would be better serviced by a refined dwarf-poet than a hulking lowbrow giant, the narrator instructs her to

Look in the glass, survey that cheek—
Where Flora has with all her roses blush'd;
The shape so tender—looks so meek—
The breasts made to be press'd, not to be crush'd—
Then turn to me—turn with obliging eyes,
No longer Nature's works, in miniature, despise.[4]

In arguing that his own littleness makes him more sexually compatible with the addressee's "tender" female body, he suggests, as seen in other little-men texts from earlier in the century, that a little man makes for a more sexually pleasing and useful love object than his taller (and, Smart implies, less refined) rivals. Concluding the poem with a sexual proposition, the narrator challenges the lady to meet him for a passionate rendezvous where he, like Fielding's Tom Thumb in his self-destructively bold wooing of Huncamunca, can put his corporeal and poetic claims to the test: "Then, scornful nymph, come forth to younger grove, / Where I defy, and challenge, all thy utmost love."[5]

Swift, Fielding, and others used the figure of the little man to sexualize the imagined belittlement of the male body associated with female consumption and companionate marriage. What Smart's poem adds to this tradition, however, is particular to the mid-to-late eighteenth century; by that point, the fascination with little men had taken on the new male prototype of the so-called man of feeling. In the characteristically inverse relation between feeling and physical stature intrinsic to little-men literature of the second half of the eighteenth century (according to which, the smaller the man, the bigger the feeling), Smart's narrator, after selling himself to the female reader as an ideal lover and writer, appeals to the popular cult of sensibility to make his suit:

> The less the body to the view,
> The soul (like springs in closer durance pent)
> Is all exertion, ever new,
> Unceasing, unextinguish'd, and unspent;
> Still pouring forth executive desire,
> As bright, as brisk, and lasting, as the vestal fire.[6]

And so goes the lover's rather tenuous argument: the shorter the man, the greater the soul, and therefore the greater and longer-lasting his sexual and literary capabilities—a thinly veiled allusion to the little male body's inexhaustible automaton-like sexual prowess, reminiscent of Fielding's Tom Thumb plays. The poem's equation of the little man with the new man of feeling thereby embodies a standard theme in eighteenth-century sentimental literature: the privileging of refined male sentiment over macho brute force. G. J. Barker-Benfield and others have characterized this development as a mid-century move away from a warlike male ideal to a more bourgeois, domesticated one, by which "[t]he culture of sensibility became a culture of reform, aiming to discipline women's consumer appetites in tasteful domesticity, but thence reforming male behavior."[7] By the end of the century, the little man, whose capacity for feeling was inversely proportionate to his physical stature, had become one especially meaningful embodiment of this new ideal.

Sentiment and the Little Male Body

The inverse relation between stature and sensibility in little-men literature of the latter half of the eighteenth century cannot be understood without attention to certain key attributes of the cult of feeling. The most stereotypical representative of this mid- to late-century phenomenon is Harley, the fictional protagonist of Henry Mackenzie's *Man of Feeling* (1771). As numerous critics have mentioned, the ocular function is crucial in the sentimental discourse of the period. Harley's most salient feature, then, is his eyes, which he uses both to see poor unfortunates and to shed tears over their plight. Adam Smith, in his *Theory of Moral Sentiments*, a crucial philosophical component of the canon of sentimental literature, claims that the act of feeling can be realized only through the act of spectatorship. As Barbara Benedict writes, Smith, "[w]hile arguing that sympathy is the source of all moral feeling . . . explains it as the individual's imaginary substitution of himself for the suffering other through spectatorship. By this conscious act of identification, the spectator feels for the sufferer as for himself,"[8] an act of spectatorial identification that, when applied to the context of little men, is not unlike the spectatorial identification between court dwarf and aristocratic spectator established by seventeenth-century portraiture (examined in chapter 1). Janet Todd has written of how the role of sentimental eyes as instigators of both crying and looking is symptomatic of the importance of the body in sentimental literature as the source and object of "constant communication."[9] One fundamental problem for any man of feeling, then, is how to both observe and emote with his body without slipping into a gross and undignified corporeal sensualism. To put it another way, the sentimental male body must be always feeling in the emotional sense of the word and, through his tears, feeling in the bodily sense of the word; at the same time, he must never experience or see others so corporeally that he might lapse into actually feeling their anatomy (that is, touching them) with his hands or being felt (that is, caressed) by others, particularly with regard to the opposite sex. In Laurence Sterne's *Tristram Shandy*, for instance, Uncle Toby is portrayed as a sentimental man who takes pity on a fly and is so anatomically and sexually naive that he does not realize he is in danger of having his genitals groped by the Widow Wadman when he invites her to touch the very spot where he received his wartime injury. For Samuel Richardson's sentimental heroines Pamela and Clarissa, their ability to feel—and the empowerment they get from it—is dependent on their not being touched by their rakish male kidnappers: Clarissa can only die after she is ultimately manhandled, whereas Pamela survives by successfully converting Mr. B, through the sentimental literature she produces in her letters, from privileging one kind of feeling (corporeal, sensual) to another (sentimental).[10] For Mackenzie's Harley, his "look[ing] steadfastly" at the body of an unfortunate prostitute leads to a back-and-forth exchange of arm holding (beginning with her taking his arm) that treads on dangerously sensual territory, so much so that his following her to a brothel, shedding tears, and giving her money look terribly suspect.[11] In Sterne's *Sentimental Journey* (1768), Yorick's encounter with the beautiful grisset who invites him to feel her pulse ("'Feel it,' said she, holding out her arm . . . I care not if all the world saw me feel it"),[12] leads to a similar tipping point between these two kinds of feeling. Benedict has argued that "[t]he literature of sentimentalism must thus separate sexual sensation from benevolence to maintain its ideal for the aesthetic and tasteful control of response. It does this by locating sensation in observation."[13] Observation, then, though corporeal in origin (located in the eyes), focused on bodies, and connected to the bodily response of crying, must be seen as a preventive for rather than a gateway to sexual feeling. As Ann Jessie Van Sant has noted, the divide between "feeling and touching" within the culture of sentiment is often a tricky one to navigate, both for the man of feeling himself and for the eighteenth-century reader.[14] The prostitute scene in *Man of Feeling*, for instance, can legitimately be read either as Benedict does, as a warning against falling from a proper emotive feeling into a dangerously sensual and corporeal kind of feeling embodied by women,[15] or as a comical satire on the interdependence between these two kinds of feeling. In the case of Josef Boruwlaski's 1788 *Memoirs of the Celebrated Dwarf* (discussed in the concluding chapter), the difference between being a man of feeling and being a corporeally "felt man" becomes an especially important one for the little male writer who would rather be seen as a passionate spectator of women than as their caressed and emasculated miniature object. If the little man is the one doing the (emotive and spectatorial) feeling of women, then he is less likely to be (corporeally) felt by them.

In its carefully circumscribed attention to the condescending observation of noteworthy bodies, the cult of feeling also engendered a new kind of compassion for so-called deformed peoples, a compassion whose beneficiaries were often dwarfs and others of unusually short stature. The smallness of their bodies seemed a perfect physical manifestation of their tragic inferiority, helplessness, and need for compassion, even as it emphasized the sentimental observer's superiority to the pathetic object of his or her gaze. In Sterne's *Sentimental Journey*, for instance, Yorick expresses compassion for dwarfs as "this poor, blighted part of my species, who have neither size nor strength to get on in the world—I cannot bear to see them trod upon."[16] As a sentimental tourist, Yorick systematically "measures" the stature of the human bodies he encounters:

> I measured everybody I saw walking in the streets. . . . Melancholy application! Especially where the size was extremely little . . . to see so many miserables, by force of accidents driven out of their own proper class into the very verge of another, which it gives me pain to write down—every third man a pigmy!—some by rickety heads and hump backs—others by bandy legs—a third set arrested by the hand of Nature in the sixth and seventh years of their growth—a fourth, in their perfect and natural state, like dwarf apple-trees; from the first rudiments and stamina of their existence, never meant to grow higher.[17]

At the same time that little male bodies were subjects of sentiment, however, they could also be a key source of the gratuitous and often cruel humor of the period, remnants of a pre-Enlightenment tradition of laughter at grotesque bodies (Rabelais's unrelenting mockery of his giant Gargantua being a prime example), which, as Simon Dickie writes, still lingered in mid-eighteenth-century jestbooks. As Dickie points out, the fact that dwarfs and hunchbacks, among other disfigured peoples, were common figures of mirth and ridicule in popular jestbooks, exhibits a "pitilessness" that contradicts or at least complicates the belief that this was the age of sentiment and sympathy.[18] Even by the end of the century, when the cult of feeling had reached its zenith, the residues of a pre-sentimental tradition of laughter at little male bodies that characterized Popiana, "A Voyage to Brobdingnag," and Fielding's Tom Thumb plays had not entirely given way to the expression of sentiment toward and by them. The dwarf incident in *Sentimental Journey* is a telling example of the persistent interplay between these two contradictory traditions. On the one hand, the reader is invited, in the same chapter, both to share Yorick's sympathy for dwarfs when he comes to the aid of one "in distress" beside a gutter ("[n]ever mind, said I; some good body will do as much for me when I am ninety") and to chuckle at the picture of a dwarf who "suffered inexpressibly on all sides" by having his view blocked by larger persons including "a tall corpulent German."[19]

Another occasion for unsentimental humor about little male bodies arises when this presumably passive object of pity loses his temper and is wittily insulted by his giant adversary: "By this time the dwarf was driven to extremes, and in his first transports, which are generally unreasonable, had told the German he would cut off his long queue with his knife—The German look'd back coolly, and told him he was welcome if he could reach it."[20] A potential occasion for sentimental feeling is thereby transformed into an antisentimental slapstick comedy of sexually violent physical feeling/reaching. The joke here is framed not only as the German's but also as an antisentimental prank on the part of Nature, Yorick remarking upon "the unaccountable sport of nature in forming such numbers of dwarfs—No doubt, she sports at certain times in almost every corner of the world; but in Paris, there is no end to her amusements—The goddess seems almost as merry as she is wise."[21] As if to demonstrate the impossibility of a complete cultural transition from the pre-sentimental tradition of dismissive laughter at and raunchy physical comedy involving little men to sentiment toward them, Oliver Goldsmith's sentimental novel *The Vicar of Wakefield* (1766) has the vicar instruct his son to read a moral parable about an unequal friendship between a status-seeking giant and a brave dwarf, in which the dwarf loses "an arm, a leg, and an eye" in fighting their enemies while the unscathed giant claims all the glory for himself.[22] The lesson that "Unequal combinations are always disadvantageous to the weaker side" is meant to arouse sympathy in its intended audience, the vicar's family, but instead has no effect on its unrefined listeners.[23]

Another stumbling block for little men in the age of feeling was the familiar stereotype established by Francis Bacon in 1625 that little and otherwise abnormally bodied men lack "natural affection." For Bacon, "[d]eformed persons are commonly even with nature; for as nature hath done ill by them, so do they by nature; being for the most part . . . 'void of natural affection'; and so they have their revenge of nature." Derision toward them, argued Bacon, has made them cunning and hard-hearted:

> Whoseover hath any thing fixed in his person that doth induce contempt, hath also a perpetual spur in himself to rescue and deliver himself from scorn. Therefore all deformed persons are extreme bold. First, as in their own defence, as being exposed to scorn; but in process of time by a general habit. Also it stirreth in them industry, and especially of this kind, to watch and observe the weakness of others, that they may have somewhat to repay.[24]

Such people, according to Bacon, are also ruthlessly self-interested and use their seemingly helpless position as a means to get ahead of their rivals undetected: "deformity is an advantage to rising" because "in their superiors it quencheth jealousy towards them . . . and it layeth their competitors and emulators asleep; as never believing they should be in possibility of advancement, till they see them in possession," invoking a connection between deformity and high social stature that physically small writers like William Hay and Josef Boruwlaski would use to their rhetorical advantage.[25] In the mid-to-late eighteenth century, this persistent stereotype translated into a belief that those perceived as deformed could never be practitioners of feeling. Although little persons were in many ways the paradigmatic objects of the sentimental gaze, they were prejudicially barred from becoming its subjects—that is, until the interventions of the sentimental little-men writings of Smart, William Hay, Sterne, and Boruwlaski.

William Hay

In his book-length examination of deformity and monstrosity in Western culture, Dennis Todd acknowledges how difficult it was for writers whose bodies were considered "deformed" to write their way out of the Baconian stereotype that the deformed were heartless, egocentric, and deceitful: "A deformed person was compelled to reveal his inner self to prove that he was not like the stereotype claimed he was, but he had been defined as so egocentric and mendacious that his very act of self-revelation was taken as evidence of his egocentricity and mendacity."[26] To make the point, Todd draws on both Pope and the somewhat lesser-known William Hay, a short, hunchbacked member of Parliament and author of *Deformity: An Essay*, an autobiographical treatise on disability, first published in 1754 and reprinted eight times over the course of the century. Correctly seeing *Deformity* as Hay's refutation of Bacon's "claim that deformed people are void of 'natural affection,'" Todd argues that "[t]he heart Hay exposes in this self-anatomy, as any reader of Pope will immediately recognize, is in its broad lineaments the 'heart' that Pope exposes in his poetry of the 1730s."[27] Missing from Todd's comparison between the two writers, however, is the significant advantage Hay enjoyed in writing at the height of the sentimental period. If, as the cult of feeling maintains, recording one's sentiments is virtuous in and of itself, then a true writer of feeling cannot rightly be accused of egocentrism or narcissism (as was Pope), and his truthfulness can be indisputably proved by the unquestionable empirical evidence of his tears, which Hay provides for his readers in plentiful but strategically not excessive amounts. When Hay writes in 1754 that "[t]hese are some of the Sensations I feel; which I have freely and fairly disclosed, that the Reader may judge, how far I am an Instance of a deformed Person wanting natural Affection," he is not only attempting to disprove Bacon's postulate about the heartlessness of deformed persons; he is explicitly referencing the contemporary discourse of feeling to excuse himself from the general rule, mentioned in the beginning of his treatise, that it is typically "offensive for Man to speak much of himself."[28] For a writer of feeling who transcribes his sentiments, "to speak much of himself" is not an egocentric offense but a benevolent moral and social virtue.

Hay's essay further subverts the Baconian hypothesis of deformity by suggesting that the moral superiority and capacity for sentimental feeling of abnormally bodied persons—and their resistance to antisentimental humor at their expense—are actually heightened, rather than impeded, by their relative isolation from society. Remarking upon his being frequently humiliated by the "mob," he writes that instead of cowering at such insults, he sees in them an opportunity for productively sentimental thought; writes Hay, "these Abuses from my Inferiors often furnish me with generous Reflexions. I sometimes recollect the expression of Brutus in Shakespear, 'Your Words pass by me as the idle Wind which I regard not.'"[29] As in the literary examples of Pamela and Clarissa, whose sentimental individualities are only augmented by their social isolation via kidnapping, the practice of feeling (as critics on the subject have observed) depended on the exaggerated autonomy of its individual subject. For Hay, if sentiment and its privileging of the anomalous individual can turn social isolation and difference into a form of empowerment (the refined person of feeling is different from and therefore better than everyone else in the unrefined, sensual, and materialistic modern world), so can that same cult of feeling empower deformed persons by romanticizing their physical uniqueness as an outward manifestation of their interior specialness.

Like Smart, Hay posits a direct relation between small size and big sensibility, but because Hay is writing a verbose, autobiographical, prose treatise (as opposed to Smart's abbreviated love poem), he is able to argue his case to an extent that Smart cannot, maintaining that "such Passions and Affections, as most naturally result from Deformity" demonstrate that

> [t]here certainly is a Consent between the Body and the Mind; and where Nature erreth in the one, she ventureth in the other; and therefore Deformity may be best considered, in this respect, as a Cause which seldom fails of the Effect, and not as a Sign, which is more

> deceivable; for as there is an Election in Man touching the Frame of his Mind, the Stars of natural Inclination are sometimes eclipsed by the Sun of Discipline and Virtue.[30]

In order to contradict Bacon's postulate that deformed men lack "natural affection," Hay paints himself not only as a man of feeling who frequently cries ("I weep," "I melt into Tears," "Tears . . . steal down my Cheek") but as an especially discriminating one whose unusually small size refines his sensibility beyond that of an ordinary man of feeling.[31] Unlike Mackenzie's overgrown and comparatively indiscriminate sentimentalist Harley, Hay does not cry at everything. In spite of his great capacity for sentiment, Hay maintains that

> I am little moved when I hear of Death, Loss, or Misfortune. . . . If I see a Person cry or beat his Breast on any such Occasion, I cannot bear him Company. . . . I read of Battles and Fields covered with Slain; of Cities destroyed by Sword, Famine, Pestilence, and Earthquake; I do not shed a Tear. . . . But there are many Things that bring Tears into my Eyes, whether I will or no; and when I reflect, I am often at a loss in searching out the secret Source from whence they flow.[32]

As a professed enemy of excess of all kinds, even in feeling, Hay dismisses the overvaluation of physical bulk in human bodies as precisely the kind of crass materialism and excessive consumption that the ideology of feeling, with its emphasis on refinement over vulgarity, opposes: "Is the Carcase the better Part of the Man? And is it to be valued by Weight, like that of Cattle in a Market?"[33] Indeed, as Hay explains it, his anticonsumerist practice of temperance and refined taste is the result of his small physique's inability to ingest as much as normal-size men, which itself is the very cause of his sentimentalism:

> I hold as Articles of Faith (but which may be condemned as Heresies in many a General Council assembled about a large Table) that the smallest Liquors are best: That there never was a good Bowl of Punch; nor a good Bottle of Champaign, Burgundy, or Claret: That the best Dinner is one Dish: That an Entertainment grows worse in proportion as the Number of Dishes increase: That a Fast is better than a Lord Mayor's Feast.[34]

As in Pope's inversion of his Grub Street critics' satire of his own corporeal and metaphorical dwarfishness (and also in the example of the proudly underpublished Gray who called himself a "shrimp" of an author), Hay associates small stature and its physical incapacity for excess with the social superiority of "highbrow" refinement, which, within the bourgeois-gentlemanly cult of feeling, trumps the excesses of lowbrow vulgarity.[35]

Hay emphasizes this inverse relation between stature and taste by comparing the admirably temperate King Henry IV with his grandson Lewis, who is characterized by "Luxury and Effeminacy," proclaiming: "[h]ow little is *Lewis*, compared to *Henry* the Great!"[36] By characterizing Lewis as "little," Hay suggests that "true" littleness has nothing to do with the size of a man's body but instead is related to a low capacity for temperance and sentiment. If small bodies are better suited to temperance, good taste, and sentiment, then littleness, in Hay's subversive formulation, is socially, aesthetically, and morally great, while greatness is socially, aesthetically, and morally little. Contrary to Lennard J. Davis and other critics of disability who have glossed Hay's essay as "reiterating (although humanizing and questioning to a degree) stereotypes about people with disabilities," Hay's treatise on deformity is downright subversive in its manipulation of the mid- to late-eighteenth-century discourse of sentiment for the purpose of establishing the little man as an empoweringly superior man of feeling whose social refinement and capacity for feeling are by definition as huge as his body is small.[37]

Tristram Shandy

Such intersections between the discourses of deformity and feeling are featured prominently in one of the most acclaimed sentimental novels of the period, Sterne's *Tristram Shandy.* As Felicity Nussbaum has written, it is in many ways a novel about disability: Tristram and Toby are disempowered and effeminized by their disabling injuries, Walter is physically and intellectually an oddball, and Tristram's deceased brother, Bobby, seems to have been "mildly retarded."[38] For Nussbaum, "[t]he allure of the irregular and discomfiting characters in the book is not unlike the perverse fascination aroused in peering at cabinets of curiousity and other exhibits of human defect enjoyed by an English public during this time. . . . In *Tristram Shandy* we find the twisted, maimed, and mutilated men among the first fictional characters whose defective bodies figure significantly as part of their characterization."[39] For Benedict, these three male protagonists whom Nussbaum defines by their deformity are also defined by their capacity for sentiment: while Toby "exemplifies sentimental delicacy," Walter "stands as 'the man of sentiment' or of 'opinion' in the book," and Tristram "blends [sentimental] confession with rhetorical virtuosity."[40] Indeed, the novel itself, like its male protagonists, is an amalgamation of disability and feeling: at once ideologically sentimental, physically odd (full of blank, black, and marbled pages and quirky visual symbols), and abruptly cut short.

Before considering how small stature and sentiment come together in *Tristram Shandy* through the body of the little man, it is important to recognize the sheer number of dwarf and little-man references in this sentimental comic novel. Tristram, for one, begins as a homunculus (a fully formed man in miniature inside the womb) who compares his own personal history to that of Tom Thumb ("[T]ho' it be but the history of Jack Hickathrift or Tom Thumb," notes Tristram, the writer of personal history "knows no more than his heels what lets and confounded hindrances he is to meet with in his way").[41] The small-bodied Walter, in decrying his son's injured nose, wishes his son had been born a dwarf like Licetus instead: "[G]ive him but a NOSE—Cripple, Dwarf, Driviller, Goosecap—(shape him as you will). . . . O *Licetus*! *Licetus*! Had I been blest with a fœtus five inches long and a half, like thee—fate might have done her worst. . . . O *Tristram*! *Tristram*! *Tristram*!"[42] Walter's Slawkenbergius tale features "a little dwarfish bandy-leg'd drummer," and the dwarfish Walter's valuation of large noses in spite of his own lack thereof suggests that it is he, of all the Shandy men, to whom the following of *Tristram Shandy*'s mock maxims most suitably applies: "A dwarf who brings a standard along with him to measure his own size . . . is a dwarf in more articles than one." In spite of their tallness, Tristram and Toby are shrunken into metaphorical little men as sentimental homunculi, while Walter is an actual little man, described as short and forever compensating for his small stature. Even Walter's preferred midwife, Dr. Slop, is described as a "little man" and introduced to the reader as an incompetent "little, squat, uncourtly figure . . . of about four feet and a half perpendicular height . . . waddling thro' the dirt upon the vertebræ of a little diminutive pony." In addition to characterizing so many of the male characters in the novel, the idea of the little man is also—according to the following sentimental reflection by the story's littlest man, Walter—emblematic of the frailty of the human condition itself and the subsequent need to treat its members with delicacy and compassion: "Man is of all others the most curious vehicle . . . 'tis of so slight a frame and so totteringly put together, that the sudden jerks and hard jostlings it unavoidably meets with in this hard journey, would overset and tear it to pieces a dozen times a day."[43]

The connection Walter posits between sentiment and small male stature is exemplified by *Tristram Shandy*'s discourse of the homunculus. The sentimental Tristram, Sterne's self-described "small hero," spends a good part of the novel as a homunculus and metaphorically remains one by evolving into a physically stunted man, deformed and shortened by having been castrated in "full three fourths of me . . . my geniture, nose, and name."[44] In narrating his origins "ab ovo," Tristram characterizes the homunculus sympathetically as a rational creature and a "little gentleman."[45] Explains Tristram:

> The HOMUNCULUS, Sir, in how-ever low and ludicrous a light he may appear, in this age of levity, to the eye of folly or prejudice; —to the eye of reason in scientifick research, he stands confess'd—a BEING guarded and circumscribed with rights:—The minutest philosophers, who, by the bye, have the most enlarged understandings, (their souls being inversely as their enquiries) shew us incontestably, That the HOMUNCULUS is created by the same hand,—engender'd in the same course of nature,—endowed with the same loco-motive powers and faculties with us.[46]

Over and against the temptation to regard the homunculus with the vulgar antisentimental humor to which other varieties of little and otherwise abnormally bodied men are so often subjected ("in how-ever low and ludicrous a light he may appear, in this age of levity, to the eye of folly or prejudice"), this little man appears to the enlightened and compassionate modern eye as a paradigmatic autonomous individual and therefore fully worthy of Tristram's and the reader's sympathetic condescension. It is important to note here that although B. L. Reid has remarked that "Sterne has conceived all his people, not only Tristram, as Homunculi,"[47] Sterne's admittedly broad application of the concept of the homunculus is actually less inclusive than Reid would have us think, for Sterne uses it to describe only the male characters in the novel; the women, by contrast, on the few occasions when their stature is discussed, are described as physically and metaphorically tall and growing taller. In the previously quoted passage, for instance, Sterne genders the homunculus as male while satirically appropriating the modern discourses of individualism and human rights, suggesting that the prototypical individual in enlightened society—"a Being guarded circumscribed with rights"—is no more than a homuncular "little gentleman" himself: an aristocratic male dwarf and a modern little man all rolled up in one. Here and throughout the novel, the homunculus epitomizes both man's paradoxical importance in modern society (in an age characterized by both reason and sentiment) and his insignificance or inferiority within it (in an age of cruel antisentimental "folly or prejudice").[48] In this, it is much like those Enlightenment philosophers whom Tristram ridicules in the very same passage as essentially "minute" in spite of their "enlarged understandings,"[49] a pun on Berkeley's *Alciphron: Or, the Minute Philosopher*, suggesting that a minute philosopher might be minute in body as well as subject matter, a satirical reversal of the age-old association of male dwarfs with excessive intellectual cultivation.

At every turn, Sterne reveals that the homunculus-size Walter's misogynistic responses to female pregnancy, such as his insistence upon the animalculist homunculus theory of generation (the belief that humans originate as anthropomorphic sperm) in contrast to the ovist theory (the belief that human life begins in the egg),[50] serve as a defense mechanism protecting him against the reality of his own "homuncular" little-man status. As Louis Landa explains, the eighteenth-century discourse of the homunculus was bound up in the competing "ovist" and "animalculist" views of prominent natural philosophers who defined the terms by which human reproduction came to be understood in the age of Enlightenment.[51] According to some, the homunculus was thought to have developed out of a so-called animalcule, the man in miniature that purportedly existed in each individual human spermatozoa. Believers in animalcules—most prominently the microscope-oriented "minute philosophers" Leeuwenhoek, Hooke, and Henry Baker—witnessed with their own eyes under the microscope what they thought to be little men swimming about in male ejaculate and concluded that man, not woman, was responsible for sexual reproduction, since the homunculus obviously developed directly out of human sperm. According to this theory, woman's role in reproduction is merely to serve as a vessel in which the animalcule must grow. It is easy to see how this theory would appeal to an anxious little man like Walter Shandy, secretly concerned that women's control over both (re)production and consumption (exemplified by Mrs. Shandy's earlier insistence upon giving birth in the commercial city of London, to which Walter initially and regretfully succumbed) might reveal man to be little more than a helpless homunculus himself.

The History of Human Heart (1749), an anonymous pre-Shandean homunculus-themed piece of eighteenth-century erotica, highlights the point by satirizing the animalcule hypothesis of generation in exaggeratedly patriarchal and misogynistic terms:

> that Hypothesis, which Supposes Generation to depend chiefly upon the Men, and that the Woman, on her Part, only furnishes a proper Nidus to nourish the Embrio. This Doctrine was more controverted, and less understood, till the ingenious Mr. Leewenhoeck, by his microscopical Observations, discovered the Animalcule in the Semen Humanum, which has put the question beyond all Controversy. Our Author supposes one of these Animalculae to be a whole Man in Miniature . . . he even supposes the Soul to animate that minute Body, and to receive the first Perception of its Existence in that State. Few Authors have enquired when the Soul animates the Foetus; the common Opinion I suppose is, that the Existence begins from the Moment of Conception, but he has gone a Step further back, and supposes it to commence while yet the Animalcule is in the Loins of the Parent.[52]

In another mock footnote, the narrator of this pre-Shandean text underscores the idea by maintaining that "Those who maintain the Hypothesis which our Author has espoused, Account for the Process of Human Generation in this manner," that the uterus is "impregnated by the Animalculae, and conveyed into the Womb, the Mouth of which, at other Times close shut, is by the Contraction of its Fibres, now open for the Reception of its new Guest."[53] The satirical effect of mock-scientific passages like these is to characterize male-centered animalcule and homunculus theories of reproduction as expressions of Enlightenment-era male anxieties over the frightening possibility of individual men's physical and metaphorical arbitrariness in relation to modern women, harking back to Swift's sexual-scientific microscopical satire of Gulliver as a woman-owned little man–pocket microscope–sexual prop in "Voyage to Brobdingnag" (discussed in chapter 3).

Thus, Walter Shandy, as a homunculus-size supporter of the phallocentric animalcule theory of reproduction, scolds both his wife and her maidservant Susannah for their height-enhancing "false" airs of statural superiority regarding the matter of reproduction, complaining that "from the very moment the mistress of the house is brought to bed, every female in it, from my lady's gentlewoman down to the cinder-wench becomes an inch taller for it; and give themselves more airs upon that single inch, than all the other inches put together." Uncle Toby perceptively replies by revealing the unflattering truth behind the little patriarch's anxieties: "I think rather . . . that 'tis we who sink an inch lower."[54] Either way, according to Walter's misogynistic explanation of women's false tallness or Toby's self-deprecating hypothesis of male shrinkage, modern women alone are responsible for making mere homunculi of modern men.

In contrast to Walter, the sentimental Toby embraces his emasculated little-man/homunculus status by sympathizing with a fly, cavorting with miniatures on the bowling green, and then trading in this childish hobbyhorse for his own metaphorical shrinkage in the reductive gaze of the Widow Wadman (when she tricks him into looking into her eye, he becomes lost in the minutiae of her iris and is consequently "undone"), who, in that famous scene of Toby's amours, threatens to turn him from a man of feeling into a felt man. It begins with Toby

> looking—and looking—then rubbing his eyes—and looking again, with twice the good nature that even Galileo look'd for a spot in the sun.
>
> —In vain! For by all the powers which animate the organ—Widow Wadman's left eye shines this moment as lucid as her right—there is neither mote, or sand, or dust, or chaff, or speck, or particle of opake matter floating in it—there is nothing, my dear paternal uncle! But one lambent delicious fire, furtively shooting out from every part of it, in all directions, into thine—
>
> —If thou lookest, uncle Toby, in search of this mote one moment longer—thou art undone.[55]

The passage continues as Tristram loses not only Toby but also himself and the reader in his magnified description of her Brobdingnagian eye:

> . . . I protest, Madam, said my uncle Toby, I can see nothing whatever in your eye.
>
> It is not in the white; said Mrs. Wadman: my uncle Toby look'd with might and main into the pupil—

Now of all the eyes, which ever were created—from your own, Madam, up to those of Venus herself, which certainly were as venereal a pair of eyes as ever stood in a head—there never was an eye of them all, so fitted to rob my uncle Toby of his repose, as the very eye, at which he was looking—it was not, Madam, a rolling eye—a romping or wanton one—nor was it an eye sparkling—petulant or imperious—of high claims and terrifying exactions, which would have curled at once that milk of human nature, of which my uncle Toby was made up—but 'twas an eye full of gentle salutation—and soft responses—speaking—not like the trumpet stop of some ill-made organ, in which many an eye I talk to, holds coarse converse—but whispering soft—like the last low accents of an expiring saint—[56]

At one point, in a bawdy aside, Tristram describes both himself and his uncle as women's candles, the household object referred to in eighteenth-century dildo literature as that with which Englishwomen "made do" before superior Italian imports were available—recalling an earlier kind of degraded and satirical eighteenth-century little man, the anthropomorphic male dildo of Swift, Fielding, and various comic-erotica of the period. By this point in the novel, Toby as a practically felt man of feeling has become the "candle" of the enamored widow "predetermined to light my uncle *Toby* neither at this end or that; but like a prodigal's candle, to light him, if possible, at both ends at once." The dying Tristram, as an emasculated woman-owned phallic prop, is devolutionarily reduced "from little to less, from less to nothing," "cut short in the midst of my days": "It is a great pity—but 'tis certain from every day's observation of man, that he may be set on fire like a candle, at either end—provided there is a sufficient wick standing out. . . . For my part, . . . I would oblige a housewife constantly to light me at the top; for then I should burn down decently to the socket"[57]—irreparably shrunken, wick and all.

In this comic sentimental novel, as in the works of Smart and Hay, the new man of feeling is the little man, but in Sterne's treatment of the theme (contrary to Smart's and Hay's), the modern little man is not empowered by his capacity for feeling but is instead disempowered, further shrunken, unsentimentally mocked, and even, in Sterne's depiction of the miniature patriarch Walter, mercilessly satirized because of it. And thus, in *Tristram Shandy*, the little man's apparent "progress" from woman-dependent court dwarf to sentimental hero has come full circle.[58] While Sterne's imagined female reader (addressed as "Madam") might, like Mrs. Shandy and Susannah, feel physically and metaphorically elevated by the comparison and even join in the unsentimental laughter at the expense of little men, Sterne's male readers, whether they choose to comply with their emasculation (like Toby) or to deny it (like Walter), are both staturally and metaphorically belittled.

six

JOSEF BORUWLASKI'S *MEMOIRS OF THE CELEBRATED DWARF*

The year 1788 saw the publication of the last significant little-man text of the century, *Memoirs of the Celebrated Dwarf*, the autobiographical account of Josef Boruwlaski, a Polish court dwarf. Boruwlaski emigrated to England to earn a living for himself and his family after creating a scandal in Poland and offending his royal mistress, the Countess Humieska, by marrying a normal-size woman. Penniless and in debt, Boruwlaski wrote his memoirs intending to sell it by subscription to members of the English nobility, from whom he also earned money by singing in concerts, both expressly in order to support himself, his wife, and, later, their child. Far from concealing his commercial aspirations, Boruwlaski begins his *Memoirs* with the admission that "On [these memoirs'] reception in the world, entirely depend my future welfare and my family's support."[1] As with Pope before him, publishing by subscription proved to be a symbolically and pragmatically convenient way for Boruwlaski to bridge the worlds of old-dwarf–old-writerly aristocratic patronage and new-dwarf–new-writerly free-market independence. This is because subscription publishing in the eighteenth century, as Paul Korshin has noted, could be seen as both a form of literary patronage (as a way for rich individuals to fund writers) and an expression of free-market writerly independence, greatly reducing and in some cases even eradicating "[t]he sense of obligation which pervades and often exacerbates the traditional patron-client relationship."[2] Fortunately for Boruwlaski, *Memoirs* proved to be a great success and made him the best-known living little man of the fin de siècle, even though he is virtually unheard of today. As Betty Adelson, one of the few critics to comment on this remarkable book, writes, Boruwlaski's *Memoirs* is "a rare enduring portrait of a dwarf who bridged a historic moment—the transition from court dwarf to exhibiting dwarf."[3] Considering the terms and circumstances of its circulation, the same could be said for Boruwlaski's position as a little male writer, à la Pope much earlier in the century. In this sense, *Memoirs* marked the end of a roughly hundred-year era of little men representation not only by its fin de siècle timing but also by its production and distribution.

Memoirs also provided the finale to a century of little-men literature in its content, by managing to encompass the century's wide and shifting range of little-men-oriented themes. Chapter 1 of this book explored the early-eighteenth-century shift in the visual representation of small male bodies from aristocratic and private dwarf representations to public and bourgeois depictions of little men, which took place while still retaining residues of its court-dwarf heritage. In *Memoirs of the Celebrated Dwarf*, Boruwlaski starts at this historically early point as a court dwarf and writer attempting to move from aristocratic dependence to middle-class independence and goes on to incorporate the century's historical trajectory of little-man representation, blending into his newfound bourgeois English identity the 1730s idea of the little man as paradigmatic companionate husband and revising that role to fit the new mid- to late-century little man of feeling. He attempts this historically sweeping rhetorical gesture by proposing, as others have done, an inversely proportional relationship between male stature and male feeling; at the same time, he describes his newfound companionate marriage in order to make himself a paradigmatic feeling patriarchal male subject as opposed to a felt object with regard to women (as discussed in chapter 5, and in contrast to Fielding's Tom Thumb plays, which satirically portray the modern companionate husband as an anthropomorphic dildo) and continually draws on the complex relationship between male stature and visual spectatorship that has manifested itself in varying ways throughout the century. Boruwlaski's *Memoirs* thus provides a thematic—as well as chronological—conclusion to the eighteenth-century English history of little-men representation.

Barbara Benedict and Kerry Duff (the only two critics besides Adelson to address Boruwlaski's *Memoirs*) have both described the paradox inherent in Boruwlaski's attempt to assimilate and establish a sentimental middle-class identity as a self-made man by selling himself as an aristocratic object of curiosity.[4] As both critics have noted, the predominant theme of Boruwlaski's *Memoirs* is his attempt to compensate for his physical and national strangeness through his mastery of the mid- to late-eighteenth-century English discourse of sentiment. Indeed, Boruwlaski concludes *Memoirs* by reflecting on the way in which his capacity for feeling is inversely proportionate to his size:

> In writing these memoirs, I not only mean to describe my size and its proportions, I would likewise follow the development of my sentiments, the affections of my soul; I would speak openly; rather tell what I felt than what I did, and demonstrate that, if I can upbraid nature with having refused me a body like that of other men, she has made me ample amends, by endowing me with a sensibility, which, it is true, displayed itself rather late, but, even in my indiscretions, spread a glow of happiness, the remembrance of which I enjoy with gratitude and a feeling of heart.[5]

Perpetually undermining Boruwlaski's self-fashioning narrative of feeling, however, is the emasculating Tom Thumb–style narrative he constructs, in which he plays the role of a miniature women's object, referred to by his female companions and owners as "Joujou" (meaning "little plaything")—and appropriately so, for, as Benedict points out, he is constantly seen not as a person but as "a phenomenon for use"—and moves at the age of fifteen from the hands of the soon-to-be-married Lady de Caorliz into the possession of the Countess Humieska.[6] Transferred from one benefactress to another, Boruwlaski's predicament mirrors the objectification of women in pre-companionate marriage, traded from one man (father) to another (husband), leaving him totally dependent on the countess, just as any young unmarried woman of the time would have been upon her father ("I had no fortune, I was totally indebted to her beneficence for my easy circumstances, I only subsisted through her bounty").[7] For a while, it seems as if his entrance into a sentimental companionate marriage provides him with the opportunity to rhetorically overcome his sexually objectified and emasculating "felt" status, but in the end, it only ends up underscoring his status as a "felt" little man like Fielding's pre-sentimental Tom Thumb. This failure is forecast by a frontispiece illustration of Boruwlaski and his wife that awkwardly straddles the chronologically and ideologically opposed artistic traditions of late-eighteenth-century sentimental domestic portraiture and seventeenth-century court-dwarf portraiture.

The rhetorical power of sentimental feeling to counteract the objectifying effects of corporeal feeling (being felt) is a lesson that Boruwlaski takes a while to learn. At first, he considers women's caresses—and his role as a felt little man—a welcome perk to his court-dwarf status. As in Fielding's "To the Same. On Her Wishing to Have a Lilliputian to Play With," Boruwlaski is happily aware that it is not his feeling heart but his portable size that makes him appealing to women and grants him physical access to them, and to their "caresses," which would otherwise be considered improper. On one occasion, Boruwlaski writes of being "agreeably surprised when I beheld about twenty beautiful women, who received me in the most tender and affectionate manner, the smallness of my stature having procured me this very particular honor."[8] Another time, he describes how during his travels, the Queen of Hungary "took me on her lap," and "much caressed me."[9] When the queen asks him about his experiences abroad, Boruwlaski confesses that he has seen nothing so "extraordinary" as that which he now beholds: "'to see so little a man on the lap of so great a woman.' This answer gained me her caresses." The Duchess of Modena, who is enchanted by Boruwlaski, takes liberties with him such that "her caresses, praises, and eagerness proved how great her enthusiasm was."[10]

Though initially flattered by all the physical "feeling" from admiring women, Boruwlaski eventually comes to disdain women's caresses as a preventive to his desires to possess them:

> "What!" said I to myself; "the most reserved women take me upon their lap; they embrace me, they bestow upon me the most tender caresses, they use me like a child! How can I hazard, in such circumstances, a declaration at which they will only laugh, whilst I shall remain covered with eternal ridicule?" It was not an easy matter to make my pride agree with my desires. The farther I was from pos-

> sessing the common size of other men, the more eagerly I wished that difference might be forgotten, and that I might be treated like them.[11]

In one scene, women's caresses are characterized as disempoweringly objectifying and affirming of his status as a mere object of enlightened female inquiry, reminiscent of Gulliver as woman's pocket microscope–cum–sexual prop in Brobdingnag. In a group of such caressing women,

> [o]ne of the company having put the question, whether Dwarfs possess the faculty of procreating? another advanced, that if they have it, their children would grow to the common size. . . . I spare my readers the particulars of that conversation, which was carried very far, and only interrupted by my weeping bitterly. . . . I had to conclude, not only that they believed themselves entitled to dispose of me without my advice, but even looked upon me *as being merely physical, without morality, on whom they might try experiments of every kind.*[12]

In this passage, the Tom Thumb romantic narrative of Boruwlaski's *Memoirs* turns from comic to pathetic, and it is at this moment that Boruwlaski sadly comes to understand how women see him—not as an unusually attractive individual man but as a Gulliverian hybrid of erotic prop and scientific specimen, not to "feel for" or feel with but to feel sensually and corporeally while at the same time observing him with a pre-sentimental kind of scientific curiosity.

In contrast to Gulliver, however, who as a women's pocket microscope and sexual prop was unable to determine the objects of his gaze (discussed in chapter 3), Boruwlaski discovers that the way to escape women's humiliating sexual and scientific curiosity about his body is to counteract their objectification of him by fashioning himself as a spectatorially empowered proponent of the feeling male gaze. This happens through Boruwlaski's discovery of the pleasures of theatrical spectatorship. No longer merely the object of women's belittling gazes, he finds that attending the theater makes him, for the first time, an empowered sentimental spectator in his own right, particularly with regard to women. He writes:

> The show itself attracted me; the concourse of spectators, but women above all, who, stirring up in me some kind of new emotions, made me attend the theater with a degree of frenzy. Till then I had lived

> almost without conceiving any difference between the sexes; but from the inquietude, the agitation, and the trouble which the presence of a woman caused in me, I could no longer conceal to myself that on this enchanting sex depends all our happiness; yet was I not able to define in what and how it might be promoted.[13]

After he has belatedly "discovered" the power over women achievable through the spectatorial feeling male gaze (having transformed himself from looked-at spectacle to sentimental theatrical spectator), Boruwlaski comes to appreciate the fact that his size enables him to attain a physical proximity to women that would otherwise be impossible and decides to take full advantage of that emboldening position: "Women, besides their continual railleries at the shortness of my stature, their pleasantries on my reservedness and circumspection, completely cured me of that timidity, which seemed, as it were, natural to my size." Notice how Boruwlaski uses the conflicting discourses of both sensibility and sensual passion to describe his discovery of the self-empowering capacity of the feeling male gaze: "Women, in my eyes, had taken quite a new form. They excited my admiration, my sensibility, my affections; but it was sufficient to be a woman, that title gave her a right to my rising passion; I was fond of the sex, without choice or distinction; I loved them all."[14] The feeling male gaze, Boruwlaski realizes, even in the artificial and idealized voyeuristic setting of the theater, can transform him from a desired women's object denied the bourgeois privilege of individuality into a desiring individual subject who denies others—in this case, the women he observes—of their individuality ("without choice or distinction").

No longer content with being the corporeally felt and looked-at object of women, Boruwlaski determines to feel and visually objectify them himself. Contemplating "how to gratify desires which every day grew more pressing," Boruwlaski decides that in spite of the obstacle presented by his stature and "pressed by the warmth of my affections, I wished *to fix my views upon a particular object.* How much was my mind mortified on reflecting upon my stature, which I considered as an insurmountable obstacle to the happiness I longed for with so much ardor!"[15] However, when Boruwlaski finally loses his virginity to none other than an actress from the theater he has been frequenting, he soon realizes, à la Fielding's Tom Thumb, that being in any kind of sensually feeling relationship with a woman only underscores his status as an "object" of female amusement:

> I was told that my little intrigue was known to everybody, and spoken of publicly; that they laughed at my discretion; and she, whom I thought the most interested in secrecy, did not scruple openly to laugh at my passion and eagerness, at the tumultuous emotions she had excited in me; that she even gloried in it, and deemed it no small proof of her merit to have provoked in a man of my size a sentiment apparently so little suitable to him. This discovery sunk me down, by humbling my pride; I thought I loved sincerely, I had hoped to be sincerely beloved; and it was not without extreme grief I saw the veil fall, and my illusion dispelled.[16]

Here, he is neither a subject nor an object of modern sentiment but a victim of old-fashioned antisentimental laughter at the deformed, according to which the affectation of any kind of feeling in a little man—as in Bacon's view of deformed people's incapacity for compassion—constitutes the very reason for his persecutors' mockery of him.

Eventually, Boruwlaski decides that the solution to this problem is to achieve a sentimental companionate marriage based on feeling and mutual admiration rather than sexual objectification. Contrary to Fielding's satire of companionate marriage in the Tom Thumb plays, in Boruwlaski's fantasy, it is not the wife but the little husband who reverses his previously objectified status by entering into a companionate partnership. Reflecting upon his disastrous affair with the actress, Boruwlaski remarks: "I then began to perceive that sentiment, reciprocal sentiment only, can give animation and liveliness to pleasures, which without it are nought." For that reason, Boruwlaski does not want his intended wife, Isalina (a woman of high stature, high birth, and low fortune) to feel him corporeally as other women have done and risk undoing his newly cultivated role as a feeling husband: "Whilst I suffered every other lady to take me on her lap, and submitted to their fondness and caresses, I was anxiously cautious lest Isalina should do the same . . . when I would have given my life to enjoy a single one of her caresses as a friend, I scorned to receive all those she would lavish on me as a child."[17] Upon relocating himself and Isalina to England, it becomes increasingly important both to Boruwlaski's newfound rhetorical strategy and to the logistics of eighteenth-century sentiment that he be the one doing the feeling and looking, rather than the one who, like a premodern court dwarf, is felt and, like the subjects of seventeenth-century court-dwarf portraiture, observed.

In an English middle-class companionate marriage filled with sentiment, Boruwlaski discovers that he can metaphorically elevate himself to the level of Isalina while at the same time making her the subordinated female object of his sentimental male gaze.[18] As he observes:

> Being now a father, having found in my wife a sincere friend, who partakes of my pains and pleasures. . . . It was, however, young Isalina's beauty, her sparkling eyes, the elegance of her figure, which struck me at first sight, and subdued my heart . . . I discovered in her a smart and brilliant wit . . . and that native meekness which was the plain index of a feeling heart![19]

And thus, in passages such as the following, Boruwlaski combines the discourses of feeling and companionate marriage to create a new identity for himself, a modern masculinity that seems to elevate him from the status of a felt female object to a feeling male subject and companion while corresponding perfectly with the new English bourgeois culture into which this displaced Polish aristocrat, as Benedict and Duff have observed, is trying to assimilate:

> my only desire was to spend my life with the object of my affection; and whereas formerly I had been determined only by the allurements of pleasure and personal satisfaction, I felt that the end at which I truly aimed was the happiness of the person to whom I was attached; and that, if I could succeed in making her happy, there would not be anything wanting to my own felicity. I had every day new occasions of applauding myself for my sentiments.[20]

Boruwlaski continues to equate companionate marriage with sensibility, setting forth a sentimental philosophy of companionate marriage in the following passages:

> Yes, it is true, I have sacrificed for this happiness—ease, riches, tranquility. It has been for me the source of a thousand inquietudes, respecting either the subsistence of myself and family, or that of my children for the future. Yet, for these eight years that I have enjoyed it, I have found that nothing in the world is preferable to the satisfaction of pouring our inquietudes, our hopes, our fears into the bosom of a

true friend united to our fate, whose tender and feeling soul relieves our pains by sharing them, and enlivens our pleasures with a far greater delight.

> [I] have discovered a very comfortable truth, that a man of feeling never regrets those actions which originate from tenderness of sentiment when unaccompanied by self-reproach. If a look on my children affect me, if a glance of a dear wife who has been so long my adored companion, and is now become a sincere friend, recall to my mind a sweet remembrance, I feel a starting tear, which would be the tear of happiness, did not other intrusive fears disturb these delightful moments.[21]

No longer a felt little man, Boruwlaski has rhetorically self-fashioned himself as an assimilated, tear-shedding, companionate husband and little man of feeling. When writing to Isalina to convince her to marry him, Boruwlaski maps out for her his rhetorical strategy: people will talk, he says, but "the wise, and even the ill-natured must be forced to own, that you had no other motive than a profound sentiment, a strong friendship, a sincere desire of making me happy."[22]

Making the by now familiar case that a bigger husband would not have the level of feeling and capacity for conjugal companionship of a little man, Boruwlaski's proposal to Isalina posits the little man as the ideal man of feeling and companionate husband:

> It is very true, that, at first sight, the idea of marrying a man of my stature will appear somewhat ludicrous; but, my charming friend, are you not already familiarized with this idea? . . . Besides, if I love you better than any other man could do . . . [if] I strive to make you amends by the greatest attentions and cares, would you not be happier than with an imperious husband, who, not knowing how to value you, even ignorant of what love is, would make you sink under the yoke of marriage, and not taste its sweets?[23]

For Boruwlaski, producing a child is not only a victory over those who see his marriage as an antisentimental joke; it also gives him a new source of bourgeois sentiment: "To the great astonishment of all those who had deemed my marriage a folly, six weeks had scarcely elapsed when she apprised me of my being destined to be a father." He writes, on another occasion, "the time came when she was brought to bed, and delivered of a pretty little girl, whose birth made me experience feelings beyond description. Then I felt, on becoming a father, that though the passion which unites us to the object of our love might before be ever so violent, yet it receives quite another energy from this new source of enjoyment." Having absorbed the discourses of feeling and companionate marriage, Boruwlaski would have the reader think that he is now completely assimilated into and empowered by what he proudly refers to as his new "middle station of life."[24] As Boruwlaski would have it, his step down in social stature (from upper to middle) is a step up in dignity, from a felt and looked-at belittled Polish aristocratic dwarf to a bourgeois, English, individual little man of feeling.

Boruwlaski's rhetorical strategy is ultimately a failure, however, not only because, as Benedict and Duff have observed, his strategic embrace of English bourgeois values is dismantled when it becomes apparent that, while he characterizes himself as a modern-day Englishman working for a living, his concerts only emphasize his objectified status—like Tom Thumb—as a dehumanized laboring object, but also because, even in their sentimental English companionate marriage, Isalina continues to think of him as a "little creature" and still refuses to see him as anything other than her "little Joujou." Writes Isalina in a letter reproduced by Boruwlaski: "But, believe me, Joujou, all this cannot alter my resolutions; though you exert yourself to have a contract of marriage in due form, to have me sign it, to take me to church, and to marry me, you shall not cease, for all that, to be my little Joujou." This persistent objectification is underscored by the actions of a young girl at one of Boruwlaski's concerts who, like Glumdalclitch in Brobdingnag, is determined to "purchase the little man like a doll' and "load him with caresses."[25] In fact, as *Memoirs* makes painfully clear, it is primarily Isalina's *sentiment* that makes her accept his marriage proposal, more out of pity than from anything approaching reciprocated love.

Thus, ironically, Boruwlaski's sentimental companionate wife's loving caresses and sentimental rhetoric are what ultimately negate his efforts to overturn his objectified and commodified status as a felt little man by appropriating the English bourgeois discourse of companionate marriage and embodying the little man of feeling. This self-representational failure of Boruwlaski's is characterized by the book's remarkable anonymous frontispiece, described on the title page as "a Copper-plate Engraving, wherein he is represented in a Family-Scene" (fig. 17). At first glance, the illustration

FIGURE 17 Anonymous, frontispiece, in Josef Boruwlaski, *Memoirs of the Celebrated Dwarf* (London, 1788). Etching. Courtesy of the James Smith Noel Collection. Photo: Robert Leitz

depicts a traditional sentimental bourgeois domestic scene—of the genre of domestic portraiture typically commissioned by middle-class families of the period—in which Boruwlaski appears as a loving companionate husband and father, surrounded by recognizable material markers of his and his family's bourgeois status and fashionability. Upon further inspection, however, Isalina's enormous hat and her centrality in the composition only emphasize her physical dominance and make Boruwlaski, who stands left of center—the traditional positioning of the dwarf in court-dwarf portraiture—appear as just another one of her accessories. As in seventeenth-century court-dwarf portraiture, the spectator is invited to identify with the dwarf as protagonist (he is, after all, the protagonist and author of the book), only, here, it is a pathetic identification, as either the object of the spectator's sentimental and compassionate or, alternatively, antisentimental and ridiculing gaze. Even his normal-size child is positioned above him, ready, like that famous Brobdingnagian baby encountering Gulliver, "to get me for a Plaything," whereupon "[t]he Mother out of pure Indulgence took me up, and put me towards the Child, who presently seized me by the Middle, and got my Head in his Mouth."[26] And thus, in the context of Boruwlaski's *Memoirs*, the family-portrait frontispiece appears as more of an old-fashioned dwarf portrait demonstrating the male dwarf's inferiority to the larger woman (and also, in this particular case, the child) he stands beside than a modern domestic portrait representing both his equality with his wife as companionate husband and his superiority to her and his child as domestic patriarch—or perhaps as an irresolvable hybrid of these two ideologically and chronologically incompatible forms of little-men representation.

In this respect, Smart's and Hay's strategic self-fashioning as mid- to late-century little men of feeling is far more rhetorically successful than Boruwlaski's. It is no coincidence, then, that Smart keeps his little-man love poem lightweight and brief, and that Hay, rather than dwelling on his relation to normal-size women, only mentions his marriage once and in a parenthetical aside, noting that "it was my Lot, many Years ago, to marry a young Lady, very piously educated, and of a very distinguished Family, and whose Virtues are an Honour to her Family, and her Sex"—as if out of the realization of what companionate marriage, pre or post feeling, can do to little men.[27] One of Hay's few mentions of his relationship to women comes in the "Post-Postscript" in which he admits that the Brobdingnagian proportions of ladies' hoop petticoats emasculate him by making him feel physically smaller and denying him spectatorship of women's bodies:

> When I am in a Coach with a Fair Lady, I am hid by Silk and Whalebone. When I sit next her at Table, my Arm is so pinioned, I can neither help her nor myself. We are deprived of the Pleasure of seeing each other; and she would scarce know I was there, if she did not

> sometimes hear me under her Wing. I am in Purgatory on the Confines of Paradise. I therefore beg one Favour, and which she may grant with Honor; that (since I despair of supplanting her . . . Lap-dog) she will allow me a Cushion to raise me above such Misfortunes.[28]

His sly joke about petticoats and lapdogs suggests that although he strategically omits the subjects of women and sexuality from the rest of the treatise, he is well aware of the literary history from earlier in the century of the metaphorical consumption of little men by Brobdingnagian and Huncamunca-like modern women.

Hay further resists situating himself within this pre-sentimental tradition of emasculating little-men representation by, in direct contrast to Boruwlaski, consciously omitting a visual self-portrait from his book. He explains his lack of a frontispiece portrait by stating: "If any Reader imagines, that . . . a print of me in the Frontispiece of this Work would give him a clearer Idea of the Subject; I have no Objection, provided he will be at the Expence of engraving. But for want of it, let him know, that I am scarce five Feet high; that my Back was bent in my Mother's Womb; and that in Person I resemble *Aesop*" and other famous hunchbacks and ugly persons, including "Mr. *Pope*."[29] Hay is intimately familiar with the abuse done to little men through visual representation, both from his own experience ("When I was a Child," Hay admits, "I was drawn like a Cupid, with a Bow and Arrow in my Hands, and a Quiver on my Shoulder; I afterwards thought this an Abuse, which ought to be corrected") and through his knowledge of Popiana ("[e]ven Mr. *Pope* was not invulnerable in this Part. For when the Dunces were foiled by his Writings, they printed a Caricature of his Figure; and it is evident that this stung him more than a better Answer; for . . . he ranks it among the most atrocious Injuries").[30] By providing the reader with a written rather than a visual portrait, and by situating his relationships with women in the margins of his text, Hay alludes to but ultimately refuses to participate in the pre-sentimental history of little-man representation going back to Velázquez and anti-Pope caricature and extending all the way to Fielding's Tom Thumb, in which Boruwlaski entangles himself. Unlike Hay, who wisely omits his picture and keeps his discussion of marriage to a bare minimum, Boruwlaski does not understand that for a little man even to appear beside a normal-size woman in the eighteenth century posits him as either a woman-owned sex object like Gulliver in Brobdingnag, a laboring companionate husband–sexual commodity like Tom Thumb or

Monsieur Thing, or a self-contradictorily aristocratic dwarf–working little man as in Popiana, establishing himself not as a feeling desirer of women but as a small felt object-writer. Hay, by contrast, understands that for little men to allow themselves to be visually represented negates their claim to the feeling male gaze by "draw[ing] the Eyes of the World too much upon them, and theirs too much from the World. For who would choose to be always looking at bad Pictures, when there is so great a Collection to be met with of good ones, especially among the Fair Sex; who, if they will not admit them to be Intimates, will permit them to be distant Admirers."[31] If there is one practical lesson to be learned from the century's history of little-men representation, then Hay (and not Boruwlaski) seems to have learned it: better for a little man of feeling to be a spectator of women, than for women to become the staturally elevated spectators of "bad Pictures" of either anachronistic court dwarfs or modern little men.

Contemporary critics of eighteenth-century gender and disability studies must begin to acknowledge the powerful metaphorical significance of physical stature to the sexual and body politics of the period, particularly the important place held in the eighteenth-century imagination by the little man as a shifting cultural signifier. For this heretofore untold story of the ubiquitous height-impaired Everyman—and his transformation over the course of a hundred years from court dwarf, to independent writer, to miniature microscope, to companionate husband, to little man of feeling—is also the story of eighteenth-century English culture itself.

NOTES

Preface

1 Peter Mandler, *The English National Character: The History of an Idea from Edmund Burke to Tony Blair* (New Haven, Conn.: Yale University Press, 2006), 164.

2 Ibid.

3 Ibid., 165.

4 Lennard J. Davis, "Dr. Johnson, Amelia, and the Discourse of Disability in the Eighteenth Century," in *"Defects": Engendering the Modern Body*, ed. Helen Deutsch and Felicity Nussbaum (Ann Arbor: The University of Michigan Press, 2000), 60.

5 Katherine Park and Lorraine J. Daston, "Unnatural Conceptions: The Study of Monsters in Sixteenth- and Seventeenth-Century England," *Past and Present* 92 (1981): 24.

6 Rosemarie Garland Thompson, Introduction to *Freakery: Cultural Spectacles of the Extraordinary Body* (New York: New York University Press, 1996), 4.

7 Barbara M. Benedict, *Curiosity: A Cultural History of Early Modern Inquiry* (Chicago: University of Chicago Press, 2001).

8 Dennis Todd, *Imagining Monsters: Miscreations of the Self in Eighteenth-Century England* (Chicago: University of Chicago Press, 1995), 141–42.

9 Self-identified dwarfs nowadays refer to dwarfs as LP, "a dwarfism-community neologism" for Little People, meaning those whose stature is less than four foot ten.

10 Betty M. Adelson, *The Lives of Dwarfs: Their Journey from Public Curiosity toward Social Liberation* (New Brunswick, N.J.: Rutgers University Press, 2005), xv, xvi. "Midget, *n.*," *OED Online*, Oxford University Press, 9 July 2009, http://dictionary.oed.com/.

11 John Jonston, *An History of the Constancey of Nature: Wherein, By comparing the latter Age with the former, it is maintained that the World doth not decay universally in respect of it Self or the Heavens, Elements, Mixt Bodies, Meteors, Minerals, Plants, Animals, nor Mand in his Age, Stature, Strength, or Faculties of his Minde, as relating to all Arts and Science* (London: 1657), 252.

12 William Derham, *Physico-Theology* (London, 1688), 329.

13 Sarah Scott, *A Description of Millenium Hall*, ed. Gary Kelly (Peterborough, Ontario: Broadview Literary Texts, 1995), 72.

14 See Adelson, *Lives of Dwarfs*, 62–65.

15 Ellen Brinks, *Gothic Masculinity: Effeminacy and the Supernatural in English and German Romanticism* (Lewisburg, Pa.: Bucknell University Press, 2003).

16 Janis Dawson, "Trade and Plumb-Cake in Lilliput: The Origins of Juvenile Consumerism and Early English Children's Periodicals," *Children's Literature in Education* 29.4 (1998): 175.

17 Ibid., 184.

18 As Adelson articulates in her preface, her project is to narrate a history of dwarf representation that stands apart from more general discussions of freaks, monstrosities, the disabled, and the deformed, into which discussions of dwarfs are so often subsumed (*Lives of Dwarfs*, xv).

1. A Visual Prehistory

1 Thomas Paine, *Rights of Man*, in *Collected Writings* (New York: Library of America, 1995), 480.

2 Ibid., 476–77. That "writer, of some antiquity," is Saint Paul; see *Corinthians* 13:1–13.

3 Leslie Fiedler, *Freaks: Myths and Images of the Secret Self* (New York: Simon & Schuster, 1979), 51.

4 Betty M. Adelson's *The Lives of Dwarfs: Their Journey from Public Curiosity toward Social Liberation* (New Brunswick, N.J.: Rutgers University Press, 2005), is the first of its kind to provide an exhaustive cultural history of little people independent of more wide-ranging discussions of "freaks" and "monstrosities" and provides an excellent account of the significant change in dwarfs' cultural status from the 1600s to the 1700s.

5 Ibid., 15.

6 Andrew Wilton, *The Swagger Portrait: Grand Manner Portraiture in Britain from Van Dyck to Augustus John, 1630–1930* (London: Tate Gallery Publications, 1992), 15.

7 Adelson, *Lives of Dwarfs*, 139.

8 Fiedler, *Freaks*, 47.

9 Yi-Fu Tuan, *Dominance and Affection: The Making of Pets* (New Haven, Conn.: Yale University Press, 1984), 157.

10 Adelson, *Lives of Dwarfs*, 13.

11 Ibid., 8.

12 Ibid., 11.

13 Lindsey Hughes, *Playing Games: The Alternate History of Peter the Great* (London: School of Slavonic and East European Studies, 2000), 13–14, 30–32.

14 Edmund Waller, "At the marriage of the Dwarfs" (London, 1645), 82.

15 John Ashton, *Social Life in the Reign of Queen Anne* (London: Chatto and Windus, 1925); and Henry Morley, *Memoirs of Bartholomew Fair* (London: Chatto and Windus, 1880).

16 Adelson, *Lives of Dwarfs*, 146.

17 Barbara M. Benedict, "Displaying Difference: Curious Count Boruwlaski and the Staging of Class Identity," *Eighteenth-Century Life* 30.3 (2006): 81.

18 See J. Murdoch and V. J. Murrell, "The Monogramist DG: Dwarf Gibson and His Patrons," *Burlington Magazine* 938 (1981): 282–89.

19 Susan Stewart, *On Longing: Narratives of the Miniature, the Gigantic, the Souvenir, the Collection* (Durham, N.C.: Duke University Press, 1993), 47, 51.

20 J. P. Dominguez, "El buffon don Sebastian de Morra," *Journal of the American Medical Association* 261.5 (February 1989): 671 (also quoted in Adelson, *Lives of Dwarfs*, 149).

21 Adelson, *Lives of Dwarfs*, 21.

22 See Wilton, *Swagger Portrait*, 64.

23 Fiedler, *Freaks*, 52.

24 Morley, *Memoirs of Bartholomew Fair*, 253.

25 "The Lucky Dwarf," in *The Pall Mall Miscellany. Containing Many Curious Pieces of Prose and Verse, with Variety of New Songs, adapted to Old Ballad Tunes and Country Dances* (London: Printed by Christopher Dickson, the Port-Office Yard, 1732), 55–58.

26 Ibid., 55.

27 Ibid., 57.

28 Ibid.

29 Ibid., 57–58.

30 Ashton, *Social Life*, 205–6.

31 Ibid., 361.

32 Morley, *Memoirs of Bartholomew Fair*, 251.

33 "The Little Man," in *The Gentleman's Bottle-Companion, Containing a Collection of Curious, Uncommon, and Humourous Songs; Most of which are Originals* (London, 1768), 7.

34 Ibid.

35 Ibid.

36 Adelson, *Lives of Dwarfs*, 23, 4.

37 Ibid., 35.

38 Adelson writes that "[t]he lessening of this subject matter in art coincided with the declining incidence and ultimate disappearance of dwarfs from the courts. Fantasy little people continued to be caricatured and used to accompany folktales and children's stories, but paintings and sculptures of dwarfs became relatively scarce in the nineteenth and twentieth centuries, with only a few first-rate portrait treatments" (ibid., 139).

39 Mark Hallet, *The Spectacle of Difference: Graphic Satire in the Age of Hogarth* (New Haven, Conn.: Yale University Press, 1999), 27.

40 As Tony Halliday writes of court portraiture in his study of the genre, "Their significance was overwhelmingly private, and depended on the identity of their individual subject. It was relatively unusual for private portraits to appear in public" (*Facing the Public: Portraiture in the Aftermath of the French Revolution* [Manchester: Manchester University Press, 1999], 2).

41 Hallet, *The Spectacle of Difference*, xiii.

42 Ibid., 27–28.

43 Louise Lippincott, "Expanding on Portraiture: The Market, the Public, and the Hierarchy of Genres in Eighteenth-Century Britain," *The Consumption of Culture, 1600–1800: Image, Object, Text*, ed. Ann Bermingham and John Brewer (London: Routledge, 1995), 83.

44 Hallet, *Facing the Public*, 27.

45 M. Dorothy George, *Hogarth to Cruikshank: Social Change in Graphic Satire* (New York: Walker and Company, 1967), 52.

46 "William Hogarth," Art of the Print, www.artoftheprint.com/artistpages/hogarth_ william_evening.htm.

47 Herbert M. Atherton says of the conceptual simplicity of such Walpole caricatures: "Walpole's character in the prints fits more of a stereotype than an individual person". . . . He is the grand corruptor, and not the corrupted. . . . His vices are those expected of an evil minister: ambition, avarice, and cunning" (*Political Prints in the Age of Hogarth: A Study of the Ideographic Representation of Politics* [Oxford: Clarendon Press, 1974], 204).

48 Ibid., 208.

49 William Shakespeare, *Julius Caesar*, 1.2.135. References are to act, scene, and line.

50 David Bindman, *Hogarth and His Times* (Berkeley: University of California Press, 1997), 156.

51 Barbara M. Benedict, *Curiosity: A Cultural History of Early Modern Inquiry* (Chicago: University of Chicago Press, 2001), 7.

52 George, *Hogarth to Cruikshank*, 162.

2. *The Dwarfing of Little-Man Pope*

1 Quoted in Maynard Mack, *Alexander Pope: A Life* (New Haven, Conn.: Yale University Press, 1985), 153.

2 "Dwarf, *n.*," *OED Online*, Oxford University Press, 20, December, 2010, http://dictionary.oed.com/ J. V. Guerinot, *Pamphlet Attacks on Alexander Pope, 1711–1744* (New York: New York University Press, 1969), 16, 187; 197; 16; 227; 254; 317, 293; 2, 4; 177; 5, 294; 44; 155, 306.

3 Guerinot, *Pamphlet Attacks on Alexander Pope*, 155, 212, 304.

4 John Barrell, "'The Dangerous Goddess': Masculinity, Prestige, and the Aesthetic in Early Eighteenth-Century Britain," *Cultural Critique* 12 (1989), 102.

5 See Helen Deutsch, *Resemblance and Disgrace: Alexander Pope and the Deformation of Culture* (Cambridge, Mass.: Harvard University Press, 1996), on Pope's responses to his critics' disparagements of his body; Dennis Todd, who argues that Pope describes his critics as monsters in order to deflect stereotypes of monstrosity from himself, in his *Imagining Monsters* (Chicago: University of Chicago Press, 1995), 217–68; and Mack, *Alexander Pope*, an essential Pope biography in which Pope's stature and deformity compose a recurrent theme.

6 Mack, *Alexander Pope*, 153.

7 See Marjorie Nicolson and G. S. Rousseau, *'This Long Disease My Life:' Alexander Pope and the Sciences* (Princeton, N.J.: Princeton University Press, 1968), 7–82. Nicolson and Rousseau mention Pope's Short Club as an allusion to his own diseased and stunted body. Noting Pope's poetic fascination with insects and other small matter, they posit elsewhere that "Perhaps some of Pope's persistent interest in 'the poetry of little things' went back, in part at least, to his own smallness" (243).

8 See Deutsch, *Resemblance and Disgrace*, 18–25; and William Kurtz Wimsatt, *The Portraits of Alexander Pope* (New Haven, Conn.: Yale University Press, 1965).

9 Quoted in Mack, *Alexander Pope*, 152.

10 Pope to Judith Cowper, 18 October (1722), *The Correspondence of Alexander Pope*, ed. George Sherburne (Oxford: Clarendon Press, 1956), 2:138; quoted in Mack, "'The Least Thing like a Man in England': Some Effects of Pope's Physical Disability on His Life and Literary Career," in *Collected in Himself: Essays Critical, Biographical, and Bibliographical on Pope and Some of His Contemporaries* (Newark: University of Delaware Press, 1982), 372.

11 Pope, *The Correspondence of Alexander Pope*, 3:444; quoted in Deutsch, *Resemblance and Disgrace*, 5.

12 Pope, "Imitations of Horace," Epistle 1.1., lines 49–50, in *The Poems of Alexander Pope*, ed. John Butt (New Haven, Conn.: Yale University Press, 1963), 613–703.

13 Pope, "An Epistle to Dr. Arbuthnot," lines 115–20, in *The Poems of Alexander Pope*, 597–612.

14 Deutsch, *Resemblance and Disgrace*, 2.

15 Ibid., 1.

16 "Resignification" is Butler's useful term for the practice of strategically and performatively changing the meaning of a signifier. See, for instance, her *The Psychic Life of Power: Theories in Subjection* (Stanford, Calif.: Stanford University Press, 1997).

17 See Anne Hall Bailey, "How Much for Just the Muse?" *The Eighteenth Century* 36.1 (1995): 33.

18 Colin Nicholson, "The Mercantile Bard," *Studies in the Literary Imagination* 38.1 (2005): 78.

19 Ibid., 81, 79.

20 Catherine Ingrassia, *Authorship, Commerce, and Gender in Early Eighteenth-Century England* (Cambridge: Cambridge University Press, 2005), 40–41.

21 Nicholson, "The Mercantile Bard," 88. Flavio Gregori, "Pope on the Margins and in the Center," *Studies in the Literary Imagination* 38.1 (2005): vi-vii.

22 Nicholas Hudson, "Challenging Eisenstein: Recent Studies in Print Culture," *Eighteenth-Century Life* 26.2 (2002): 86.

23 Margaret J. M. Ezell, *Social Authorship and the Advent of Print* (Baltimore: Johns Hopkins University Press, 1999), 12.

24 Dustin Griffin, *Literary Patronage in England* (Cambridge: Cambridge University Press, 1996), 9.

25 Ibid., 124.

26 Ibid., 124, 125.

27 Guerinot, *Pamphlet Attacks on Alexander Pope*, xxxviii.

28 See Pope, *The Poems of Alexander Pope*, 604.

29 Guerinot, *Pamphlet Attacks on Alexander Pope*, xliii.

30 Ibid., 254.

31 Ibid., 154.

32 Ibid., 5, 2.

33 Ibid., 17.

34 Benedict, "Displaying Difference: Curious Count Boruwlaski and the Staging of Class Identity," *Eighteenth-Century Life* 30.3 (2006): 81.

35 Guerinot, *Pamphlet Attacks on Alexander Pope*, 229, 230–31.

36 Claudia N. Thomas, *Alexander Pope and His Eighteenth-Century Women Readers* (Carbondale: Southern Illinois University Press, 1994).

37 Guerinot, *Pamphlet Attacks on Alexander Pope*, 81, 177, 178.

38 Also quoted in Deutsch, *Resemblance and Disgrace*, 40.

39 Guerinot, *Pamphlet Attacks on Alexander Pope*, 210, 218, 220.

40 Alexander Pope, "Rondeau," in *Minor Poems*, ed. Norman Ault and John Butt (London: Methuen & Co., 1954), 61.

41 Alexander Pope, "Pope to Lady Mary Wortley Montagu," October 1716, in *The Correspondence of Alexander Pope*, 1:365.

42 "Woman," in *The Dryden-Tonson Miscellanies, 1684–1709*, ed. Stuart Gillespie and David Hopkins (London: Routledge, 2008), 6:354, 355.

43 I thank an anonymous reader for this suggestion that Pope used his littleness as a sign of his uniqueness as a writer.

44 "Of a Dwarf Courting a Bright Lady," in *The Dryden-Tonson Miscellanies*, 6:556–57.

45 Guerinot, *Pamphlet Attacks on Alexander Pope*, 294, 293.

46 Ibid., 317, 318.

47 See Leslie Fiedler, *Freaks: Myths and Images of the Secret Self* (New York: Simon & Schuster, 1979), 51–52.

48 Quoted in Adelson, *Lives of Dwarfs*, 15.

49 Joseph Addison, "*The Spectator*, No. 99, Saturday, June 23," in *The Spectator in Four Volumes* (London: J. M. Dent & Sons, 1961), 1:306.

50 Adelson, *Lives of Dwarfs*, 8.

51 Thomas Gray, "Letter LXXX, Mr. Gray to Mr. Walpole," February 26, 1768, in *The Works of Thomas Gray* (Oxford: Talboys and Wheeler, 1825), 306.

52 Shaun Regan, "Print Culture in Transition: Tristram Shandy, The Reviewers, and the Consumable Text," *Eighteenth-Century Fiction*, 14.3–4 (2002): 290–91.

53 David Hume, quoted in James Noggle, "Literary Taste as Counter-Enlightenment in Hume's *History of England*," *SEL* 44.3 (Summer 2004): 617, 627.

54 Ibid., 634.

55 Martha Woodmansee, "The Interests in Disinterestedness: Karl Phillipp Moritz and the Emergence of the Theory of Aesthetic Autonomy in Eighteenth-Century Germany," *Modern Language Quarterly* 45.1 (1984): 41.

56 Guerinot, *Pamphlet Attacks on Alexander Pope*, 99.

57 Pope, *Minor Poems*, 271.

58 John Dennis, "A True Character of Mr. Pope and his Writings," in *The Critical Works of Dennis*, ed. Edward Niles Hooker (Baltimore: The Johns Hopkins University Press, 1943), 2:103, 104. In his attack, Dennis writes that Pope is "in Shape a *Monkey*," and a monkey "in his every Action; in his senseless Chattering, and his merry Grimaces, in his doing hourly Mischief and hiding himself, in the variety of his Ridiculous Postures, and his continual Shiftings, from Place to Place, from Persons to Persons, from Thing to Thing. But whenever he Scribbles, he is emphatically a *Monkey*, in his awkward servile Imitations" (104). Dennis also describes Pope as "a Creature not of our Original, nor of our Species" (105).

59 As in the anonymous anti-Pope pamphlet *A Compleat Collection of all the Verses, Essays Letters and Advertisements, Which Have been occasioned by the Publication of Three Volumes of Miscellanies, by Pope and Company*.

60 Andrew Wilton, *The Swagger Portrait: Grand Manner Portraiture in Britain from Van Dyck to Augustus John, 1630–1930* (London: Tate Gallery Publications, 1992), 64; Fiedler, *Freaks*, 72–73.

61 Alexander Pope, "Pope to John Caryll, Jr., 1 March 1712," in *The Monthly Magazine; or, British Register* 24.2 (London: 1808), 515.

62 Guerinot, *Pamphlet Attacks on Alexander Pope*, 167.

63 For an analysis of Tyson's mistakes, see Londa Schiebinger, "Nature's Unruly Body: The Limits of Scientific Description," in *Regimes of Description: In the Archive of the Eighteenth Century* (Stanford, Calif.: Stanford University Press, 2005), 31–33.

64 Edward Tyson, *The Anatomy of a Pygmy, Compared with that of a Monkey, an Ape, and a Man* (London, 1699), title page. For more on Linnaeus's distinction, see Julia Douthwaite, "*Homo ferus*: Between Monster and Model," *Eighteenth-Century Life* 21.2 (1997): 178.

65 See Fiedler, *Freaks*, 47.

66 Guerinot, *Pamphlet Attacks on Alexander Pope*, 303–4.

67 Ibid., 304.

68 Pope, *Minor Poems*, 268.

69 Abigail Williams, "Patronage and Whig Literary Culture in the Early Eighteenth Century," in *"Cultures of Whiggism": New Essays on English Literature and Culture in the Long Eighteenth Century*, ed. David Womersley (Newark: University of Delaware Press, 2005), 149.

70 Alexander Pope, "No. XCI. Thursday, June 25," *The Guardian* (London, 1713), 44.

71 Ibid., 45.

72 For example, Mack writes that for Pope, as a "hunchback and dwarf, such comforting communities [as the Short Club] were realizable only in imagination," while Roger Lund argues that Pope in these pieces creates "an imaginary world [not unlike the real one] where laughing at cripples is so widespread and so acceptable, that even dwarfs feel compelled to laugh at one another" (Mack, "The Least Thing Like a Man," 374; Lund, "Laughing at Cripples: Ridicule, Deformity, and the Argument from Design," *Eighteenth-Century Studies* 39.1 [2005]: 111).

73 Alexander Pope, "No. XCII. Friday, June 26," *The Guardian* (London, 1713), 48.

74 See, for instance, Lund, "Laughing at Cripples," 110.

75 Pope, "No. XCII. Friday, June 26," 52.

76 Alexander Pope, "No. CVIII. Wednesday, July 15," *The Guardian* (London, 1713), 122.

77 Pope, "No. XCII. Friday, June 26," 51–52 (my italics).

78 Ibid., 49.

79 Ibid.

80 Ibid.

81 Writes pro-Ancient William Temple: "The force of all that I have met with upon this subject, either in talk or writings is, first, as to knowledge, that we must have more than the ancients, because we have the advantage both of theirs and our own, which is commonly illustrated by the similitude of a dwarf's standing upon a giant's shoulders, and seeing farther than he" ("Essay Upon the Ancient and Modern Learning" [London, 1690], in *Five Miscellaneous Essays by Sir William Temple*, ed. Samuel Holt Monk [Ann Arbor: University of Michigan Press, 1963], 38). The expression began in the twelfth century with Bernard de Chartres and was revived in 1676 by Isaac Newton, who wrote in a letter to Robert Hooke, "If I have seen farther than others, it is because I was standing on the shoulders of giants" (letter to Robert Hooke, 5 February 1676, in *Correspondence of Isaac Newton*, ed. H. W. Turnbull [Cambridge: Cambridge University Press, 1959], 1:416).

82 Pope, "No. CVIII. Wednesday, July 15," 121.

3. *Little Man–Microscope in Brobdingnag*

1 Jonathan Lamb, "Modern Metamorphoses and Disgraceful Tales," in *Things*, ed. Bill Brown (Chicago: University of Chicago Press, 2004), 209.

2 Marjorie Nicolson, "The Microscope and the English Imagination," *Smith College Studies in Modern Languages* 16.4 (July 1955). The essay was published a year later in Nicolson's book *Science and Imagination* (Ithaca, N.Y.: Great Seal Books, 1956), 155–234. While studies of general science, the Royal Society, and Enlightenment ideology in *Gulliver's Travels* abound (particularly regarding the third section), few since Nicolson have considered how the microscope in particular figures into Swift's scientific satire. One exception is Christopher Fox, who argues that Gulliver plays the part of a microscopical specimen in Brobdingnag ("How to Prepare a Noble Savage," in *Inventing Human Science: Eighteenth-Century Domains*, ed. Christopher Fox, Roy Porter, and Robert Wokler [Berkeley: University of California Press, 1995], 1–30). Fox's argument adds a welcome new dimension to Nicolson's but fails to account for the physicality of the microscope, its particular status in the eighteenth century, and Gulliver's resemblance to it. Noteworthy analyses of general science in *Gulliver's Travels* include Frederick Smith on Brobdingnag and *Philosophical Transactions of the Royal Society* ("Science, Imagination, and Swift's Brobdingnagians," *Eighteenth-Century Life* 14.1 [February 1990]: 100–112); David Renaker on science and satire in Laputa ("Swift's Laputians as a Caricature of the Cartesians," *PMLA* 94.5 [1979]: 936–44); and Douglas Lane Patey ("Swift's Satire on 'Science' and the Structure of *Gulliver's Travels*," *ELH* 58.4 [Winter 1991]: 809–39).

3 Jonathan Swift, *Gulliver's Travels*, ed. Peter Dixon and John Chalker (New York: Penguin Books, 1967), 151.

4 Ibid., 130, 148.

5 The box was also a common and inhumane method of transportation for dwarf performers in traveling freak shows; see Aline MacKenzie Taylor, "Sights and Monsters and Gulliver's Voyage to Brobdingnag," *Tulane Studies in English* 7 (1957): 29–83.

6 Swift, *Gulliver's Travels*, 149.

7 See, for example, Paul-Gabriel Boucé, "Gulliver Phallophorus and the Maids of Honour in Brobdingnag," *Bulletin de la Société d'Études Anglo-Américaines des XVIIe et XVIIIe Siècles* 53 (November 2001): 81–98; Laura Brown, "Reading Race and Gender: Jonathan Swift," in *Critical Essays on Jonathan Swift*, ed. Frank Palmeri (New York: G. K. Hall & Co., 1993), 121–42; and Ruth Salvaggio, "Swift's Disruptive Woman," in *Enlightened Absence: Neoclassical Configurations of the Feminine* (Urbana: University of Illinois Press, 1988), 77–104.

8 Writes Nicolson, "In England, the period 1660–85 saw the emergence of the microscope from a stage of mere novelty into an important adjunct to the investigations of the Royal Society, then saw a period of intense enthusiasm for its possibilities, followed by a period of waning interest and of comparative disuse of the microscope among scientists, accompanied by a growing interest

in the microscope among laymen" ("The Microscope and the English Imagination," 8). Later, Nicolson explains how "[f]or a time the microscope ceased to be an important scientific instrument and became the plaything of the aristocracy—most of all, of the 'ladies'" (ibid., 22). Compared with the telescope, the microscope "naturally made the greater appeal. It was . . . easily obtainable and at a price not prohibitive; it could easily be used by amateurs and its 'discoveries' were immediate and readily intelligible. It became in a short time the ladies' toy. As contemporary advertisements indicate, commercial manufacturers found in the women of the day an important additional source of revenue: exquisite glasses were available for them, in specially prepared cases, which might easily be carried in the place of snuff-boxes; and the charming *virtuosae* of the day delighted in the new fad" (ibid., 41–42).

9 Robert Boyle, quoted in J. Paul Hunter, "Robert Boyle and the Epistemology of the Novel," *Eighteenth-Century Fiction* 2.4 (July 1990): 284.

10 Robert Hooke, *Micrographia* (London, 1665), xxvii.

11 Joseph Roach, "The Artificial Eye: Augustan Theater and the Empire of the Visible," in *The Performance of Power: Theatrical Discourse and Politics*, ed. Sue-Ellen Case and Janelle Reinelt (Iowa City: University of Iowa Press, 1991), 131, 133.

12 For more on the connection between Hooke's *Micrographia* and the philosophy of Francis Bacon, see Svetlana Alpers, *The Art of Describing: Dutch Art in the Seventeenth Century* (Chicago: University of Chicago Press, 1983), 73.

13 This fascinating topic is addressed in Marian Fournier, *The Fabric of Life: Microscopy in the Seventeenth Century* (Baltimore: Johns Hopkins University Press, 1996); Catherine Wilson, *The Invisible World: Early Modern Philosophy and the Invention of the Microscope* (Princeton, N.J.: Princeton University Press, 1997); Christopher Herbert Lüthy, "Matter and Microscopes in the Seventeenth Century" (PhD diss., Harvard University, 1995); and James B. McCormick, M.D., *Eighteenth-Century Microscopes: A Synopsis of History and Workbook* (Lincolnwood, Ill.: Scientific Heritage, 1987).

14 Hooke, *Micrographia*, iv.

15 McCormick, *Eighteenth-Century Microscopes*, 12.

16 Quentin Skinner, pointing out that the Royal Society, far from being "the conscious center of all genuinely scientific endeavour" was "'something much more like a gentlemen's club' meeting in coffee-houses and private lodgings"; quoted in Michael Hunter, *Science and Society in Restoration England* (Cambridge: Cambridge University Press, 1981), 33.

17 Michael Hunter, *The Royal Society and Its Fellows 1660–1700: The Morphology of an Early Scientific Institution* (London: The British Society for the History of Science, 1982), 44, 35.

18 Michael Hunter, *Science and the Shape of Orthodoxy: Intellectual Change in Late Seventeenth-Century Britain* (Woodbridge, Suffolk, U.K.: Boydell Press, 1995), 155.

19 Larry Stewart, *The Rise of Public Science: Rhetoric, Technology, and Natural Philosophy in Newtonian Britain* (Cambridge: Cambridge University Press, 1992), 101.

20 Wilson, *The Invisible World,* 228.

21 Fournier, *The Fabric of Life,* 8.

22 Susannah Centlivre, *The Basset Table,* in *Female Playwrights of the Restoration: Five Comedies,* ed. Paddy Lyons and Fidelis Morgan (London: Everyman, 1991), 261, 3:i.

23 Ibid.

24 See Maurice Daumas, *Scientific Instruments of the Seventeenth and Eighteenth Centuries* (New York: Praeger Publishers, 1972), for an in-depth commentary on the English instrument-making workshops of the seventeenth and eighteenth centuries.

25 McCormick, *Eighteenth-Century Microscopes,* 41.

26 Maxine Berg, *Luxury and Pleasure in Eighteenth-Century Britain* (Oxford: Oxford University Press, 2005), x.

27 Adam Smith, quoted in Berg, *Luxury and Pleasure,* 21.

28 Berg, *Luxury and Pleasure,* 24.

29 Ibid., 267, 268.

30 Harriet Guest, *Small Change: Women, Learning, Patriotism, 1750–1810* (Chicago: University of Chicago Press, 2000), 73.

31 Ibid.

32 Swift, "November 15 1710," in *Journal to Stella,* ed. Harold Williams, (Oxford: Clarendon Press, 1963), 1:97.

33 Hooke, "Discourse Concerning Telescopes and Microscopes; with a short Account of Their Inventors, read in February 1691–2," in *Philosophical Experiments of the Late Eminent Dr. Robert Hooke and Other Eminent Virtuoso's in His Time* (London, 1726), 5.

34 Hooke, *Micrographia,* i.

35 Swift, *Gulliver's Travels,* 54.

36 Ibid., 142, 135.

37 Ibid., 130.

38 For more on misogyny in "A Voyage to Brobdingnag" and elsewhere in Swift, see Laura Brown, "Reading Race and Gender," in Palmeri, *Critical Essays on Jonathan Swift*; Salvaggio, "Swift's Disruptive Woman"; Margaret Anne Doody, "Swift among the Women," in *Critical Essays on Jonathan Swift,* ed. Frank Palmeri (New York: G. K. Hall & Co., 1993), 13–37; Felicity A. Nussbaum, "Gulliver's Malice: Gender and the Satiric Stance," in *Gulliver's Travels: Complete, Authoritative Text with Biographical and Historical Contexts, Critical History, and Essays from Five Contemporary Critical Perspectives,* ed. Christopher Fox (Boston: Bedford Books of St. Martin's Press, 1995), 318–34; Nora F. Crow, "Swift and the Woman Scholar," in *Pope, Swift, and Women Writers,* ed. Donald C. Mell (Newark: University of Delaware Press, 1996), 222–38; Louise K. Barnett, "Betty's Freckled Neck: Swift, Women, and Women Readers," *1650–1850: Ideas, Aesthetics, and Inquiries in the Early Modern Era* 4 (1998): 233–45; and Ellen Pollak, *The Poetics of Sexual Myth: Gender and Ideology in the Verse of Swift and Pope* (Chicago: University of Chicago Press, 1985).

39 Swift, *Gulliver's Travels*, 153, 134.

40 Ibid., 139, 151.

41 Hoh-Cheung Mui and Lorna H. Mui, *Shops and Shopkeeping in Eighteenth-Century England* (London: McGill-Queens University Press, 1989).

42 Swift, *Gulliver's Travels*, 150.

43 Elizabeth Kowaleski-Wallace, *Consuming Subjects: Women, Shopping, and Business in the Eighteenth Century* (New York: Columbia University Press, 1997), 61. For more on the advent of female consumerism in the eighteenth century, see Ann Bermingham and John Brewer, eds., *The Consumption of Culture, 1600–1800: Image, Object, Text* (London: Routledge, 1995); Lorna Weatherhill, *Consumer Behavior and Material Culture in Britain, 1660–1760* (London: Routledge, 1996); and Guest, *Small Change*, 1–94.

44 Swift, *Gulliver's Travels*, 151–52.

45 John Locke, *Essay Concerning Human Understanding* (New York: Penguin Books, 1964), 119–22.

46 The name Glumdalclitch gives Gulliver, Grildrig, highlights his position in Brobdingnag as a women's prop. Gulliver translates this name as "what the Latins call *nanunculus*, the Italians *homunceletino*, and the English *mannikin*" (Swift, *Gulliver's Travels*, 134). Paul Odell Clark, drawing from Swift's and Stella's "little language," translates "Grildrig" as "Girl-thing" (*Gulliver Dictionary* [New York: Haskell House Publishers, 1979], 20).

47 As Gulliver wonders upon encountering his first Brobdingnagian, "What could I expect but to be a morsel in the mouth of the first among these enormous barbarians who should happen to seize me?" (Swift, *Gulliver's Travels*, 125). During the same meal with the queen, the court dwarf (arguably a stand-in for Swift himself) delights in reminding Gulliver that he is a mere morsel in the eyes of the queen by dropping Gulliver into a bowl of cream and inserting him into a marrow bone on her plate.

48 Ibid., 145.

49 Ibid., 157, 158.

50 This is a stark contrast to his adventures in Lilliput, where he uses his enormous member (much admired by the Lilliputians) to put out a fire on the queen's tiny palace.

51 Catherine Wilson, "Visual Surface and Visual Symbol: The Microscope and the Occult in Early Modern Science," *Journal of the History of Ideas* 49.1 (January–March 1988): 103.

52 Joseph Addison, "*The Tatler*, January 12, 1709," in *The Works of Joseph Addison*, ed. Henry G. Bohn (London: George Bell and Sons, 1901), 2:72; Alexander Pope, "Essay on Man," in *The Poems of Alexander Pope*, ed. John Butt (New Haven, Conn.: Yale University Press, 1965), 511 ("Why has not Man a microscopic eye? / For this plain reason, Man is not a Fly. / Say what the use, were finer optics giv'n, / T'inspect a mite, not comprehend the heav'n?" For more on Locke and microscopy, see Wilson, *Invisible World*, chapter 7.

53 See Peter Wagner, "The Discourse on Sex—Or Sex as Discourse: Eighteenth-

Century Medical and Paramedical Erotica," in *Sexual Underworlds of the Enlightenment*, ed. G. S. Rousseau and Roy Porter (Chapel Hill: University of North Carolina Press, 1988), 53.

54 See also the tongue-in-cheek manner in which the comic-erotic 1722 poem "Monsieur Thing's Origin" (Cheapside, 1722) frames the conflict between dildo and penis as a matter of "Art" versus "Nature" and the similarly comical disparagement of dildos as "false ware" in the anonymous 1706 poem "Dildoides" (in *Dildoides*, reprint [Kingston, R.I.: Biscuit City Press, 1980], 9), which is often attributed to Samuel Butler (see A. H. De Quehen, "An Account of Works Attributed to Samuel Butler," *The Review of English Studies* 33.131 [August 1982]: 262–77).

55 John Wilmot, Earl of Rochester, "Signior Dildo," in *The Works of John Wilmot Earl of Rochester*, ed. Harold Love (Oxford: Oxford University Press, 1999), 253. For more on literary representations of dildos—anthropomorphic and inanimate alike—in the seventeenth and eighteenth centuries, see Emma Donoghue, *Passions between Women: British Lesbian Culture, 1668–1801* (New York: Harper Collins, 1993); Harold Weber, "'Drudging in Fair Aurelia's Womb': Constructing Homosexual Economies in Rochester's Poetry," *The Eighteenth Century* 33.2 (Summer 1992): 99–117; and Jeffrey Kahan, "Violating Hippocrates: Dildoes and Female Desire in Thomas Nashe's 'The Choice of Valentines,'" *Para*doxa* 2.2 (1996): 204–16.

56 See Sheila Shaw, "The Rape of Gulliver: Case Study of a Source," *PMLA* 90.1 (January 1975): 64.

57 "Monsieur Thing's Origin: Or Seignior D___'s Adventures in Britain" (Cheapside, 1722), 20–21.

58 "The Bauble: A Tale" (London, 1721), 5.

59 Ibid., 3.

60 Lisa Anscomb, "'A Close, Naked, Natural Way of Speaking': Gendered Metaphor in the Texts of Margaret Cavendish and the Royal Society," *In-Between: Essays & Studies in Literary Criticism* 9.1–2 (2000): 168.

61 Denise Tillery, "The Plain Style in the Seventeenth Century: Gender and the History of Scientific Discourse," *The Journal of Technical Writing and Communication*, 35.3 (2005): 277.

62 Richard Nate, "'Plain and Vulgarly Express'd': Margaret Cavendish and the Discourse of the New Science," *Rhetorica* 19.4 (2001): 404, 403–17.

63 Steven Shapin, "Who Was Robert Hooke?" in *Robert Hooke: New Studies*, ed. Michael Hunter and Simon Schaffer (Woodbridge, Suffolk, U.K.: The Boydell Press, 1989), 261.

64 Robert Hooke, *Micrographia*; quoted in Alpers, *The Art of Describing*, 74.

65 James Randall Jacob, *Robert Boyle and the English Revolution: A Study in Social and Intellectual Change* (New York: Burt Frankline & Co., 1977), 144, 145.

66 Henry Oldenburg, quoted in Michael Hunter, *Science and Society in Restoration England*, 53.

67 Christopher Flint, "Speaking Objects: The Circulation of Stories in Eighteenth-Century Prose Fiction," *PMLA* 113.2 (March 1998): 212.

68 Ibid.

69 Bill Brown, "Thing Theory," in *Things* (Chicago: University of Chicago Press, 2004), 5.

70 Swift, *Gulliver's Travels*, 158.

71 Louise Barnett, "Swift, Women, and Women Readers: A Feminist Perspective on Swift's Life," in *Representations of Swift*, ed. Brian A. Connery (Newark: University of Delaware Press, 2002), 192.

72 Stephen Colclough, *Consuming Texts: Readers and Reading Communities, 1695–1870* (New York: Palgrave Macmillan, 2007), 57; Naomi Tadmor, "'In the even my wife read to me': Women, Reading and Household Life in the Eighteenth Century," in *The Practice and Representation of Reading in England*, ed. James Raven, Helen Small, and Naomi Tadmor (Cambridge: Cambridge University Press, 1996), 162–74.

73 Susan Stewart, *On Longing: Narratives of the Miniature, the Gigantic, the Souvenir, the Collection* (Durham, N.C.: Duke University Press, 1993), 41, 40.

74 Swift, *Gulliver's Travels*, 191.

4. The Labor of Little Men

Epigraphs: Alexander Pope, "The Rape of the Lock," in *The Poems of Alexander Pope*, ed. John Butt (New Haven, Conn.: Yale University Press, 1965), 79, Canto 1, Line 11; and Henry Fielding, *"Tom Thumb" and "The Tragedy of Tragedies,"* ed. L. J. Morrissey (Berkeley: University of California Press, 1970), 230, 2.2.7–8. Future references to this play are to act, scene, and line number of this edition.

1 Cradock eventually became the inspiration for the idealized wife in Fielding's *Amelia*.

2 Henry Fielding, "To the Same. On Her Wishing to Have a Lilliputian to Play With," in *Miscellanies by Henry Fielding, Esq*, ed. Henry Knight Miller (Oxford: Clarendon Press, 1972), 1:72.

3 Ibid., lines 1–2. Gulliver describes the first Lilliputian he encounters as "a human creature not six inches high"; Jonathan Swift, *Gulliver's Travels*, ed. Peter Dixon and John Chalker (New York: Penguin Books, 1967), 56.

4 Fielding, "To the Same," lines 37–38.

5 Ibid., lines 39–40.

6 In addition to the extra act, *The Tragedy of Tragedies* was printed with an introduction and footnotes by the alleged author, H. Scriblerus Secundus, a joke at the expense of the celebrated Scriblerians.

7 Henry Fielding, *Tom Thumb*, in *"Tom Thumb" and "The Tragedy of Tragedies,"* epilogue, lines 23–28. Unless stated otherwise, all subsequent citations of Fielding's Tom Thumb plays, *Tom Thumb* and *The Tragedy of Tragedies*, refer to act, scene, and line numbers in Morrissey, *"Tom Thumb" and "The Tragedy of Tragedies."*

8 "Thump, *v.*," *OED Online*, Oxford University Press, 20, December, 2010, http://dictionary.oed.com/.

9 Recent Fielding criticism has had surprisingly little to say about the author's interest in sexual and marital relations between little men and normal-size women. Criticism on the Tom Thumb plays, from 1918 to the present day, has been concerned primarily with reading the plays either as burlesques of Restoration tragedy or as satires of Walpole and the royal family. For recent analyses of the plays, see Sheridan Baker, "Political Allusion in Fielding's Author's Farce, Mock Doctor, and Tumble-Down Dick," *PMLA* 77 (1962): 221–31; Jill Campbell, *Natural Masques: Gender and Identity in Fielding's Plays and Novels* (Stanford, Calif.: Stanford University Press, 1995); Thomas R. Cleary, *Henry Fielding: Political Writer* (Ontario: Wilfred Laurier University Press, 1984); T. W. Craik, "Fielding's 'Tom Thumb' Plays," in *Augustan Worlds*, ed. J. C. Hilson, M. M. B. Jones, and J. R. Watson (New York: Barnes & Noble Books, 1978), 165–74; Robert D. Hume, *Henry Fielding and the London Theater, 1728–1737* (Oxford: Clarendon Press, 1988); Bertrand A. Goldgar, *Walpole and the Wits: The Relation of Politics to Literature, 1722–1742* (Lincoln: University of Nebraska Press, 1976); James T. Hillhouse, preface to *The Tragedy of Tragedies; Or the Life and Death of Tom Thumb the Great, with the Annotations of H. Scriblerus Secundus* (New Haven, Conn.: Yale University Press, 1918), vii-viii; J. Paul Hunter, *Occasional Form: Henry Fielding and the Chains of Circumstance* (Baltimore: The Johns Hopkins University Press, 1975), 40; Peter Lewis, *Fielding's Burlesque Drama: Its Place in the Tradition* (Edinburgh: Edinburgh University Press, 1987), 118; and Samuel L. Macey, "Fielding's *Tom Thumb* as the Heir to Buckingham's *Rehearsal*," *Texas Studies in Literature and Language* 10.3 (Fall 1968): 405–14.

10 See Elizabeth Kowaleski-Wallace, *Consuming Subjects: Women, Shopping, and Business in the Eighteenth Century* (New York: Columbia University Press, 1997), 6. Other recent studies of consumption in eighteenth-century literature and culture include James Cruise, *Governing Consumption: Needs and Wants, Suspended Characters, and the "Origins" of Eighteenth-Century English Novels* (Lewisburg, Pa.: Bucknell University Press, 1999); Ann Bermingham and John Brewer, eds., *The Consumption of Culture, 1600–1800: Image, Object, Text* (London: Routledge, 1995); John Brewer and Roy Porter, eds., *Consumption and the World of Goods* (London: Routledge, 1993); Malcolm Waters, ed., *Modernity: Critical Concepts*, (London: Routledge, 1999); Lorna Weatherhill, *Consumer Behavior and Material Culture in Britain, 1660–1760* (London: Routledge, 1988); Nandini Bhattacharya, *Reading the Splendid Body: Gender and Consumerism in Eighteenth-Century British Writing on India* (Newark: University of Delaware Press, 1998); and Charlotte Sussman, *Consuming Anxieties: Consumer Protest, Gender, and British Slavery, 1713–1833* (Stanford, Calif.: Stanford University Press, 2000).

11 Kowaleski-Wallace, *Consuming Subjects*, 4–5.

12 See Gayle Rubin's feminist revision of Claude Lévi-Strauss's analysis of the kinship system and the incest taboo, "The Traffic in Women: Note on the 'Political Economy' of Sex," in *Feminist Literary Theory and Criticism*, ed. Sandra M. Gilbert and Susan Gubar (New York: W. W. Norton & Company, 2007), 392–413.

13 Lawrence Stone, *The Family, Sex, and Marriage in England: 1500–1800* (New York: Harper & Row, 1977), 325, 330.

14 Ibid., 330.

15 Susan Staves, *Married Women's Separate Property in England, 1660–1833* (Cambridge, Mass.: Harvard University Press, 1990), 131–61.

16 "To the Ladies" (1703), cited in Stone, *The Family, Sex, and Marriage*, 340.

17 Katherine Sobba Green, *The Courtship Novel, 1740–1820: A Feminized Genre* (Kentucky: University Press of Kentucky, 1991), 71.

18 Niklas Luhmann, *Love as Passion: The Codification of Intimacy*, trans. Jeremy Gaines and Doris L. Jones (Stanford, Calif.: Stanford University Press, 1982), 114, 100.

19 Ibid., 10.

20 *Onania* (London, 1718), 8, 9.

21 Fielding, *Tom Thumb*, 1.3.55, 2.10.44.

22 According to Georges-Louis Lesage, a Frenchman who traveled through England in 1713–14: "there were always some women in St. James's Park, London, carrying baskets full of dolls which seemed to be in great demand with the younger ladies. Instead of legs, the dolls sported a cylinder, covered with cloth, which was about six inches long and one inch wide"; cited in Peter Wagner, "The Discourse on Sex—Or Sex as Discourse: Eighteenth-Century Medical and Paramedical Erotica," in *Sexual Underworlds of the Enlightenment*, ed. G. S. Rousseau and Roy Porter (Chapel Hill: University of North Carolina Press, 1988), 53.

23 Writes Wagner, "Lesage reports in an anecdote that a young woman found her purchase too big and ordered a smaller one. But the saleswoman insisted on being paid in advance, arguing that she would not be able to sell it, if ever the young lady changed her mind, since only big ones were being asked for" (ibid.).

24 As Paul-Gabriel Boucé notes, the tendency in eighteenth-century English literature to characterize the dildo as an object of French or Italian origin is "a constant linguistic and moralistic reflex in eighteenth-century England: anything 'naughty' may safely be ascribed to those lecherous Continentals" ("Aspects of Sexual Tolerance and Intolerance in XIIIth-Century England," *The British Journal for Eighteenth-Century Studies* 3 [1980]: 180).

25 While *anthropomorphic* dildo poetry has yet to be recognized as a subgenre unto itself, there have been a number of critical writings on seventeenth- and eighteenth-century dildo literature in general. Roughly speaking, these critical analyses tend to fall into one of two categories: those that situate dildo literature in the context of contemporaneous cultural anxieties over depopulation and masturbation (see Wagner, "The Discourse on Sex," and Boucé, "Aspects of Sexual Tolerance and Intolerance") and those that explore the feminist and antifeminist implications of texts in which artificial penises are characterized as superior to real ones (see Emma Donoghue, *Passions between Women: British Lesbian Culture, 1668–1801* [New York: Harper Collins Press, 1993]; Harold Weber, "'Drudging in Fair Aurelia's Womb': Constructing Homosexual

Economies in Rochester's Poetry," *The Eighteenth Century* 33.2 [Summer 1992]: 99–117; and Jeffrey Kahan, "Violating Hippocrates: Dildoes and Female Desire in Thomas Nashe's 'The Choice of Valentines,'" *Para*doxa* 2.2 [1996]: 204–16).

26 A. H. De Quehen questions Samuel Butler's authorship of the poem in "An Account of Works Attributed to Samuel Butler," *The Review of English Studies* 33.131 (August 1982): 262–77.

27 "Dildoides," in *Dildoides*, reprint (Kingston, R.I.: Biscuit City Press, 1980), 3, 4.

28 Karl Marx, *Capital: A Critique of Political Economy*, trans. Ben Fowkes (Penguin Books, 1976)) 164; "Dildoides," 1.

29 "Dildoides," 10.

30 Harold Love disputes the traditional attribution of "Signior Dildo" to Rochester in "A Restoration Lampoon in Transmission and Revision: Rochester's (?) 'Signior Dildo,'" *Studies in Bibliography* 46, ed. David L. Vander Meulen (Charlottesville: University of Virginia Press, 1993), 250–62.

31 John Wilmot, Earl of Rochester, "Signior Dildo" and "Disputed Works," in *The Works of John Wilmot Earl of Rochester*, ed. Harold Love (Oxford: Oxford University Press, 1999), 253–55.

32 Ibid., 253, 255–56, 254.

33 "Monsieur Thing's Origin: Or Seignior D___'s Adventures in Britain" (Cheapside, 1722), 10.

34 Ibid., 11.

35 Ibid.

36 Ibid., 14.

37 See Karl Marx, *Grundrisse*, trans. Martin Nicolaus (London: Penguin Books,1993), 94; and Karl Marx, *Capital: A Critique of Political Economy, Volume 1*, trans. Ben Fowkes (London: Penguin Books, 1976), 291.

38 Marx, *Capital*, 505, 465.

39 "Monsieur Thing's Origin," 16.

40 Marx, *Capital*, 271.

41 Ibid.

42 Simon Schaffer, "Enlightened Automata," in *The Sciences in Enlightened Europe*, ed. William Clark, Jan Golinski, and Simon Schaffer (Chicago: University of Chicago Press, 1999), 126.

43 Quoted in Schaffer, "Enlightened Automata," 129.

44 Barbara M. Benedict, "Encounters with the Object: Advertisements, Time, and Literary Discourse in the Early Eighteenth-Century Thing-Poem," *Eighteenth-Century Studies* 40.2 (2007), 203.

45 Ibid., 205.

46 *Daily Journal*, London, June 9, 1722.

47 "Just published, Monsieur Thing; or Seignior D__do's Adventures in Great Britain," *Daily Journal*, London, June 9, 1722.

48 Fielding, *Tom Thumb*, 2.3.15–18, 2.3.32–33.

49 Fielding, *The Tragedy of Tragedies*, 2.4.19–24.

50 Lewis, *Fielding's Burlesque Drama*, 123; and Hunter, *Occasional Form*, 29.

51 Fielding, *The Tragedy of Tragedies*, 1.3.50, 1.3.53–58.

52 "Brickdusta" *n*.," *OED Online*, Oxford University Press, 20, December, 2010, http://dictionary.oed.com/.

53 The ballads' title pages read: "Tom Thumbe, his Life and Death: Wherein is declared many Marvailous Acts of Manhood, full of wonder, and strange merriments" ("Tom Thumb, His Life and Death," in *Remains of the Early Popular Poetry of England*, ed. W. Carew Hazlitt [London, 1866], 167). For a reading of Richard Johnson's *History of Tom Thumb*, a seventeenth-century prose version of the ballads, see Anne Lake Prescott, "The Odd Couple: Gargantua and Tom Thumb," in *Monster Theory: Reading Culture*, ed. Jeffrey Jerome Cohen (Minneapolis: University of Minnesota Press, 1996), 75–91. Little is known about the precise origins of these Tom Thumb ballads, but W. Carew Hazlitt provides an informative literary history. Hazlitt surmises that Tom Thumb dates back to the late sixteenth century, citing a reference to a "Treatise of Tom Thumme" in Nashe's *Pierce Penilesse His Supplication to the Divell* (1592). Hazlitt cites subsequent references dating from Ben Jonson's mention of Tom Thumb falling into a pudding in *The Fortunate Isles* (1624) to William Wagstaffe's satirical "Comment upon the History of Tom Thumb" (1711). The life of the Tom Thumb Two legend continued long after Fielding's plays. Eliza Haywood and William Hatchett set Fielding's *The Tragedy of Tragedies* to music in *The Opera of Operas* (1733), which is generally faithful to Fielding's dialogue, with the addition of various songs. Jonathan Swift mentions Tom Thumb in "A Tale of a Tub," in *The Writings of Jonathan Swift*, ed. Robert A. Greenberg and William B. Piper (New York: Norton, 1973), 299), as does Laurence Sterne in *Tristram Shandy: An Authoritative Text, the Author on the Novel, Criticism*, ed. Howard Anderson (New York: Norton, 1980), 26. In the mid- to late-eighteenth century, children's chapbooks appeared with titles such as *Tom Thumb's Folio: Or a New Penny Play-Thing for Little Giants to which is Prefixed an Abstract of the Life of Mr. Thumb and an Historical Account of the Wonderful Deeds He Performed* (1789). The nineteenth and twentieth centuries saw P. T. Barnum's renowned dwarf performer General Tom Thumb and children performing in so-called Tom Thumb weddings. Susan Stewart provides a succinct history of the Tom Thumb legend in *On Longing: Narratives of the Miniature, the Gigantic, the Souvenir, the Collection* (Baltimore: The Johns Hopkins University Press, 1988).

54 In *The Tragedy of Tragedies*, a giantess named Glumdalca joins the cast of lovers and rivals and falls instantly in love with Tom Thumb, who does not reciprocate. Launching yet another little-man–big-woman scenario, the king falls in love with the giantess at first sight.

55 The two versions of the play differ slightly in their resolution of Tom Thumb's fate: in *Tom Thumb*, our little hero is eaten by the cow before the marriage can take place; in *The Tragedy of Tragedies*, the cow consumes him immediately after the wedding. Yet in spite of these differences, one crucial fact remains consistent: in both plays, Fielding makes clear that Tom Thumb dies before he and Huncamunca have a chance to consummate their marriage.

56 Kowaleski-Wallace, *Consuming Subjects*, 34.

57 See Ruth Perry, "Colonizing the Breast: Sexuality and Maternity in Eighteenth-Century England," *Journal of the History of Sexuality* 2.2 (October 1991): 204–34.

58 Mary Peace, "The Economy of Nymphomania: Luxury, Virtue, Sentiment and Desire in Mid-Eighteenth-Century Medical Discourse," in *At the Borders of the Human: Beasts, Bodies, and Natural Philosophy in the Early Modern Period*, ed. Erica Fudge, Ruth Gilbert, and Susan Wiseman (London: Macmillan Press, 1999), 239–58, 244.

59 Fielding, *Tom Thumb*, 2.4.6–12.

60 Fielding, *The Tragedy of Tragedies*, 2.4.9–11. "Mumble" *v.*," *OED Online*, Oxford University Press, 20, December, 2010, http://dictionary.oed.com/.

61 Fielding, *The Tragedy of Tragedies*, 2.2.20–23.

62 Carol Houlihan Flynn, *The Body in Swift and Defoe* (Cambridge: Cambridge University Press, 1990), 149.

63 Henry Fielding, *The History of Tom Jones, a Foundling* (Hanover, Conn.: Wesleyan University Press, 1975), 241.

64 Dagmar Burkhart, "Archeology of Female Cannibalism: Slavenka Drakulić's Novel *Divine Hunger*," *Russian Literature* 59.1 (2006): 3.

65 Carla Freccero, "Cannibalism, Homophobia, Women: Montaigne's 'Des Cannibales' and 'De l'amitié,'" in *Women, "Race," and Writing in the Early Modern Period*, ed. Margo Hendricks and Patricia Parker (London: Routledge, 1994), 75.

66 Ibid., 77.

67 Fielding, *The Tragedy of Tragedies*, 2.10.62–70.

68 Ibid., 2.8.19–21.

69 Ibid., 1.3.32–34.

70 Ibid., 2.7.28–33.

71 Ibid., 2.10.41–46.

72 Fielding, *The History of Tom Jones*, 159.

73 Henry Fielding, *The Female Husband*, in *The Female Husband and Other Writings*, ed. Claude E. Jones (Liverpool: Liverpool University Press, 1960), 32.

74 Ibid., 43. See Daniel Defoe, *Conjugal Lewdness: or, Matrimonial Whoredom* (London: 1727).

75 Fielding, *The Female Husband*, 46.

76 Ibid., 47.

5. *The Little Man of Feeling*

1 Arthur Sherbo, *Christopher Smart: Scholar of the University* (Ann Arbor: Michigan State University Press, 1967), 61.

2 Christopher Smart, "The Author Apologizes to a Lady, for His Being a Little Man," *The Student* (Oxford, October 5, 1750), 26.

3 Ibid., 27.

4 Ibid.

5 Ibid., 28.

6 Ibid., 27.

7 G. J. Barker-Benfield, *The Culture of Sensibility: Sex and Society in Eighteenth-Century Britain* (Chicago: University of Chicago Press, 1992), xxvi.

8 Barbara M. Benedict, *Framing Feeling: Sentiment and Style in English Prose Fiction, 1745–1800* (New York: AMS Press, 1994), 3.

9 Janet Todd, *Sensibility: An Introduction* (London: Methuen, 1986), 99.

10 I am purposefully invoking the interpretation of Pamela as domestic fiction writer and Mr. B. as reader made by Nancy Armstrong in *Desire and Domestic Fiction: A Political History of the Novel* (Oxford: Oxford University Press, 1987).

11 Henry Mackenzie, *The Man of Feeling*, ed. Brian Vickers (Oxford: Oxford University Press, 1987), 37.

12 Laurence Sterne, *A Sentimental Journey through France and Italy*, in *"A Sentimental Journey" and "Continuation of the Bramine's Journal" with Related Texts*, ed. Melvyn New and W. G. Day (Indianapolis: Hackett Publishing Company, 2006), 75.

13 Benedict, *Framing Feeling*, 14.

14 Ann Jessie Van Sant, *Eighteenth-Century Sensibility and the Novel: The Senses in Social Context* (Cambridge: Cambridge University Press, 1993), 93, 97.

15 Benedict, *Framing Feeling*, 14.

16 Sterne, *A Sentimental Journey*, 85.

17 Ibid., 83.

18 Simon Dickie, "Hilarity and Pitilessness in the Mid-eighteenth Century: English Jestbook Humor," *Eighteenth-Century Studies*, 37.1 (2003): 1–22.

19 Sterne, *A Sentimental Journey*, 84, 85.

20 Ibid., 86.

21 Ibid., 83.

22 Oliver Goldsmith, *The Vicar of Wakefield* (London: Penguin Books, 1982), 86.

23 Ibid., 85.

24 Francis Bacon, "On Deformity," in *Francis Bacon: A Critical Edition of the Major Works*, ed. Brian Vickers (Oxford: Oxford University Press, 1996), 426.

25 Ibid., 426–27.

26 Dennis Todd, *Imagining Monsters: Miscreations of the Self in Eighteenth-Century England* (Chicago: University of Chicago Press, 1995), 249.

27 Ibid., 234, 237.

28 William Hay, *Deformity: An Essay*, ed. Kathleen James-Cavan (Victoria, B.C.: University of Victoria, 2004), 122, 93.

29 Ibid., 98.

30 Ibid., 115.

31 Ibid., 115, 118, 121

32 Ibid., 116–17.

33 Ibid., 96.

34 Ibid., 106.

35 For an analysis of sentimentalism as a bourgeois adaptation of aristocratic refinement, see Robert Markley, "Sentimentality as Performance: Shaftesbury,

Sterne, and the Theatrics of Virtue," in *The New Eighteenth Century: Theory, Politics, English Literature*, ed. Felicity Nussbaum and Laura Brown (London: Methuen, 1987), 210–30.

36 Ibid., 119, 120.

37 Lennard J. Davis, "Dr. Johnson, Amelia, and the Discourse of Disability in the Eighteenth Century," in *"Defects": Engendering the Modern Body*, ed. Helen Deutsch and Felicity Nussbaum (Ann Arbor: The University of Michigan Press, 2000), 60.

38 Felicity Nussbaum, *The Limits of the Human: Fictions of Anomaly, Race, and Gender in the Long Eighteenth Century* (Cambridge: Cambridge University Press, 2003), 105.

39 Ibid.

40 Benedict, *Framing Feeling*, 69.

41 Laurence Sterne, *The Life and Opinions of Tristram Shandy, Gent.*, in *Tristram Shandy: An Authoritative Text, the Author on the Novel, Criticism*, ed. Howard Anderson (New York: W. W. Norton & Company, 1979), 26.

42 Sterne, *Tristram Shandy*, 216.

43 Ibid., 202, 74–75, 202.

44 Ibid., 6, 261.

45 Ibid., 2 ("so young a traveler, my little gentleman had got to his journey's end miserably spent").

46 Ibid.

47 B. L. Reid, "Sterne and the Absurd Homunculus," *Virginia Quarterly Review* 43.1 (Winter 1967): 77.

48 Admits Tristram later in the chapter, "[I] am a mortal of so little consequence in the world, it is not much matter what I do" (Sterne, *Tristram Shandy*, 9).

49 Ibid., 2.

50 Louis Landa, "The Shandean Homunculus: The Background of Sterne's 'Little Gentleman,'" in *Restoration and Eighteenth-Century Literature: Essays in Honor of Alan Dugald McKillop* (Chicago: University of Chicago Press, 1963), 51.

51 Ibid., 51. For other commentaries on the sexual politics of *Tristram Shandy*, see Barbara M. Benedict, "'Dear Madam': Rhetoric, Cultural Politics and the Female Reader in Sterne's *Tristram Shandy*," *Studies in Philology* 89.4 (1992): 485–98; Martha F. Bowden, "The Interdependence of Women in *Tristram Shandy*: A Chapter of Eyes, Sausages, and Sciatica," *English Language Notes* 31.4 (1994): 41–47; Michael Hardin, "Is There a Straight Line in This Text?: The Homoerotics of *Tristram Shandy*," *Orbis Litterarum* 54.3 (June 1999): 185–202; Elizabeth Kraft, "Laurence Sterne and the Chiasmus of Double Desire," *Shandean* 11 (1999–2000): 55–62; Bonnie Blackwell, "Tristram Shandy and the Theater of the Mechanical Mother," *English Literary History* 68.1 (2001): 81–133; and Robert Darby, "'An Oblique and Slovenly Initiation': The Circumcision Episode in *Tristram Shandy*," *Eighteenth-Century Life* 27.1 (2003): 72–84.

52 *The History of the Human Heart; Or, the Adventures of a Young Gentleman* (New York: Garland Publishing, 1974), 15–16.

53 Ibid., 17.
54 Sterne, *Tristram Shandy*, 206.
55 Ibid., 408.
56 Ibid., 408–9.
57 Ibid., 390, 346, 347, 390.
58 I am thankful to Richard Gray for pointing this out.

6. *Memoirs of the Celebrated Dwarf*

1 Josef Boruwlaski, *Memoirs of the Celebrated Dwarf* (London, 1788), 1. *Memoirs* was published with Boruwlaski's French and a translator's English on facing pages. The full title page reads *MEMOIRS OF THE CELEBRATED DWARF, JOSEPH BORUWLASKI, A POLISH GENTLEMAN; CONTAINING a faithful and curious Account of his BIRTH, EDUCATION, MARRIAGE, TRAVELS and VOYAGES; WRITTEN BY HIMSELF; Translated from the French By Mr.* DES CARRIERES. *With a Copper-plate Engraving, wherein he is represented in a Family-Scene.* LONDON, *1788*.

2 Paul J. Korshin, "Types of Eighteenth-Century Literary Patronage," *Eighteenth-Century Studies* 7.4 (1974): 464.

3 Betty Adelson's book *The Lives of Dwarfs: Their Journey from Public Curiosity toward Social Liberation* (New Brunswick, N.J.: Rutgers University Press, 2005), 20. The only others I have found are Barbara Benedict's "Displaying Difference: Curious Count Boruwlaski and the Staging of Class Identity," *Eighteenth-Century Life* 30.3 (2006): 78–106, and Kerry Duff's "Biographies of Scale," *Disabilities Studies Quarterly* 25.4 (2005).

4 Duff, "Biographies of Scale," 3; and Benedict, "Displaying Difference," 79.
5 Boruwlaski, *Memoirs of the Celebrated Dwarf*, 69–70.
6 Benedict, "Displaying Difference," 85.
7 Boruwlaski, *Memoirs of the Celebrated Dwarf*, 54–55.
8 Ibid., 15.
9 Ibid., 14.
10 Ibid., 15.
11 Ibid., 67.
12 Ibid., 31–33 (my italics).
13 Ibid., 61.
14 Ibid., 65.
15 Ibid., 67 (my italics).
16 Ibid., 73.
17 Ibid., 75, 53.
18 The class and rank of Boruwlaski's subscribers can be ascertained by a quick glance at the beginning of the alphabetized subscriber list: "His Royal Highness the PRINCE OF WALES, DUTCHESS Dowager of Ancaster, Earl of Aylesford, Countess Dowager of Aylesford, Earl of Aylesbury, Hon. Mr. Annesley, *Oxford*, A. Adair, Esq., Mr. E. Addison, Mr James Everard Arundell, *Salisbury*, Dr.

Andrieu, *Paris,* Dr. Ash, Miss Asker, Mr. Ayton, Countess of Bute, Right Hon. Lady Diana Beauclerk, Count de Bruhl, Miss de Bruhl, Lady Bloomsbury, Lady Bligh . . ." (ibid., i).

19 Ibid., 75.

20 Ibid., 52.

21 Ibid., 151, 142–43.

22 Ibid., 65.

23 Ibid., 66.

24 Ibid., 86, 88, 153.

25 Ibid., 70, 82–83, 102.

26 Jonathan Swift, *Gulliver's Travels,* ed. Peter Dixon and John Chalker (New York: Penguin Books, 1967), 87.

27 William Hay, *Deformity: An Essay,* ed. Kathleen James-Cavan (Victoria, B.C.: University of Victoria, 2004), 124.

28 Ibid., 139.

29 Ibid., 94–95.

30 Ibid., 112–13, 96–97.

31 Ibid., 100.

BIBLIOGRAPHY

Addison, Joseph. "*The Spectator,* No. 99, Saturday, June 23." In *"The Spectator" in Four Volumes,* vol. 1: 306. London: J. M. Dent & Sons, 1961.

———. "*The Tatler,* January 12, 1709." In *The Works of Joseph Addison,* edited by Henry G. Bohn, vol. 2. London: George Bell and Sons, 1901.

Adelson, Betty M. *The Lives of Dwarfs: Their Journey from Public Curiosity toward Social Liberation.* New Brunswick, N.J.: Rutgers University Press, 2005.

Alpers, Svetlana. *The Art of Describing: Dutch Art in the Seventeenth Century.* Chicago: University of Chicago Press, 1983.

Anscomb, Lisa. "'A Close, Naked, Natural Way of Speaking': Gendered Metaphor in the Texts of Margaret Cavendish and the Royal Society." *In-Between: Essays & Studies in Literary Criticism* 9.1–2 (2000): 161–77.

Armstrong, Nancy. *Desire and Domestic Fiction: A Political History of the Novel.* Oxford: Oxford University Press, 1987.

Ashton, John. *Social Life in the Reign of Queen Anne.* London: Chatto and Windus, 1925.

Atherton, Herbert M. *Political Prints in the Age of Hogarth: A Study of the Ideographic Representation of Politics.* Oxford: Clarendon Press, 1974.

Bacon, Francis. "On Deformity." In *Francis Bacon: A Critical Edition of the Major Works*, edited by Brian Vickers, 426–27. Oxford: Oxford University Press, 1996.

Bailey, Anne Hall. "How Much for Just the Muse?" *The Eighteenth Century* 36.1 (1995): 24–37.

Baker, Sheridan. "Political Allusion in Fielding's Author's Farce, Mock Doctor, and Tumble-Down Dick." *PMLA* 77 (1962): 221–31.

Barker-Benfield, G. J. *The Culture of Sensibility: Sex and Society in Eighteenth-Century Britain.* Chicago: University of Chicago Press, 1992.

Barnett, Louise. "Betty's Freckled Neck: Swift, Women, and Women Readers." *1650–1850: Ideas, Aesthetics, and Inquiries in the Early Modern Era* 4 (1998): 233–45.

———. "Swift, Women, and Women Readers: A Feminist Perspective on Swift's Life." In *Representations of Swift*, edited by Brian A. Connery, 181–94. Newark: University of Delaware Press, 2002.

Barrell, John. "'The Dangerous Goddess': Masculinity, Prestige, and the Aesthetic in Early Eighteenth-Century Britain." *Cultural Critique* 12 (1989): 101–31.

"The Bauble: A Tale." London, 1721.

Benedict, Barbara M. *Curiosity: A Cultural History of Early Modern Inquiry.* Chicago: University of Chicago Press, 2001.

———. "'Dear Madam': Rhetoric, Cultural Politics and the Female Reader in Sterne's *Tristam Shandy*." *Studies in Philology* 89.4 (1992): 485–98.

———. "Displaying Difference: Curious Count Boruwlaski and the Staging of Class Identity." *Eighteenth-Century Life* 30.3 (2006): 78–106.

———. "Encounters with the Object: Advertisements, Time, and Literary Discourse in the Early Eighteenth-Century Thing-Poem." *Eighteenth-Century Studies* 40.2 (2007): 193–207.

———. *Framing Feeling: Sentiment and Style in English Prose Fiction, 1745–1800.* New York: AMS Press, 1994.

Berg, Maxine. *Luxury and Pleasure in Eighteenth-Century Britain.* Oxford: Oxford University Press, 2005.

Bermingham, Ann, and John Brewer, eds. *The Consumption of Culture, 1600–1800: Image, Object, Text.* London: Routledge, 1995.

Bhattacharya, Nandini. *Reading the Splendid Body: Gender and Consumerism in Eighteenth-Century British Writing on India.* Newark: University of Delaware Press, 1998.

Bindman, David. *Hogarth and His Times.* Berkeley: University of California Press, 1997.

Blackwell, Bonnie. "Tristam Shandy and the Theater of the Mechanical Mother." *English Literary History* 68.1 (2001): 81–133.

Boruwlaski, Josef. *Memoirs of the Celebrated Dwarf.* London, 1788.

Boucé, Paul-Gabriel. "Aspects of Sexual Tolerance and Intolerance in XIIIth-Century England." *The British Journal for Eighteenth-Century Studies* 3.1980: 173–91.

———. "Gulliver Phallophorus and the Maids of Honour in Brobdingnag." *Bulletin de la Société d'Études Anglo-Américaines des XVIIe et XVIIIe Siècles*, no. 53 (November 2001): 81–98.

Bowden, Martha F. "The Interdependence of Women in *Tristam Shandy*: A Chapter of Eyes, Sausages, and Sciatica." *English Language Notes* 31.4 (1994): 41–47.

Brewer, John, and Roy Porter, eds. *Consumption and the World of Goods.* London: Routledge, 1993.

Brinks, Ellen. *Gothic Masculinity: Effeminacy and the Supernatural in English and German Romanticism.* Lewisburg, Pa.: Bucknell University Press, 2003.

Brown, Bill. "Thing Theory." In *Things*, 1–22. Chicago: University of Chicago Press, 2004.

Brown, Laura. "Reading Race and Gender: Jonathan Swift." In *Critical Essays on Jonathan Swift*, edited by Frank Palmeri, 121–42. New York: G. K. Hall & Co., 1993.

Burkhart, Dagmar. "Archeology of Female Cannibalism: Slavenka Drakulić's Novel Divine Hunger." *Russian Literature* 59.1 (2006): 1–24.

Butler, Judith. *The Psychic Life of Power: Theories in Subjection.* Stanford, Calif.: Stanford University Press, 1997.

Campbell, Jill. *Natural Masques: Gender and Identity in Fielding's Plays and Novels.* Stanford, Calif.: Stanford University Press, 1995.

Centlivre, Susannah. *The Basset Table.* In *Female Playwrights of the Restoration: Five Comedies*, edited by Paddy Lyons and Fidelis Morgan, 235–92. London: Everyman, 1991.

Clark, Paul Odell. *Gulliver Dictionary.* New York: Haskell House Publishers, 1979.

Cleary, Thomas R. *Henry Fielding: Political Writer.* Ontario: Wilfred Laurier University Press, 1984.

Colclough, Stephen. *Consuming Texts: Readers and Reading Communities, 1695–1870.* New York: Palgrave Macmillan, 2007.

Craik, T. W. "Fielding's 'Tom Thumb' Plays." In *Augustan Worlds*, edited by J. C. Hilson, M. M. B. Jones, and J. R. Watson, 165–74. New York: Barnes & Noble Books, 1978.

Crow, Nora F. "Swift and the Woman Scholar." In *Pope, Swift, and Women Writers*, edited by Donald C. Mell, 222–38. Newark: University of Delaware Press, 1996.

Cruise, James. *Governing Consumption: Needs and Wants, Suspended Characters, and the "Origins" of Eighteenth-Century English Novels.* Lewisburg, Pa.: Bucknell University Press, 1999.

Darby, Robert. "'An Oblique and Slovenly Initiation': The Circumcision Episode in *Tristam Shandy*." *Eighteenth-Century Life* 27.1 (2003): 72–84.

Daumas, Maurice. *Scientific Instruments of the Seventeenth and Eighteenth Centuries.* New York: Praeger Publishers, 1972.

Davis, Lennard J. "Dr. Johnson, Amelia, and the Discourse of Disability in the Eighteenth Century." In *"Defects": Engendering the Modern Body*, edited by Helen Deutsch and Felicity Nussbaum, 54–74. Ann Arbor: The University of Michigan Press, 2000.

Dawson, Janis. "Trade and Plumb-Cake in Lilliput: The Origins of Juvenile Consumerism and Early English Children's Periodicals." *Children's Literature in Education* 29.4 (1998): 175–94.

Defoe, Daniel. *Conjugal Lewdness: or, Matrimonial Whoredom.* London, 1727.

De Quehen, A. H. "An Account of Works Attributed to Samuel Butler." *The Review of English Studies* 33.131 (August 1982): 262–77.

Dennis, John. "A True Character of Mr. Pope and his Writings." In *The Critical Works of Dennis*, edited by Edward Niles Hooker, vol. 2: 103–8. Baltimore: Johns Hopkins University Press, 1943.

Derham, William. *Physico-Theology.* London, 1688.

Deutsch, Helen. *Resemblance and Disgrace: Alexander Pope and the Deformation of Culture.* Cambridge, Mass.: Harvard University Press, 1996.

Dickie, Simon. "Hilarity and Pitilessness in the Mid-eighteenth Century: English Jestbook Humor." *Eighteenth-Century Studies* 37.1 (2003): 1–22.

"Dildoides." In *Dildoides.* Reprint. Kingston, R.I.: Biscuit City Press, 1980.

Dominguez, J. P. "El buffon don Sebastian de Morra." *Journal of the American Medical Association* 261.5 (February 1989).

Donoghue, Emma. *Passions between Women: British Lesbian Culture, 1668–1801.* New York: Harper Collins, 1993.

Doody, Margaret Anne. "Swift among the Women." In *Critical Essays on Jonathan Swift*, edited by Frank Palmeri, 13–37. New York: G. K. Hall & Co., 1993.

Douthwaite, Julia. "*Homo ferus*: Between Monster and Model." *Eighteenth-Century Life* 21.2 (1997): 176–202.

Duff, Kerry. "Biographies of Scale." *Disabilities Studies Quarterly* 25.4 (Fall 2005).

Ezell, Margaret J. M. *Social Authorship and the Advent of Print.* Baltimore: Johns Hopkins University Press, 1999.

Fiedler, Leslie. *Freaks: Myths and Images of the Secret Self.* New York: Simon & Schuster, 1979.

Fielding, Henry. *The Female Husband.* In *The Female Husband and Other Writings*, edited by Claude E. Jones, 29–51. Liverpool: Liverpool University Press, 1960.

———. *The History of Tom Jones, a Foundling.* Hanover, Conn.: Wesleyan University Press, 1975.

———. "To the Same. On Her Wishing to Have a Lilliputian to Play With." In *Miscellanies by Henry Fielding, Esq.*, edited by Henry Knight Miller, vol. 1: 72–74. Oxford: Clarendon Press, 1972.

———. *"Tom Thumb" and "The Tragedy of Tragedies."* Edited by L. J. Morrissey. Berkeley: University of California Press, 1970.

Flint, Christopher. "Speaking Objects: The Circulation of Stories in Eighteenth-Century Prose Fiction." *PMLA* 113.2 (March 1998): 212–26.

Flynn, Carol Houlihan. *The Body in Swift and Defoe.* Cambridge: Cambridge University Press, 1990.

Fournier, Marian. *The Fabric of Life: Microscopy in the Seventeenth Century.* Baltimore: Johns Hopkins University Press, 1996.

Fox, Christopher. "How to Prepare a Noble Savage." In *Inventing Human Science: Eighteenth Century Domains*, edited by Christopher Fox, Roy Porter, and Robert Wokler, 1–30. Berkeley: University of California Press, 1995.

Freccero, Carla. "Cannibalism, Homophobia, Women: Montaigne's 'Des Cannibales' and 'De l'amitié." In *Women, "Race," and Writing in the Early Modern Period*, edited by Margo Hendricks and Patricia Parker. London: Routledge, 1994.

George, M. Dorothy. *Hogarth to Cruikshank: Social Change in Graphic Satire.* New York: Walker and Company, 1967.

Goldgar, Bertrand A. *Walpole and the Wits: The Relation of Politics to Literature, 1722–1742.* Lincoln: University of Nebraska Press, 1976.

Goldsmith, Oliver. *The Vicar of Wakefield.* London: Penguin Books, 1982.

Gray, Thomas. "Letter LXXX, Mr. Gray to Mr. Walpole," February 26, 1768. In *The Works of Thomas Gray,* 306. Oxford: Talboys and Wheeler, 1825.

Green, Katherine Sobba. *The Courtship Novel, 1740–1820: A Feminized Genre.* Lexington: University Press of Kentucky, 1991.

Gregori, Flavio. "Pope on the Margins and in the Center." *Studies in the Literary Imagination* 38.1 (2005): i-xliv.

Griffin, Dustin. *Literary Patronage in England.* Cambridge: Cambridge University Press, 1996.

Guerinot, J. V. *Pamphlet Attacks on Alexander Pope, 1711–1744.* New York: New York University Press, 1969.

Guest, Harriet. *Small Change: Women, Learning, Patriotism, 1750–1810.* Chicago: University of Chicago Press, 2000.

Hallet, Mark. *The Spectacle of Difference: Graphic Satire in the Age of Hogarth.* New Haven, Conn.: Yale University Press, 1999.

Halliday, Tony. *Facing the Public: Portraiture in the Aftermath of the French Revolution.* Manchester, U.K.: Manchester University Press, 1999.

Hardin, Michael. "Is There a Straight Line in This Text?: The Homoerotics of Tristam Shandy." *Orbis Litterarum* 54.3 (June 1999): 185–202.

Hay, William. *Deformity: An Essay.* Edited by Kathleen James-Cavan. Victoria, B.C.: University of Victoria, 2004.

Hillhouse, James T. Preface to *The Tragedy of Tragedies; Or the Life and Death of Tom Thumb the Great, with the Annotations of H. Scriblerus Secundus,* vii-viii. New Haven, Conn.: Yale University Press, 1918.

The History of the Human Heart; Or, the Adventures of a Young Gentleman. New York: Garland Publishing, 1974.

Hooke, Robert. "Discourse Concerning Telescopes and Microscopes; with a short Account of Their Inventors, read in February 1691–2." In *Philosophical Experiments of the Late Eminent Dr. Robert Hooke and Other Eminent Virtuosos in His Time,* 257–64. London, 1726.

———. *Micrographia.* London, 1665.

Hudson, Nicholas. "Challenging Eisenstein: Recent Studies in Print Culture." *Eighteenth-Century Life* 26.2 (2002): 83–95.

Hughes, Lindsey. *Playing Games: The Alternate History of Peter the Great.* London: School of Slavonic and East European Studies, 2000.

Hume, Robert D. *Henry Fielding and the London Theater, 1728–1737.* Oxford: Clarendon Press, 1988.

Hunter, J. Paul. *Occasional Form: Henry Fielding and the Chains of Circumstance.* Baltimore: The Johns Hopkins University Press, 1975.

——. "Robert Boyle and the Epistemology of the Novel." *Eighteenth-Century Fiction* 2.4 (July 1990): 275–91.

Hunter, Michael. *The Royal Society and Its Fellows 1660–1700: The Morphology of an Early Scientific Institution.* London: The British Society for the History of Science, 1982.

——. *Science and Society in Restoration England.* Cambridge: Cambridge University Press, 1981.

——. *Science and the Shape of Orthodoxy: Intellectual Change in Late Seventeenth-Century Britain.* Woodbridge, Suffolk, U.K.: Boydell Press, 1995.

Ingrassia, Catherine. *Authorship, Commerce, and Gender in Early Eighteenth-Century England.* Cambridge: Cambridge University Press, 2005.

Jacob, James Randall. *Robert Boyle and the English Revolution: A Study in Social and Intellectual Change.* New York: Burt Frankline & Co., 1977.

Jonston, John. *An History of the Constancey of Nature: Wherein, By comparing the latter Age with the former, it is maintained that the World doth not decay universally in respect of it Self or the Heavens, Elements, Mixt Bodies, Meteors, Minerals, Plants, Animals, nor Mand in his Age, Stature, Strength, or Faculties of his Minde, as relating to all Arts and Science.* London, 1657.

"Just published, Monsieur Thing; or Seignior D__do's Adventures in Great Britain." *Daily Journal.* London, June 9, 1722.

Kahan, Jeffrey. "Violating Hippocrates: Dildoes and Female Desire in Thomas Nashe's 'The Choice of Valentines.'" *Para*doxa* 2.2 (1996): 204–16.

Korshin, Paul J. "Types of Eighteenth-Century Literary Patronage." *Eighteenth-Century Studies* 7.4 (1974): 453–73.

Kowaleski-Wallace, Elizabeth. *Consuming Subjects: Women, Shopping, and Business in the Eighteenth Century.* New York: Columbia University Press, 1997.

Kraft, Elizabeth. "Laurence Sterne and the Chiasmus of Double Desire." *Shandean* 11 (1999–2000): 55–62.

Lamb, Jonathan. "Modern Metamorphoses and Disgraceful Tales." In *Things,* edited by Bill Brown, 193–226. Chicago: University of Chicago Press, 2004.

Landa, Louis. "The Shandean Homunculus: The Background of Sterne's 'Little Gentleman.'" In *Restoration and Eighteenth-Century Literature: Essays in Honor of Alan Dugald McKillop,* 49–68. Chicago: University of Chicago Press, 1963.

Lewis, Peter. *Fielding's Burlesque Drama: Its Place in the Tradition.* Edinburgh: Edinburgh University Press, 1987.

Lippincott, Louise. "Expanding on Portraiture: The Market, the Public, and the Hierarchy of Genres in Eighteenth-Century Britain." *The Consumption of Culture, 1600–1800: Image, Object, Text,* edited by Ann Bermingham and John Brewer, 75–88. London: Routledge, 1995.

"The Little Man." In *The Gentleman's Bottle-Companion, Containing a Collection of Curious, Uncommon, and Humourous Songs; Most of which are Originals.* London, 1768.

Locke, John. *Essay Concerning Human Understanding.* New York: Penguin Books, 1964.

Love, Harold. "A Restoration Lampoon in Transmission and Revision: Rochester's (?) 'Signior Dildo.'" *Studies in Bibliography* 46, edited by David L. Vander Meulen, 250–62. Charlottesville: University of Virginia Press, 1993.

"The Lucky Dwarf." In *The Pall Mall Miscellany. Containing Many Curious Pieces of Prose and Verse, with Variety of New Songs, adapted to Old Ballad Tunes and Country Dances*, 55–58. London: Printed by Christopher Dickson, the Port-Office Yard, 1732.

Luhmann, Niklas. *Love as Passion: The Codification of Intimacy.* Translated by Jeremy Gaines and Doris L. Jones. Stanford, Calif.: Stanford University Press, 1982.

Lund, Roger. "Laughing at Cripples: Ridicule, Deformity, and the Argument from Design." *Eighteenth-Century Studies* 39.1 (2005): 91–114.

Lüthy, Christopher Herbert. "Matter and Microscopes in the Seventeenth Century." PhD diss., Harvard University, 1995.

Macey, Samuel L. "Fielding's *Tom Thumb* as the Heir to Buckingham's *Rehearsal*." *Texas Studies in Literature and Language* 10.3 (Fall 1968): 405–14.

Mack, Maynard. *Alexander Pope: A Life.* New Haven, Conn.: Yale University Press, 1985.

———. "'The Least Thing like a Man in England': Some Effects of Pope's Physical Disability on His Life and Literary Career." In *Collected in Himself: Essays Critical, Biographical, and Bibliographical on Pope and Some of His Contemporaries*, 372–92. Newark: University of Delaware Press, 1982.

Mackenzie, Henry. *The Man of Feeling.* Edited by Brian Vickers. Oxford: Oxford University Press, 1987.

Mandler, Peter. *The English National Character: The History of an Idea from Edmund Burke to Tony Blair.* New Haven, Conn.: Yale University Press, 2006.

Markley, Robert. "Sentimentality as Performance: Shaftesbury, Sterne, and the Theatrics of Virtue." In *The New Eighteenth Century: Theory, Politics, English Literature*, edited by Felicity Nussbaum and Laura Brown, 210–30. London: Methuen, 1987.

Marx, Karl. *Capital: A Critique of Political Economy, Volume 1.* Translated by Ben Fowkes. London: Penguin Books, 1976.

———. *Grundrisse.* Translated by Martin Nicolaus. London: Penguin Books, 1993.

McCormick, James B., M.D. *Eighteenth-Century Microscopes: A Synopsis of History and Workbook.* Lincolnwood, Ill.: Science Heritage, 1987.

"Monsieur Thing's Origin: Or Seignior D___'s Adventures in Britain." Cheapside, 1722.

Montagu, Lady Mary Wortley. "Verses Address'd to the Imitator of the First Satire of the Second Book of Horace. By a Lady." 1733.

Morley, Henry. *Memoirs of Bartholomew Fair.* London: Chatto and Windus, 1880.

Mui, Hoh-Cheung, and Lorna H. Mui. *Shops and Shopkeeping in Eighteenth-Century England.* London: McGill-Queens University Press, 1989.

Murdoch, J., and V. J. Murrell, "The Monogramist DG: Dwarf Gibson and His Patrons." *Burlington Magazine* 938 (1981): 282–89.

Nate, Richard. "'Plain and Vulgarly Express'd': Margaret Cavendish and the Discourse of the New Science." *Rhetorica* 19.4 (2001): 403–17.

Newton, Isaac. Letter to Robert Hooke, 5 February 1676. In *Correspondence of Isaac*

Newton, edited by H. W. Turnbull. Vol. 2. Cambridge: Cambridge University Press, 1960. Nicholson, Colin. "The Mercantile Bard." *Studies in the Literary Imagination* 38.1 (2005): 77–94.

Nicolson, Marjorie. "The Microscope and the English Imagination." *Smith College Studies in Modern Languages* 16.4 (July 1955): 1–92.

———. *Science and the Imagination.* Ithaca, N.Y.: Great Seal Books, 1956.

Nicolson, Marjorie, and G. S. Rousseau. *"This Long Disease My Life": Alexander Pope and the Sciences.* Princeton, N.J.: Princeton University Press, 1968.

Noggle, James. "Literary Taste as Counter-Enlightenment in Hume's *History of England*." *SEL* 44.3 (Summer 2004): 617–38.

Nussbaum, Felicity A. "Gulliver's Malice: Gender and the Satiric Stance." In *Gulliver's Travels: Complete, Authoritative Text with Biographical and Historical Contexts, Critical History, and Essays from Five Contemporary Critical Perspectives*, edited by Christopher Fox, 318–34. Boston: Bedford Books of St. Martin's Press, 1995.

———. *The Limits of the Human: Fictions of Anomaly, Race, and Gender in the Long Eighteenth Century.* Cambridge: Cambridge University Press, 2003.

"Of a Dwarf Courting a Bright Lady." In *The Dryden-Tonson Miscellanies*, edited by Stuart Gillespie and David Hopkins, vol. 6: 556–57. London: Routledge, 2008.

Onania. London, 1718.

Paine, Thomas. *Collected Writings.* New York: Library of America, 1995.

Park, Katherine, and Lorraine J. Daston. "Unnatural Conceptions: The Study of Monsters in Sixteenth- and Seventeenth-Century England." *Past and Present* 92 (1981): 20–54.

Patey, Douglas Lane. "Swift's Satire on 'Science' and the Structure of *Gulliver's Travels*." *ELH* 58.4 (Winter 1991): 809–39.

Peace, Mary. "The Economy of Nymphomania: Luxury, Virtue, Sentiment and Desire in Mid-Eighteenth-Century Medical Discourse." In *At the Borders of the Human: Beasts, Bodies, and Natural Philosophy in the Early Modern Period*, edited by Erica Fudge, Ruth Gilbert, and Susan Wiseman, 239–58. London: Macmillan, 1999.

Perry, Ruth. "Colonizing the Breast: Sexuality and Maternity in Eighteenth-Century England." *Journal of the History of Sexuality* 2.2 (October 1991): 204–34.

Pollak, Ellen. *The Poetics of Sexual Myth: Gender and Ideology in the Verse of Swift and Pope.* Chicago: University of Chicago Press, 1985.

Pope, Alexander. *The Correspondence* of *Alexander Pope.* Edited by George Sherburn. 5 vols. Oxford: Clarendon Press, 1956.

———. "An Epistle to Dr. Arbuthnot." In *The Poems of Alexander Pope*, edited by John Butt, 597–612. New Haven, Conn.: Yale University Press, 1965.

———. "Essay on Man." In *The Poems of Alexander Pope*, edited by John Butt, 501–48. New Haven, Conn.: Yale University Press, 1965.

———. "Imitations of Horace," Epistle 1.1. In *The Poems of Alexander Pope*, edited by John Butt, 613–703. New Haven, Conn.: Yale University Press, 1965.

———. "The Lamentation of Glumdalclitch, for the Loss of Grildig. A Pastoral." In *Minor Poems*, edited by Norman Ault and John Butt, 271. London: Methuen & Co., 1954.

——. *Minor Poems.* Edited by Norman Ault and John Butt. London: Methuen & Co., 1954.
——. "No. XCI. Thursday, June 25." *The Guardian.* London, 1713.
——. "No. XCII. Friday, June 26." *The Guardian.* London, 1713.
——. "No. CVIII. Wednesday, July 15." *The Guardian.* London, 1713.
——. "The Rape of the Lock." In *The Poems of Alexander Pope,* edited by John Butt, 218–42. New Haven, Conn.: Yale University Press, 1965.
——. "Rondeau." In *Minor Poems,* edited by Norman Ault and John Butt, 61. London: Methuen & Co., 1954.
——. "To Quinbus Flestrin the Man Mountain. An Ode. By Titty Tit, Esq; Poet Laureate to his Majesty of Lilliput. Translated into English." In *Minor Poems,* edited by Norman Ault and John Butt, 268. London: Methuen & Co., 1954.
Prescott, Anna Lake. "The Odd Couple: Gargantua and Tom Thumb." In *Monster Theory: Reading Culture,* edited by Jeffrey Jerome Cohen, 75–91. Minneapolis: University of Minnesota Press, 1996.
Regan, Shaun. "Print Culture in Transition: Tristam Shandy, The Reviewers, and the Consumable Text." *Eighteenth-Century Fiction* 14.3–4 (2002): 289–309.
Reid, B. L. "Sterne and the Absurd Homunculus." *Virginia Quarterly Review* 43.1 (Winter 1967): 71–95.
Renaker, David. "Swift's Laputians as a Caricature of the Cartesians." *PMLA* 94.5 (1979): 936–44.
Roach, Joseph. "The Artificial Eye: Augustan Theater and the Empire of the Visible." In *The Performance of Power: Theatrical Discourse and Politics,* edited by Sue-Ellen Case and Janelle Reinelt, 131–45. Iowa City: University of Iowa Press, 1991.
Rubin, Gayle. "The Traffic in Women: Note on the 'Political Economy' of Sex." In *Feminist Literary Theory and Criticism,* edited by Sandra M. Gilbert and Susan Gubar, 392–413. New York: W. W. Norton & Company, 2007.
Salvaggio, Ruth. "Swift's Disruptive Woman." In *Enlightened Absence: Neoclassical Configurations of the Feminine,* 77–104. Urbana: University of Illinois Press, 1988.
Schaffer, Simon. "Enlightened Automata." In *The Sciences in Enlightened Europe,* edited by William Clark, Jan Golinski, and Simon Schaffer, 126–65. Chicago: University of Chicago Press, 1999.
Schiebinger, Londa. "Nature's Unruly Body: The Limits of Scientific Description." In *Regime of Description: In the Archive of the Eighteenth Century,* 25–41. Stanford, Calif.: Stanford University Press, 2005.
Scott, Sarah. *A Description of Millenium Hall.* Edited by Gary Kelly. Peterborough, Ontario: Broadview Literary Texts, 1995.
Shakespeare, William. *Julius Caesar,* 1.2.135.
Shapin, Steven. "Who Was Robert Hooke?" In *Robert Hooke: New Studies,* edited by Michael Hunter and Simon Schaffer, 253–85. Woodbridge, Suffolk, U.K.: The Boydell Press, 1989.
Shaw, Sheila."The Rape of Gulliver: Case Study of a Source." *PMLA* 90.1 (January 1975): 62–68.

Sherbo, Arthur. *Christopher Smart: Scholar of the University.* Ann Arbor: Michigan State University Press, 1967.

Smart, Christopher. "The Author Apologizes to a Lady, for His Being a Little Man." *The Student.* Oxford, October 5, 1750.

Smith, Frederick. "Science, Imagination, and Swift's Brobdingnagians." *Eighteenth-Century Life* 14.1 (February 1990): 100–112.

Staves, Susan. *Married Women's Separate Property in England, 1660–1833.* Cambridge, Mass.: Harvard University Press, 1990.

Sterne, Laurence. *The Life and Opinions of Tristam Shandy, Gent.* In *Tristam Shandy: An Authoritative Text, the Author on the Novel, Criticism,* edited by Howard Anderson, xiii-458. New York: W. W. Norton & Company, 1979.

———. *A Sentimental Journey through France and Italy.* In *"A Sentimental Journey" and "Continuation of the Bramine's Journal" with Related Texts,* edited by Melvyn New and W. G. Day, 1–174. Indianapolis, Ind.: Hackett Publishing Company, 2006.

Stewart, Larry. *The Rise of Public Science: Rhetoric, Technology, and Natural Philosophy in Newtonian Britain.* Cambridge: Cambridge University Press, 1992.

Stewart, Susan. *On Longing: Narratives of the Miniature, the Gigantic, the Souvenir, the Collection.* Baltimore: The Johns Hopkins University Press, 1988.

Stone, Lawrence. *The Family, Sex, and Marriage in England: 1500–1800.* New York: Harper & Row, 1977.

Sussman, Charlotte. *Consuming Anxieties: Consumer Protest, Gender, and British Slavery, 1713–1833.* Stanford, Calif.: Stanford University Press, 2000.

Swift, Jonathan. *Gulliver's Travels.* Edited by Peter Dixon and John Chalker. New York: Penguin Books, 1967.

———. "November 15 1710." In *Journal to Stella,* edited by Harold Williams, vol. 1. Oxford: Clarendon Press, 1963.

Tadmor, Naomi. "'In the even my wife read to me': Women, Reading and Household Life in the Eighteenth Century." In *The Practice and Representation of Reading in England,* edited by James Raven, Helen Small, and Naomi Tadmor, 162–74. Cambridge: Cambridge University Press, 1996.

Taylor, Aline MacKenzie. "Sights and Monsters and Gulliver's Voyage to Brobdingnag." *Tulane Studies in English* 7 (1957): 29–83.

Temple, William. "Essay Upon the Ancient and Modern Learning." In *Five Miscellaneous Essays by Sir William Temple,* edited by Samuel Holt Monk. Ann Arbor: University of Michigan Press, 1963.

Thomas, Claudia N. *Alexander Pope and His Eighteenth-Century Women Readers.* Carbondale: Southern Illinois University Press, 1994.

Thompson, Rosemarie Garland. Introduction to *Freakery: Cultural Spectacles of the Extraordinary Body.* New York: New York University Press, 1996.

Tillery, Denise. "The Plain Style in the Seventeenth Century: Gender and the History of Scientific Discourse." *Journal of Technical Writing and Communication* 35.3 (2005): 273–89.

Todd, Dennis. *Imagining Monsters: Miscreations of the Self in Eighteenth-Century England.* Chicago: University of Chicago Press, 1995.

Todd, Janet. *Sensibility: An Introduction.* London: Methuen, 1986.

"Tom Thumb, His Life and Death." In *Remains of the Early Popular Poetry of England,* edited by W. Carew Hazlitt, 167–92. London, 1866.

Tuan, Yi-Fu. *Dominance and Affection: The Making of Pets.* New Haven, Conn.: Yale University Press, 1984.

Tyson, Edward. *The Anatomy of a Pygmy, Compared with that of a Monkey, an Ape, and a Man.* London, 1699.

Van Sant, Ann Jessie. *Eighteenth-Century Sensibility and the Novel: The Senses in Social Context.* Cambridge: Cambridge University Press, 1993.

Wagner, Peter. "The Discourse on Sex—Or Sex as Discourse: Eighteenth-Century Medical and Paramedical Erotica." In *Sexual Underworlds of the Enlightenment,* edited by G. S. Rousseau and Roy Porter, 46–68. Chapel Hill: University of North Carolina Press, 1988.

Waller, Edmund. "At the marriage of the Dwarfs." London, 1645.

Waters, Malcolm, ed. *Modernity: Critical Concepts.* London: Routledge, 1999.

Weatherhill, Lorna. *Consumer Behavior and Material Culture in Britain, 1660–1760.* London: Routledge, 1996.

Weber, Harold. "'Drudging in Fair Aurelia's Womb': Constructing Homosexual Economies in Rochester's Poetry." *The Eighteenth Century* 33.2 (Summer 1992): 99–117

"William Hogarth." Art of the Print, http://www.artoftheprint.com/artistpages/hogarth_william_evening.htm.

Williams, Abigail. "Patronage and Whig Literary Culture in the Early Eighteenth Century." In *"Cultures of Whiggism": New Essays on English Literature and Culture in the Long Eighteenth Century,* edited by David Womersley, 149–72. Newark: University of Delaware Press, 2005.

Wilmot, John, Earl of Rochester. "Signior Dildo." In *The Works of John Wilmot, Earl of Rochester,* edited by Harold Love. Oxford: Oxford University Press, 1999.

Wilson, Catherine. *The Invisible World: Early Modern Philosophy and the Invention of the Microscope.* Princeton, N.J.: Princeton University Press, 1997.

———. "Visual Surface and Visual Symbol: The Microscope and the Occult in Early Modern Science." *Journal of the History of Ideas* 49.1 (January-March 1988): 85–108.

Wilton, Andrew. *The Swagger Portrait: Grand Manner Portraiture in Britain from Van Dyck to Augustus John, 1630–1930.* London: Tate Gallery Publications, 1992.

Wimsatt, William Kurtz. *The Portraits of Alexander Pope.* New Haven, Conn.: Yale University Press, 1965.

"Woman." In *The Dryden-Tonson Miscellanies, 1684–1709,* edited by Stuart Gillespie and David Hopkins, vol. 6: 354, 355. London: Routledge, 2008.

Woodmansee, Martha. "The Interests in Disinterestedness: Karl Phillipp Moritz and the Emergence of the Theory of Aesthetic Autonomy in Eighteenth-Century Germany." *Modern Language Quarterly* 45.1 (1984): 22–47.

INDEX

a

b

C

d

e

f

g

h

i

j

k

l

m

n

o

p

r

s